INTIMACY AND SEXUALITY IN THE AGE OF SHAKESPEARE

James M. Bromley argues that Renaissance texts circulate knowledge about a variety of non-standard sexual practices and intimate life narratives, including non-monogamy, anal eroticism, masochism, and cross-racial female homoeroticism. Rethinking current assumptions about intimacy in Renaissance drama, poetry, and prose, the book blends historicized and queer approaches to embodiment, narrative, and temporality. An important contribution to Renaissance literary studies, queer theory, and the history of sexuality, the book demonstrates the relevance of Renaissance literature to today. Through close readings of William Shakespeare's "problem comedies," Christopher Marlowe's *Hero and Leander*, plays by Beaumont and Fletcher, Thomas Middleton's *The Nice Valour*, and Lady Mary Wroth's sonnet sequence *Pamphilia to Amphilanthus* and her prose romance *The Urania*, Bromley re-evaluates notions of the centrality of deep, abiding affection in Renaissance culture and challenges our own investment in a narrowly defined intimate sphere.

JAMES M. BROMLEY is Assistant Professor of English at Miami University. He has published essays on intimacy, sexual practice, and Renaissance literature in *Early Modern Literary Studies*, *Studies in Philology*, and *Modern Philology*. He is the winner of the 2011 Martin Stevens Award for Best New Essay in Early Drama Studies from the Medieval and Renaissance Drama Society.

INTIMACY AND SEXUALITY IN THE AGE OF SHAKESPEARE

JAMES M. BROMLEY

Miami University

CAMBRIDGE UNIVERSITY PRESS
Cambridge, New York, Melbourne, Madrid, Cape Town,
Singapore, São Paulo, Delhi, Tokyo, Mexico City

Cambridge University Press
The Edinburgh Building, Cambridge CB2 8RU, UK

Published in the United States of America by Cambridge University Press, New York

www.cambridge.org
Information on this title: www.cambridge.org/9781107015180

First published 2012

Printed in the United Kingdom at the University Press, Cambridge

A catalogue record for this publication is available from the British Library

Library of Congress Cataloguing in Publication data
Bromley, James M., 1978–
Intimacy and sexuality in the age of Shakespeare / James M. Bromley.
p.   cm.
Includes index.
ISBN 978-1-107-01518-0 (hardback)
1. English literature – Early modern, 1500–1700 – History and criticism.   2. Sex in literature.
3. Intimacy (Psychology) in literature.   4. Self in literature.   5. Homosexuality in literature.
I. Title.
PR428.S48B76   2011
820.9′353809031 – dc23   2011043834

ISBN 978-1-107-01518-0 Hardback

Contents

Illustrations

Acknowledgements

It is perhaps apt that a book about forms of affection in Renaissance texts should first pause to express my thanks for the relationships that have sustained me since this project's inception at Loyola University Chicago. I continue to profit immeasurably from Suzanne Gossett's rigorous reading of my work and her unique and indefatigable way of pushing me to grow as a scholar and writer. Christopher Castiglia, a model of clarity and insight, helped me to see what this project was actually about. With his broad understanding of Renaissance literary production, James Biester nurtured the inclusion of non-dramatic texts of the period in this project. Jeffrey Masten unstintingly offered his engagement with the work on this project, and my gratitude for his unflagging encouragement and mentorship of me as a scholar is, to adapt a phrase, too little payment for so great a debt.

At Miami University, I am never forgetful of how fortunate I am to have intelligent and supportive colleagues. This book has incalculably benefitted from my conversations with Katharine Gillespie, Elisabeth Hodges, and other members of Miami's interdisciplinary Early Modern Collective. I am much obliged to Mary Jean Corbett and Kaara Peterson, who, with keen eyes, proofread the text. At various stages, work on this project was supported by a fellowship from the Arthur J. Schmitt Foundation and by Summer Research and Assigned Research Appointments from Miami University.

I also wish to extend my appreciation to the far-flung early modern scholars who have helped shape this work. A valued interlocutor and indispensable friend, Will Stockton read the entire manuscript with the same acuity that he demonstrates in his own work, and this book and my thinking about Renaissance sexuality are better because of him. I thank Gary Taylor for permission to consult the Oxford Middleton edition of *The Nice Valour* prior to its publication. Richard Strier read part of Chapter 3 in his capacity as editor of *Modern Philology*, and it is much improved as a result. Fran Dolan generously gave me constructive commentary on a draft of

Chapter 4. At many times and in different locales, thoughtful and friendly conversations with Will Fisher, Vin Nardizzi, and Michael Schoenfeldt have invigorated my thinking about early modern literature. I have also reaped much from discussion by audiences and seminar participants at the Modern Language Association Convention; the annual meetings of the Renaissance Society of America, the Shakespeare Association of America, and the Group for Early Modern Cultural Studies; and the Elizabethan Theatre Conference.

I am grateful for the support of Sarah Stanton at Cambridge University Press, and the comments from Rick Rambuss and an anonymous reader have strengthened and enriched this book. Celeste Newbrough provided the index.

Finally, Laura LeMone has taught me more about the varieties of affection than anyone I have ever met. For her patience and kindness, I dedicate this book to her.

Previously published material in Chapter 1 is reprinted by permission of the publishers from "'Let it suffise': sexual acts and narrative structure in *Hero and Leander*", in *Queer Renaissance Historiography: Backward Gaze*, edited by Vin Nardizzi, Stephen Guy-Bray and Will Stockton. An earlier version of Chapter 3 appeared as "Social Relations and Masochistic Sexual Practice in *The Nice Valour*" in *Modern Philology* (2010).

NOTE

Where I am not quoting from a modern edition of a text, I have retained early modern spelling and punctuation. For clarity, however, I have silently modernized *i/j*, *u/v*, and long *s*, and where macrons indicate the suspension of a letter I have re-inserted the letter.

Introduction: Interiority, futurity, and affective relations in Renaissance literature

In his 1583 *The Anatomy of Abuses*, Philip Stubbes famously charged that drama taught audiences how to "play the Sodomits, or worse."[1] Stubbes's capacious "or worse," I would suggest, refers to certain affective relations that eventually became illegible under the rubrics of modern intimacy. In this book, I map the circulation of knowledge about these queer affections, not only in the plays that Stubbes targets, but also in poetry and prose written between 1588 and 1625. During the sixteenth and seventeenth centuries, the intimate sphere coalesced around relations characterized by two elements: interiorized desire and futurity. Interiorized desire locates the truth about the self and sexuality inside the body, thereby organizing and limiting the body's pleasures based on a hierarchized opposition between depths and surfaces. Access to futurity involves the perceived sense of a relationship's duration and its participation in legitimate social and sexual reproduction. These changes, of which Stubbes's charge is one of many indices, laid the foundation for modern understandings of normative intimacy as coextensive with long-term heterosexual monogamy. Coupling, and more specifically marriage, was invested with value as a site where affection was desirable – as opposed to a primarily economic and political arrangement with emotional bonds as a secondary concern – through its figuration as *the* interpersonal relation with the proper combination of interiorized desire and access to futurity. Other interpersonal relations were excluded from the category, becoming instead what I call "failures of intimacy," despite being characterized by affect, care, and pleasure for those involved, sometimes to a greater degree than relations typically understood as intimate in modern Western culture.

Nothing about the heterosexual couple inherently implies the automatic presence of affect, care, or pleasure, any more than any other form of relationality. Yet modern Western culture's relational economy assumes precisely the opposite in its conferral of cultural prestige and value on long-term heterosexual monogamy. In his landmark discussion in the first volume of *The History of Sexuality*, Michel Foucault argues that during the eighteenth and nineteenth centuries, there was "a centrifugal movement with respect to heterosexual monogamy" wherein "the legitimate couple, with its regular sexuality, had a right to more discretion."[2] I demonstrate that in the Renaissance, while the heterosexual couple was still actively, loudly, one might even say indiscreetly, asserting itself over alternate forms of relationality, it was nevertheless possible to challenge the authority of couple form intimacy. Various literary texts of the period critiqued the consolidation of intimacy around long-term heterosexual monogamy and instead invested value in alternate forms of intimacy, including short-term, situational relations; non-monogamous and polyamorous sexual practices; erotic practices that involve non-normative understandings of the body's pleasures, such as masochism; and beyond. In this book, I analyze Renaissance texts where these "failures of intimacy" do not fail to provide satisfaction and pleasure to those involved in them. Empowering readers to reimagine their own intimate lives, these literary texts offer a counterdiscourse to the period's marital advice conduct books and other texts that attempt to naturalize the consolidation of intimacy around monogamous coupling. This counterdiscourse is present even when texts ostensibly demonize alternate forms of intimacy, as a greater flexibility in Renaissance narrative allowed readers to resist what appears to be textual foreclosure on transgressive intimate practices. Insisting on diversity within relational life, the texts I discuss not only scrutinized the heterosexual couple's attempts to co-opt intimacy's signifying powers; they also sustained otherwise denigrated affections in the representational spaces they opened up for them.

By attending to the early modern contraction of the intimate sphere and to the changing status of alternate forms of intimacy in the period, I hope to move queer studies of the Renaissance beyond what Jonathan Goldberg and Madhavi Menon complain has been the field's tendency to "search for protoidentities" and toward a fuller analysis of the systems through which cultures of the past have understood affection and sexual practices.[3] This investigation has revealed rearrangements and realignments between and among those sexual practices and relationships that Western culture valorized and labeled as proper, civilized, natural, or decent, and those that Western culture abjected and dismissed as perverse, unnatural, threatening, or illicit. In the process, I make strategically ahistorical use of the concept of heteronormativity, which Lauren Berlant and Michael Warner describe as deriving from "a constellation of practices that everywhere disperses heterosexual privilege as a tacit but central organizing index of social membership."[4] This dispersal through modern culture is so wide that "social and economic discourses, institutions, and practices that don't feel especially sexual or familial collaborate to produce as a social norm and ideal an extremely narrow context for living."[5] More specifically, membership in a heterosexual couple, usually though not exclusively in marriage, organizes modern experiences as diverse as having health insurance, holding hands in public, and inheriting an estate. In my discussion of Renaissance texts, I use "normative" in its most general sense to refer to behaviors that were culturally prescribed through both punishment and reward. Around these behaviors, there accumulated a set of expectations that contoured the life narratives imaginable and representable in the texts of the period. Marriage's co-optation of the intimate sphere can still be deemed a normalizing process even if it was not based in the statistical analysis of populations that produces modern normative categories, because marital discourse attempted to direct the ways in which individuals understood and evaluated their relational experiences.

It is important, however, to emphasize that heteronormativity is not reducible to all cross-gender sexual practices, nor does it mean it is not appropriable by homosexuals, as evidenced by the recent dominance within gay political advocacy of the movement to legalize same-sex marriage, which, in the pursuit of equalizing access, has all too often uncritically embraced and desired the expansion of marriage's power to confer legal and cultural legitimacy and distribute economic benefits.[6] Instead, the concept heteronormativity points to the effects that making the intimacy of heterosexual coupling culturally sacrosanct has on diverse constituencies, including unmarried persons, gay men, lesbians, practitioners of S/M, those who consume pornography outside of the home, and beyond. I use the term "failures of intimacy" to describe certain bonds in Renaissance texts, not exclusively because they are same-sex, then, though gender certainly plays a role; their non-relation to interiority, to futurity, or to both has excluded them from the category of intimacy. What is more, these alternatives often strike at the logic of other cultural institutions, again not always or entirely because of gender, but because of the form of relationality involved. Though Berlant and Warner develop the concept in a post-Enlightenment, American context, the term "heteronormative" is useful to me in approaching pre-modern English texts because it helpfully locates the politicization of supposedly private affection and sexual practices due to their embeddedness in other cultural practices and sites. This normalization process was contingent, resisted, and uneven, and I pay particular attention to the moments in texts where this process of normalization is somehow interrupted or interruptible. This interruption allows an author to valorize forms of elective affinity that are not necessarily patterned on marriage and to disrupt the equation of intimacy with interpsychic connectedness and long-term monogamy.

It may seem paradoxical to use a concept like normativity ahistorically in order to situate intimacy, interiority, and narrative in historically-specific contexts. I do not mean the past to function as purely otherness or, conversely, a modernity waiting to be born. Madhavi Menon has recently called for new approaches to the literature of the past that do not assume "that the history of sexuality is always the history of difference between past and present."[7] Yet the conceptual replacement of difference with sameness would also lead to "forgetting the messiness of both time and desire."[8] Sameness can be the basis for fixity and coherence, which, according to Menon, abject the queer. Histories that bring sameness and difference together in uneasy and unexpected forms of interaction would maintain a complex, queer, even promiscuous relationship between past and present. Consequently, I strategically, if imperfectly, use "Renaissance" to attend to strains of contestation working against the consolidation of the intimate sphere and "early modern" to acknowledge elements that resemble modernity.

What is more, explicitness about the complex interaction between past and present, at least for this topic, should remind us that intimacy, embedded in politics, is in flux, contestable, and rewritable. For good or ill, such rewritings show up in the stories we tell and how we tell them. I am not only discussing a historical process that mattered to the people who produced and originally consumed these texts; this study has implications for modern readers of these texts and actors and directors of the dramatic texts that I discuss. It implicitly engages the debate on same-sex marriage and civil unions in the United States and within the European Union by opening up the social, economic, and legal investment in marriage and coupling to historical and ethical scrutiny. Those who advocate against same-sex marriage frequently offer a "slippery slope" argument that same-sex marriage will lead to polygamy and interspecies marriage. Such arguments are curiously reminiscent of Stubbes's "or worse," and are rightly denounced as ridiculous and illogical. Nevertheless, both sides in this current debate take marriage's desirability for granted, for the advocates of same-sex marriage often answer the "slippery slope" argument by distancing themselves from and even denigrating the lives of those who do not organize their affection around long-term monogamous coupling. Even civil unions, valid in the UK and parts of the US, and *pactes civils de solidarité* in France have not prompted radical relational innovation. If anything, there has been an entrenchment of the role of coupling, monogamy, and interiority in affective relations. Few voices defend alternate forms of relationship and the rights of the people who partake in them. This book asks us to consider the costs and benefits of accepting a more expansive intimate sphere by gesturing toward the similarities and differences between these present controversies and those encoded in texts of the past. These texts all continue to circulate, and they have the possibility to do so more widely now than in the Renaissance given modern electronic reproduction and transmission. Along with the affections and pleasures they represent, they are available to modern readers as scripts for intimacy, which can be appropriated and transformed to fit the present.

HISTORICIZING "INTIMACY"

According to the *Oxford English Dictionary*, the noun "intimacy" and the adjective "intimate" entered the English language during the sixteenth century and eventually came to signify a culturally valuable subset of social relations apart from the general category of relationality. The terms that would confer value on certain forms of relationality would be contested, but one of the ways dominant Western culture has defined the intimate involves subordinating one aspect of the etymological derivation of "intimacy" to another. The intimate became easily associated with inwardness because of its derivation from the Latin superlative *intimus*, or in-most. But the Latin term can also mean proximal when it describes relationships between things. For example, Tacitus, in his *Historiae*, describes the clemency that the emperor Otho showed to the consul, Marius Celsus, for having been loyal to Galba, the previous emperor whom Otho overthrew: "Nec Otho quasi ignosceret sed, ne hostem metueret, conciliationes adhibens, statim inter *intimos* amicos habuit."[9] Sir Henry Savile, in his 1598 translation printed as *The Ende of Nero and Beginning of Galba*, renders the passage: "Otho, not as remitting a fault, but admitting the defence as just and vertuous, straightway put him in place *nearest* about him."[10] Translating "*intimos*" as "nearest," Savile figures their relationship in terms of a spatial proximity with corporeal resonances.

   Proximity and profundity are distinct ways of understanding a relationship. Whereas "inmost" would bypass surfaces altogether in favor of depths, proximity remains on the level of the surface because the word implies the possibility of abutment. The "proximal," however, has fallen by the wayside in the history of intimacy and the "inmost" has been emphasized. This definitional bias may have something to do with the homograph "intimate," the verb meaning "to suggest indirectly." Predating the adjective "intimate" in English, though similarly derived from the Latin *intimus*, "to intimate," with its suggestion of subtlety, involves expressing interiority, but in a way that leaves the inward largely undisturbed by exteriority. When one intimates something, one casts a listener in the role of a detective; when precisely what is being intimated is discovered, the listener becomes part of an inner circle of knowledge, and that knowledge is then interiorized by the person receiving the information. Thus, "to intimate" is not actually to bring something internal out, but instead, to expand the internal sphere at the expense of the external world.

In modern Western culture's assessment of forms of relationality that signify as intimacy, that which is "inmost" is that which counts as "close." In this way, intimacy requires two psyches to connect, which may or may not produce any physical contact. Not valuable on its own terms, whatever physical closeness occurs would be a function or expression of the psychic connection. With its roots in interiority emphasized, the adjective "intimate" has been deployed to subordinate the world of surfaces, especially corporeal ones, to that of depths, as when partners who come to know each others' thoughts, feelings, hopes, and dreams are described as having an "intimate" relationship. In contrast, an anonymous sexual encounter, by its very nature, involves little to no interpersonal knowledge and is rarely considered intimate because such an encounter privileges the bodily experience of sexual pleasure over psychic connectedness and intersubjective knowledge. In the linguistic history of uses of the word "intimate," the proximal and the superficial, in the sense of dealing with bodily surfaces, remain unexplored roots of the adjective "intimate." If this root were brought to bear on relationality, interpersonal connections that occur primarily between bodies, rather than minds, might be reconsidered as valuable forms of intimacy.

The relational is neither static nor unaffected by historical change or political ideology. As this relationship between inwardness and intimacy crystallized, the scope of "intimacy" began to take its modern, highly circumscribed form. This narrow intimate sphere excludes what Daniel Juan Gil has termed "asocial relations" – that is, relations that do not fit neatly in the public or private spheres. While Gil usefully defamiliarizes intersubjective relations by looking at those that do not fit into modern models of intimacy, he claims they constitute "an early modern *rival* to intimacy," rather than alternate forms of intimacy, thereby suggesting that intimacy and its opposites emerged fully formed with clear definitional boundaries.[11] In contrast, I argue that the boundaries of intimacy were fluid and negotiated, only eventually condensing into modern intimacy, itself subject to contestation. The relations I discuss, then, are alternatives to marriage and coupling, but they are not always already outside the potential bounds of the intimate sphere in the Renaissance. Specifically, the types of relations that could be referred to as "intimate" – thereby conveying a sense of the value and pleasure derived by those involved – included erotic, non-erotic, cross-gender, and same-gender relations. In one of the earliest literary printed references to intimacy, Brian Melbancke uses the word in *Philotimus* (1583) to describe the closeness Aurelia has granted and then refused to Philotimus. It refers to a heterosexual relation, but Philotimus – whose name echoes the Latin superlative "intimus" and means "most loving" – says Aurelia has treated him as one of her "moste intimate frends" because he has received her favor and attention, not because they have had sex.[12] Yet Melbancke's use of the adjective "intimate" indicates that friendship, a relation that straddled the erotic and non-erotic in the period, was a recognized part of the intimate sphere. Kingsmill Long, in his translation of John Barclay's Latin romance *Argenis* (1625), similarly associates same-sex friendship with intimacy when he describes the warrior-statesman Arsidas as "an intimate friend to Poliarchus," the male protagonist who loves the romance's title character.[13]

Intimacy's association with heterosexual relations and its grounding in interiority were mutually reinforcing historical processes, but these processes were inchoate in Renaissance culture. To illustrate this, we can turn to John Milton's *Samson Agonistes* (1671), where Samson describes his urge to marry the Woman of Timna as arising "from intimate impulse," a phrase that encodes his inward sense that this marriage would be part of God's plan to help him deliver Israel from Philistine rule.[14] Samson's use of the word "intimate" reiterates the word's heteroerotic meanings encoded in the example from *Philotimus* but leaves behind the traditional use of the word to refer to male friendship. Yet, if we take for granted the connection between heterosexual marriage, intimacy, and inwardness, our understanding of Samson's use of "intimate" remains incomplete. Even as Samson summons the "intimate" to describe the inward origins of a cross-gender sexual relation, his marriage to the Woman of Timna cannot be completely extracted from his social relation to the Israelites and his place in God's plan for the Israelite nation. Thus, drawing on the Protestant model of experiencing an interiorized devotion to and relation with God, Milton uses "intimate" to refer to impulses that are private and interior; yet these impulses are also social and historical, coming from an external source, in a way that does not line up with many currently dominant assumptions about the intimate.

THE RISE OF AFFECTION IN MARRIAGE

Working against this complexity in the meaning of "intimate," the contraction of the intimate sphere privileged marriage as a primary locus for affection over other forms of relationality. Lawrence Stone's *The Family, Sex, and Marriage in England, 1500–1800*, providing much of the foundation for the history of marriage, notes that the nuclear family, rather than the extended family, was the common domestic unit in England; that individuals delayed marriage for some years after puberty, waiting until their twenties when they could better afford to establish a household; and that, though the nuptiality rate, at around eighty to ninety percent, varying by class and gender, was lower than in non-Western societies, marriage was commonly expected if not the common experience.[15] Marriage's statistical commonality only partly indicates its place within the relational field; Stone's account also tracks the period's increasing emphasis on "intensified affective bonding of the nuclear core at the expense of neighbors and kin."[16] Valerie Traub notes that even Stone's critics among social historians agree with him on the eventual dominance of marital companionship. During the period, she argues, "erotic desire for a domestic partner, in addition to desire for a reproductive, status-appropriate mate, became a *requirement for* (not just a happy byproduct of) the bonds between husband and wife."[17] This sense that marriage ought to be the place to experience companionship and desire governs the effacement of affectivity and value in other relational forms.

The Anglican Church's official pronouncements from the period newly emphasize the desirability of affection within marriage, and they index the role of the English Reformation in these changes in the intimate sphere. The *Homily of the State of Matrimony* (1563) reads that marriage "is instituted of God to the intent that man and woman should live lawfully in a perpetual friendly fellowship, to bring forth fruit, and to avoid fornication."[18] These three features – companionship, reproduction, and the legitimate experience of sexual pleasure – recur throughout the period's textual reflections on marriage, but companionship's importance in this formula emerges from Protestantism's increasing, though not entirely novel, emphasis on individual devotion to and relation with God. As it functioned in the triadic definition of marriage, fellowship linked two married persons together by desires experienced as interior to the body, the same space in which many Reformation thinkers placed the experience of religious devotion. Just as the idea that devotion could take place on the level of psychic depth was not new, neither was the idea that marital fellowship could take place there, but the Reformation provided a framework for a new investment of that space, and the emotional life that could be discursively situated there, with value.

Discussions of marital fellowship also often borrowed formulas of ideal friendship from classical texts, such as Aristotle's *Nicomachean Ethics* and Cicero's *De Amicitia*, which were concurrently being used by authors, such as Michel de Montaigne and Francis Bacon, to idealize friendship as a culturally valuable form of non-marital affection. Ideal friendship was supposed to connect two, and only two, friends on an internal, psychic level – the Aristotelian formulation of "one soul in two bodies." The mythic and iconic friends were almost always male couples – Damon and Pythias, Orestes and Pylades, Titus and Gisippus, and Achilles and Patroclus, to name a few among friendship's pantheon. Writers about friendship frequently warned readers against multiple friendships because the wills and affections of more than two men could not truly and unfeignedly be brought into accord; it was apparently inconceivable that three or more bodies be inhabited by one soul. As a result, the cultural value and prestige of friendship was not transferable to any relational forms other than affective dyads.

When early modern writers on marriage mined the discourse of friendship, instead of viewing marital affection as a subspecies of friendship, as Aristotle and other classical authors had, they cast friendship as a competing form of affection in order to obscure this borrowing and elevate marriage. As Jeffrey Masten has shown, the classical friendship tradition was embedded in same-sex affection and eroticism, and therefore the appropriation of this discourse to articulate marital fellowship produced in the period a resemblance between homo- and heteroeroticism that, to modern eyes, seems alien partly because of this recasting.[19] The changing status of the story of Damon and Pythias illustrates the eventual competition of same-sex friendship with marriage and heterosexual relations in the period. In Thomas Elyot's *The Boke Named the Governor* (1531) and Richard Edwards's play *Damon and Pythias* (1564), the pair are utopian tyranny-busters, but later playwrights satirize their philosophy of friendship and its relationship to heterosexual desire. In the puppet show in *Bartholomew Fair* (1614), for example, Ben Jonson conflates the "Hero and Leander" and "Damon and Pythias" stories, and the audience is treated to the spectacle of Damon and Pythias fighting with each other and with Leander over Hero, a ribald

portrayal that contrasts with the high idealism of Edwards's play. In Beaumont and Fletcher's *The Coxcomb* (1609), the iconicity of Damon and
Pythias contributes to the play's mockery of Antonio, whose friend, Mercury, has fallen in love with Antonio's wife, Maria. Antonio tries to help him
seduce Maria, thinking this service will put him in friendship's pantheon:
"We two will be . . . as famous for our friendship – / . . . / as ever *Damon*
was and *Pytheas*, or *Pylades* and *Orestes*, or any two that ever were."[20] His
iconicity is not that of a friend, but that of a fool. The laughter at Antonio this play elicits thinly disguises the fear that under friendship's guise a
cuckolder could obtain access to a man's wife.

   This reconfiguration of friendship discourse did not proceed smoothly.
In *The Two Gentlemen of Verona* and *The Two Noble Kinsmen*, for example,
heterosexual coupling seeks to secure itself at the expense of friendship,
but in the process the plays raise questions about marriage as a locus of
affection by persistently mourning the friendship that marriage would
displace. Friendship's insistence on equality conflicted with the patriarchal
inequality that was already written into marriage and was not displaced
by the increased emphasis on marital affection. Nevertheless, friendship's
emphasis on inwardness contributed to marriage's regulation of sexuality.
Though marital fellowship was supposed to connect the truest, deepest
parts of two people, the desire for fellowship required management so that
such desire was oriented toward only the spouse in the proper quantity
and spirit. When Edmund Tilney discusses how women are affected by
this inward bond in *The Flower of Friendship* (1568), he is explicit that this
fellowship requirement solicits desire and constrains the number of objects
at which such desire can be directed:

The first thing . . . which the married woman must labour to intende, the first
thing which she must withall hir force, applie hir whole minde unto, and the first
thing which she must hartilye put in execution, is to lyke, and love well. For reason
doth binde us, to love them, wyth whome we must eate, and drinke, whome we
must only accompany, of whose joyes, and sorrowes, welth, and woe, we must be
partakers, for whome we also forsake parents, friendes, and all, cleaving onely to
them, for no shorter time, then during lyfe.[21]

Even though they are essential to the bond of marriage and rationalized by
the exclusivity of marriage, desires nevertheless must be managed. While
this management was theoretically supposed to apply to both partners,
more often than not, the husband was to manage the wife's desire. Frances
Dolan explains, "for one spouse, marriage and selfhood are mutually constitutive and for the other marriage and selfhood are radically incompatible."[22]

Despite Tilney's assertion that it makes sense for a woman to form a deep bond only with her husband because she is not allowed other relations once married, women cannot be trusted with their own interiority:

In this long, and troublesome journey of matrimonie, the wise man . . . by little and little must gently procure that he maye also steale away hir private will, and appetite, so that of two bodies there may be made one onelye hart, which she will soone doe, if love raigne in hir, and without this agreeable concord matrimonie hath but small pleasure, or none at all, and the man, that is not lyked, and looved of his mate, holdeth his lyfe in continuall perill, his goodes in great jeopardie, his good name in suspect, and his whole house in utter perdition.[23]

The corporeal heart is the space wherein the "private will" is interiorized, but this rhetoric subordinates corporeality to interiority, for the body is a kind of discursive raw material whose value lies in articulating the will as a more significant aspect of personhood. Not only does monogamy seem to require a well-regulated interiority according to Tilney, but monogamy further requires that only the husband's interiorized desires be eventually reflected in his wife's interiority. In short, the one soul in these two bodies is the husband's.

Tracing shifts in the emotional content of marriage, social historians have ignored the profound changes that such shifts produced in attitudes toward other interpersonal relationships. This present study investigates dramatic and non-dramatic literary manifestations of the effect of the rise of marriage on other, less well-understood relational possibilities in the Renaissance. The institutional matrix systematically recording marriages and marital transgressions far exceeded anything available for other relations, except perhaps those involving exchange of wealth. With the vast archive of official culture, it is tempting to assume Renaissance culture's unhesitating investment in marriage and to calibrate our histories accordingly. Traub cautions us that such a methodology covers over the same history that the rise of marriage attempted to efface. She argues for an alternate approach to eroticism: "by refusing to position marriage as the stable point of origin for all analysis, we can address with greater flexibility the varying relations of eroticism to the social structures within which it has been expressed and regulated."[24] Our social histories time after time represent the culture as far more relationally homogenous than it was, but if everyone already agreed with Tilney about marriage and behaved accordingly, *The Flower of Friendship* would not exist. Outside of religious and legal discourses, there are traces of a culture that imagined a greater variety of social relations than did official culture. My analysis does not assume the historical inevitability or the desirability of centralizing relational life around marriage and coupling because such an assumption necessarily remarginalizes the understandings of the body, desire, interiority, identity, and futurity that were articulated within non-marital or non-monogamous contexts. Instead of casting these relations as failed approximations of marriage, I focus on the pleasure or value individuals within Renaissance culture found in an array of relations that did not take their cues from long-term monogamy.

This contraction of the intimate sphere drew from and furthered the reconfiguration of embodiment and interiority that took place in the early modern period. Traub even suggests "that under the regime of domestic heterosexuality, heterosexual desire was constructed in order for marriage itself to remain socially desirable."[25] I would extend Traub's assertion by arguing that such a construction was possible because of the inculcation within early modern culture of an understanding that desires of all kinds were experienced in a way internal to the body. This understanding of embodiment was not an early modern invention, but the experience of desire as a function of interiorized subjectivity helped to naturalize and normalize a connection between marriage and affection on a large scale during the early modern period. A subset of interiorized desire – heterosexual and unidirectional – became normative to support the increasing dominance of marriage as Traub indicates. Yet the construction of other interiorized non-marital, non-heterosexual desires also supported marriage, as fear of such desires disciplined the individual to submit to the regulations of the institution of marriage. Though it was possible for other forms of relationality to be based on affection, such relations were understood to falsely mimic the true, natural, and fulfilling affection that was only found in marriage.

The possibility that desire might have been constructed for certain social ends was raised by Michel Foucault, who wrote in *The History of Sexuality* that he sought "to analyze the practices by which individuals were led to focus their attention on themselves, to decipher, recognize, and acknowledge themselves as subjects of desire, bringing into play between themselves and themselves a certain relationship that allows them to discover, in desire, the truth of their being, be it natural or fallen."[26] At least from a psychoanalytic perspective, modern subjectivity seems to operate largely in the way he describes, but this is indeed the effect of a historical process. Materialist and historicist treatments of subjectivity, such as those by Francis Barker, Catherine Belsey, Jonathan Dollimore, Stephen Greenblatt, and Julian Yates have challenged the universality of the interiorized subject in the Renaissance and have argued that inwardness has changed in its figuration and cultural status through time.[27] Thomas Wright's *The Passions of the Minde* (1601) supports the idea that Renaissance and modern subjectivity are non-identical. Wright mentions that "three sortes of actions proceede from mens souls, some are internall and immateriall, as the actes of our wits & willes: others be mere externall and materiall, as the actes of our senses, seeing, hearing, moving, &c: others stand beetwixt these twoo extreames, and border upon them both."[28] In a passage that privileges disembodied interiority – actions proceed from the soul, some of which are "mere externall and materiall" – Wright ends up positing a category that is simultaneously between and bordering and, as such, collapses the bifurcation erected by the first two categories, which represent "extreames." As David Hillman has argued, "in the early modern era what we now call inwardness or interiority was inseparable from the interior of the body."[29] When Wright later indicates that "the very seate of all Passions, is the heart," the reference to the heart is corporeal, even as a metaphorical, disembodied meaning is beginning to emerge.[30] Later, when he reminds the reader that "passions ingender humors, and humours bred passions," Wright is drawing on a Renaissance conception of inwardness more materialist than our own.[31] Moreover, changes in understandings of corporeality, Hillman goes on to write, created anxiety rather than investment in inwardness as a locus of truth about the self: "the early modern obsession with inwardness should be taken as a symptom of a *loss* of a sense of access to the interior."[32] Inwardness was imaginable in the Renaissance only under vexed, contested, and changing circumstances.

I would argue that one effect of these changes in selfhood was to regulate intimate life and representations of affection. When operating via a hierarchy of internal over external spheres, criticism lacks the conceptual wherewithal to deal with relations that, for example, reverse this hierarchy, make the external and internal equivalent, or completely avoid the distinction altogether. Discussing the conceptual division of interiority and exteriority as it emerges in the period, Katharine Eisaman Maus argues that inwardness derives from the need to judge among different kinds of relationships, especially in urban spaces: "the new urbanite needed to learn to manage a wider spectrum of familiarities: from almost anonymous interactions with unknown persons, to casual attachments with acquaintances, to the intimate relationships among family members and close friends."[33]

The understanding of intimacy on which Maus relies is distinctly modern, and she sees the *need to manage* various relationships as a cause rather than an effect of the deployment of inwardness. When inwardness is advanced as the locus of truth about a person's identity, a way of differentiating and hierarchizing intersubjective bonds is a side-effect: relationships grounded in inwardness and characterized by the interchange of otherwise concealed knowledge subordinate those that are not because the former are connected with a space that, within the psychic depth model of personality, is considered a fundamental aspect of personhood. Thus, this managerial need to differentiate among relationships based on knowledge spills over from the ascendancy of the psychic depth model of subjecthood. Opacity in casual or anonymous relationships is only something requiring management when the level of connection valued between individuals is an inward one. If Renaissance England was not unequivocally invested in this model of personality, it is possible to imagine that the city brought bodies together in such a way as to offer at least the opportunity for intimacy to be understood in terms of corporeal proximity and even anonymity rather than intersubjective knowledge. As the possibility for casual encounters rises in the crowded, anonymous city, so does it become increasingly possible to imagine such encounters as pleasurable and even essential to city life, but only insofar as the model of interiorized subjectivity remains at bay, for it swoops in to denigrate such relations as superficial, insubstantial, and undesirable.

There are, however, more specific ideological consequences for grounding relationality in terms of a particular understanding of subjectivity as interiorized. One such end has been to aid marriage, insofar as it is advanced as a relation of individuals on the level of psychic depth, in its colonization of intimate life. If interiority is the privileged realm of experience, then marriage grounded in interiorized desire seems more necessary, for it is in such a relationship, so the story goes, that the self can reach its fullest potential. Yet inward selfhood, as it enables a form of relationality in which to nurture that self, comes at a price. Francis Barker claims that locating the truth about the self inwardly limits that self's bodily experiences by producing a "discoursing subject which is sceptical of its body and guilty of its sexuality."[34] In a system where the most valued forms of relationality are those that conform to a model of psychic depth, many of the pleasures of the body and its surfaces, as well as the forms of relationality in which these pleasures can be experienced, are often unthinkable or at the very least culturally unacceptable, assumed to be immature, immoral, unfulfilling, even pathological.

Psychoanalysis has played for the modern world an unrivalled role in shaping this model of psychic depth and its relationship to sexuality. For Freud, psychic depth entrenches a particular organization of the pleasures of the body and concomitantly privileges affective relations that conform to this understanding of pleasure. In *Three Essays on the Theory of Sexuality*, Freud defines the "normal sexual aim . . . as the union of the genitals in the act known as copulation which leads to a release of sexual tension and a temporary extinction of the sexual instinct."[35] The body's pleasures are subordinate to the interior hydraulics of tensions and instincts arising from the libido on whose behalf the body performs sexual acts. Indeed, the subordinated body's performance seems merely to replicate the workings of that interior world. Furthermore, insofar as psychoanalysis accounts for a subject with sexual aims and an object to which those aims are directed, its account of healthy sexuality is calibrated for the pleasures possible when only two are present for sexual activity. Healthy sexuality appears to take place with a heterosexual couple, as Freud emphasizes genital union in a way that implies the insertion of a penis into a vagina. Also highly phallocentric, this narrative presumes a subject for whom "the discharge of sexual products" can signify the release of interiorized sexual tension.[36] Thus, this account of healthy sexual pleasures is geared toward the sexual pleasure of heterosexual males interested in having one female partner at a time. Despite some ambivalence about whether the genitals just contribute their share or are primary, Freud's account indicates that sexual development subordinates the body's pleasures to genital pleasures, specifically those available to men. Other pleasures are the detritus of psychological development.

This emphasis on psychic health, however, represents only one side of the Freudian coin, as Freud expends much energy discussing the pathological, where it becomes clearer that interiority in psychoanalysis has the ostensible goal of contracting the pleasures available to the body. Consequently, forms of relationality that make different uses of the body are exempla of psychic disturbance. For Freud, perversions are either temporal or spatial: "Perversions are sexual activities which either (a) extend, in an anatomical sense, beyond the regions of the body that are designed for sexual union, or (b) linger over the intermediate relations to the sexual object which should normally be traversed rapidly on the path towards the final sexual aim."[37] I will return to the temporal perversions, but for now, I will focus on the spatial. In using the body for pleasure incorrectly, spatial perversions disturb the narrative of sexual health in which the pleasures of the body are properly shaped, arranged, organized, solicited, and constrained. Substituting the union of the genitals in copulation with some other erotic act – from fondling to anal sex, from voyeurism to masochism – involves perversely privileging an erotogenic zone other than the genitals. If we are to believe that psychic health is achievable, and there is much to say that Freud himself was unsure of this, the relational contexts that are characterized by the experience of non-standard pleasures, then, involve a person remaining to his or her detriment in a state of arrested psychic development. Recognizing that Freud's work has often been taken as more straightforward in its relationship to normative pleasure than it actually is, Leo Bersani and Adam Phillips have claimed that "psychoanalysis has mis-led us into believing, in its quest for normative life stories . . . that intimacy is by definition personal intimacy."[38] Consequently, affective relations that involve the pleasurable "misuse" of the body, at least according to the strands within the psychoanalytic tradition to which Bersani and Phillips object, cannot signify as intimate.

Whether Freud himself believed psychic health was illusory is less relevant in approaching Renaissance texts than the fact that voices from the period speak about experiences of pleasure, relationality, and sex according to a logic incongruent with the psychoanalytic account as it has sometimes been universalized. While I do not resist allowing psychoanalysis to inflect my account when it can offer assistance, this economy of psychic depth and health was not culturally dominant in the Renaissance, which in turn may have allowed cultural value to accrue to a broad array of affective relations that currently are understood as non-normative. There is no evidence to support the common assumption that sexual activity has universally been about the satisfaction of interiorized desires and the release of sexual tension through ejaculation and orgasm. In fact, material circumstances affect sexual practices and attitudes toward them. In a detailed passage that merits quoting at length, G. R. Quaife notes that clothing may have influenced sexual practice in the Renaissance in such a way that fondling may have been fairly common and tolerated:

The clothing worn by prospective sexual partners in part may have influenced the nature and sequence of love-making. The male usually wore breeches that were loosely tied at the waist and the female covered her lower body with a smock and one or more petticoats. The upper body was covered by a more complex lace bodice. Consequently, the male had almost immediate access to the girl below the waist by the single act of flinging up her smock, and therefore during intercourse the girl was always naked from the waist down. The simple disrobing was to 'pull up her clothes' above her middle, and 'to untie his breeches.' Perhaps it was this ease of access that accounted for the dominant form of advanced sexual activity, the manual stimulation of the penis, clitoris, and vagina. Many a wench took her man 'by the privy members and rolled them up and down in her hands', and was similarly accessible to her lover – even on horseback.[39]

Renaissance clothing allowed for what Freud would describe as normal sexual activity, genital union, though it prevented much interpersonal contact with the upper body. However, as Quaife shows, clothing promoted another means for non-penetrative sexual pleasure. These alternate sexual practices may have been satisfying without always having been organized around orgasm and ejaculation. Moreover, while the avoidance of pregnancy through non-penetrative sexual activity is available to married and unmarried persons alike, the availability of non-reproductive sexual practices may have fostered greater sexual contact among unmarried, possibly non-monogamous partners in the wake of the stigma of illegitimacy in the Renaissance.

This somewhat more permissive attitude toward sexuality outside of marriage changed in the face of increasing insistence that sexual acts culminate in orgasm, and the attendant threat of illegitimate reproduction meant marriage would have a greater monopoly on sexual acts, pleasure, and ultimately relationality itself. Henry Abelove's analysis of demographic data suggests that the common phenomenon Quaife describes was not always demonized in the Renaissance, even though the pursuit of pleasure via non-penetrative acts would achieve the status of a perversion in modern psychoanalysis. In eighteenth-century England, Abelove writes, "sexual intercourse so-called . . . [became] discursively and phenomenologically central in many ways that it had never been before [and] . . . nonreproductive sexual behaviors came under extraordinary negative pressure."[40] The historical process Abelove describes is the normalization of sexual acts based on the satisfaction, through the release of orgasm, of interiorized desires. With sex organized around acts that carry a higher potential for reproduction, the stigma of illegitimacy makes marriage even more central to the sexual economy. The ascendancy of marriage may have thus been implicated in a material change in sexual practice and an epistemological-historical change in the status of desire as motivating sexual acts. The assertion that desire is historical, rather than universal, then, allows one to show how a certain relational form achieved dominance over a broader field of interpersonal relations. More importantly, the historicization of desire reveals in the early modern period an evaporating diversity – of pleasures, of satisfying relational forms – that often goes unrecognized when one assumes pleasure can only be found where there is desire and its satisfaction. This evaporation is an effect of the increasing cultural investment in interiority as the locus of truth about the subject; in the analysis of representations of affection from the past, it is important to remember that this investment in inwardness was at most partial in Renaissance culture, and thus it would have been possible for Renaissance authors to valorize a wide array of affective relations.

NARRATIVES OF INTIMACY

Along with interiorized desire, access to futurity through long-term monogamy and, often, reproduction characterizes modern normative intimacy. A flexible, polyvocal narrative style in the Renaissance, however, enabled authors to valorize alternate intimate economies not governed by futurity even alongside representations of normative forms of intimacy. The circulation of texts shapes a society's understanding of relationality because texts offer readers scripts for their own relational lives, whether that society is the United States at the turn of the twenty-first century or England at the turn of the seventeenth. The long-term couple form's narratives have played such a delimiting role in modern understandings of intimacy that it is difficult to appreciate temporary, situational affection. In his social history of intimacy, Anthony Giddens writes that "romantic love . . . provides for a long-term life trajectory, oriented to an anticipated, yet malleable future."[41] For coupling, romantic love is the "happily ever after" narrative *par excellence* wherein the value of intimacy is equated with its permanence, and relational forms with no interest in permanence are undesirable. The possible value of short-term affective relations prompts us to ask, in Roland Barthes's words, "why is it better to *last* than to *burn*?"[42] I bring this question to bear on Renaissance texts' representations of intimacies unassimilable to the norms governing long-term monogamy.

In their texts, authors can imagine either a heterogeneity of relational possibilities or a constricted field of affective relations. Lauren Berlant has noted that the latter has occurred in modernity such that "desires for intimacy that bypass the couple or the life narrative it generates have no alternative plots."[43] Berlant calls for the generation of alternate plots in new texts, a mission whose value I would not contest. However, texts already in circulation encode these alternate plots, while reading practices that focus on closure ignore or render these possibilities unintelligible. I agree with D. A. Miller that acts of meaning-making based on closure produce an interpretive tautology that renders closure's definitive status unassailable: "once the ending is enshrined as an all-embracing cause in which the elements of a narrative find their ultimate justification, it is difficult for analysis to assert anything short of total coherence."[44] In other words, that which occurs in the middle of a narrative and which does not contribute to the achievement of closure becomes, to use Peter Brooks's terms, "postponement and error."[45] The eradication of elements of "postponement and error" stabilize narrative closure, but, within many standard accounts of narrative, they have no value in and of themselves.

In moments of narrative closure, certain affective relations, such as the monogamous couple form, are guaranteed futurity, and, in the process, temporary or situational intimacies are emptied of their value, an emptying reinforced by reading strategies that privilege closure. Narrative is related to intimacy in part by way of Freud's account of temporal perversions. For Freud, the sexual act follows a narrative trajectory structured by a rigid causality: "the normal sexual aim is regarded as being the union of the genitals in the act known as copulation which leads to a release of the sexual tension and a temporary extinction of the sexual instinct."[46] Miller describes the way Freud's sexual model has been translated into narrative theory's characterization of closure as a kind of release. He distinguishes between two aspects of narrative: the narratable, or the dynamic elements of a plot that propel it; and the non-narratable, or the static elements of a plot, including closure. The task some narrative theorists ask of closure is the "ridding the text of all traces of the narratable," but Miller argues that a text cannot completely achieve this goal.[47] Just as closure in narrative is supposed to extinguish the narratable, so non-pathological sexuality is supposedly guided by the principle that the moment of orgasm through genital copulation accompanies the momentary extinction of the same instinct that first propelled the sexual activity.

For Freud the temporal perversions "linger over the intermediate relations to the sexual object which should normally be traversed rapidly on the path towards the final sexual aim."[48] This lingering disturbs the narrative structure of normal sexual activity. Nevertheless, normalcy frequently remains fantasmatic: "Even in the most normal sexual process, we may detect rudiments which, if they had developed would lead to the deviations described as perversions."[49] The complications, complexities, and contradictions Freud introduces into his own model at least temporarily allow the perversions to exist non-pathologically and, consequently, suggest the fictiveness of narrativizing sexuality exclusively in terms of the orgasmic closure of genital copulation. If we translate these possibilities into the terms of narrative theory, Freud's work opens up a space for a

reading practice in which it is desirable to attend to elements of a text that
do not contribute to the intensification of closural satisfaction and may,
in fact, be part of an alternative economy of pleasure, satisfaction, and
affection.

Recent work on queer temporality and futurity can help readers excavate
these alternate narrative and intimate economies. Lee Edelman has argued
that heterosexual reproduction figures centrally in political calls to action
in which a better future is imagined through "the pervasive invocation
of the Child as the emblem of futurity's unquestioned value."[50] Insofar as
"that Child remains the perpetual horizon of every acknowledged politics,"
sexual reproduction delimits the terms through which political action can
be undertaken or even imagined.[51] This political order, Edelman argues,
has placed queerness in opposition to futurity: "Far from partaking of this
narrative movement toward a viable political future . . . the queer comes
to figure the bar to every realization of futurity, the resistance, internal
to the social, to every social structure or form."[52] Translating Edelman's
argument into more explicitly literary terms, I would suggest that queerness
resists narrative closure from within a text because closure supposedly
secures futurity. Closure seeks to guarantee such futurity by representing or
gesturing toward marriage, the offspring who, legitimated by that marriage,
propagate the social order, or death, which allows the social order to be
passed on to the next generation. Reading practices that equate closure
with textual endorsement assent to closure's tacit norms, including the
enshrinement of the long-term couple form. Thus, alternate approaches,
which do not replicate the normalizing processes of closure, are called for
in order to attend to these non-normative relationalities.

Not all of the power resides with the author's encoding. While many
of the texts that I discuss direct the reader toward an appreciation of their
representations of the non-normative, sometimes even representing such a
dissident reader as narrator or character, Alan Sinfield rightly notes that it is
"a mistake to regard the grain (always) as a property of the text" and not of
a hegemonic critical tradition.[53] Even when they are not explicitly pointed
to a counternarrative by an author or a text, readers still can perform a kind
of *bricolage* with the unassimilable, transgressive, and pleasurable elements
that are even part of representations hostile to queer affections.[54] Thus, the
meaning-making practice I am articulating is situated at the interaction
of text and reader or audience member. As long as a text circulates, this
bricolage is possible because readers and audience members can experiment
with its intimate scripts to discover and perform new pleasures and forms
of relationality.

L Iue with me and be my Loue,
And we will all the pleasures proue .
That hilles and vallies, dales and fields,
And all the craggy mountaines yeeld.

There will we fit vpon the Rocks,
And fee the Shepheards feed their flocks,
By fhallow Riuers, by whofe fals
Melodious birds fing Madrigals.

There will I make thee a bed of Rofes,
With a thoufand fragrant pofes,
A cap of flowers. and a Kirtle
Imbiodered all with leaues of Mirtle.

A belt of ftraw and Yuye buds,
With Corall Clafps and Amber ftuds,
And if thefe pleafures may thee moue,
Then liue with me, and be my Loue.

Louers anfwere.

IF that the World and Loue were young,
And truth in euery fhepheards toung,
Thefe pretty pleafures might me moue,
To liue with thee and be thy Loue.

Figure 1 *The Passionate Pilgrim* (London, 1599) signature D5r–v. Reproduced by permission of the Huntington Library, San Marino, California, and ProQuest. Further reproduction is prohibited without permission. Image produced by ProQuest as part of *Early English Books Online.*

LITERARY INVITATIONS TO INTIMACY

To illustrate these points about inwardness, futurity, and the early modern contest over intimacy as they emerge in literary texts, I turn to the poems currently known as Christopher Marlowe's "The Passionate Shepherd to His Love" and Sir Walter Ralegh's "The Nymph's Reply to the Shepherd." Familiar to students of Renaissance poetry and students of poetry in general, both poems meditate on the possibility of creating a life with another person based on an affective bond. The earliest of the printed versions of these poems appears in William Jaggard's 1599 miscellany, *The Passionate Pilgrim*, as an untitled four-stanza poem inviting its addressee to lavish and sensual pleasures followed by a one-stanza reply (Figure 1). In Nicholas Ling's 1600 *England's Helicon*, the invitation and reply both have six stanzas (Figure 2). The three editions of *The Passionate Pilgrim* by 1612 and three Renaissance manuscripts with similar four-stanza versions of the invitation suggest that the long and short versions had currency in the period. *The Passionate Pilgrim* version's specific historical and ideological effects are as important as but not reducible to those in the *England's Helicon* version. When

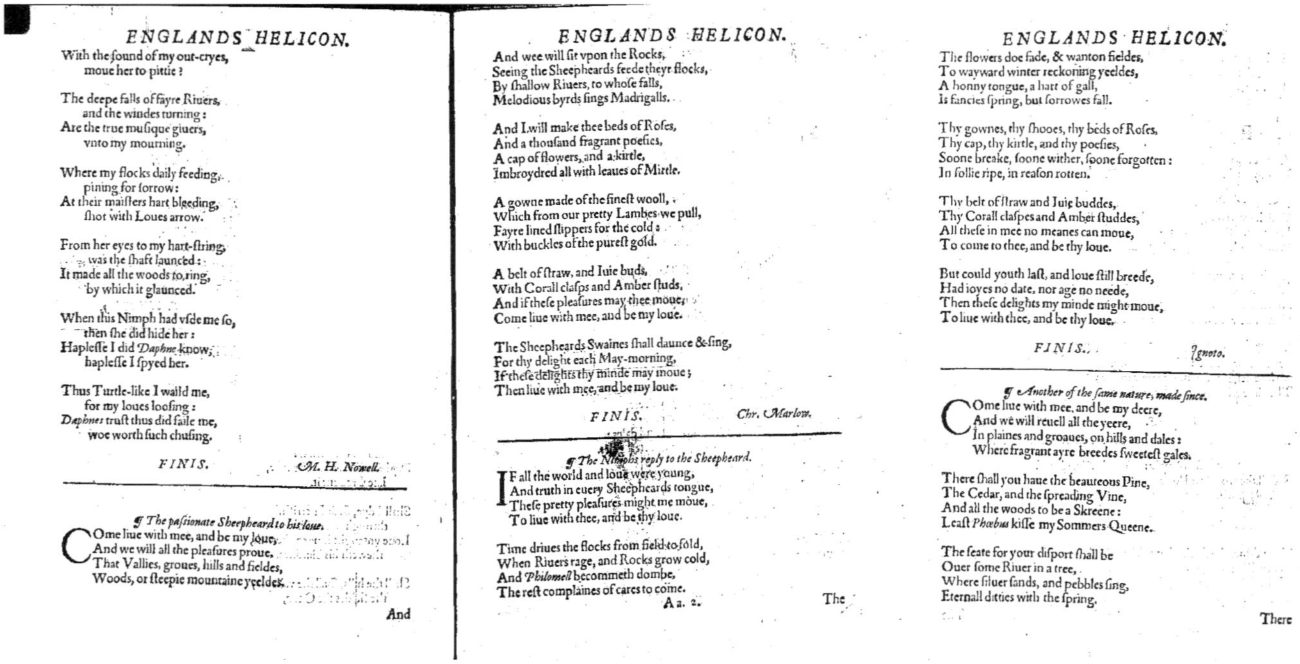

With the found of my out-cryes,
    moue her to pittie?

The deepe falls of fayre Riuers,
    and the winde turning:
Are the true mufique giuers,
    vnto my mourning.

Where my flocks daily feeding,
    piping for forrow:
At their mafters hart bleeding,
    fhot with Loues arrow.

From her eyes to my hart-ftring,
    was the fhaft launced:
In made all the woods to ring,
    by which I glaunced.

When this Nimph had vide me fo,
    then fhe did hide her:
Hapleffe I did *Daphne* know,
    hapleffe I fpyed her.

Thus Turtle-like I will me,
    for my loues loofing:
Daphne truft thus did faile me,
    woe worth fuch chufing.

FINIS.   M. H. Nowell.

¶ *The paffionate Sheepheardto his loue.*

Ome liue with mee, and be my loue,
And we will all the pleafures proue,
That Vallies, groues, hills and fieldes,
Woods, or fteepie mountaine yeeldes.

And

And wee will fit vpon the Rockes,
Seeing the Sheepheards feede their flocks,
By fhallow Riuers, to whofe falls,
Melodious byrds fings Madrigalls.

And I will make thee beds of Rofes,
And a thoufand fragrant pofies,
A cap of flowers, and a kirtle,
Imbroydred all with leaues of Mirtle.

A gowne made of the fineft wooll,
Which from our pretty Lambes we pull;
Fayre lined flippers for the cold:
With buckles ofthe pureft gold.

A belt of ftraw, and Iuie buds,
With Corall clafps and Amber ftuds,
And if thefe pleafures may thee moue,
Come liue with mee, and be my loue.

The Sheepheards Swaines fhall daunce &fing,
For thy delight each May-morning,
If thefe delights thy minde may moue;
Then liue with mee, and be my loue.

FINIS.   Chr. Marlow.

¶The Nimphs reply to the Sheepheard.

IF all the world and loue were young,
And truth in euery Sheepheards tongue,
Thefe pretty pleafures might me moue,
To liue with thee, and be thy loue.

Time driues the flocks from fielde to fold,
When Riuers rage, and Rocks grow cold,
And *Philomell* becommeth dombe,
The reft complaines of cares to come.

Aa. 2.   The

The flowers doe fade, & wanton fieldes,
To wayward winter reckoning yeldes,
A hony tongue, a hart of gall,
Is fancies fpring, but forrowes fall.

Thy gownes, thy fhooes, thy beds of Rofes,
Thy cap, thy kirtle, and thy pofies,
Soone breake, foone wither, foone forgotten:
In follie ripe, in reafon rotten.

Thy belt of ftraw and Iuie buddes,
Thy Corall clafpes and Amber ftuddes,
All thefe in mee no meanes can moue,
To come to thee, and be thy loue.

But could youth laft, and loue ftill breede,
Had ioyes no date, nor age no neede,
Then thefe delights my minde might moue,
To liue with thee, and be thy loue.

FINIS.   Ignoto.

¶ *Another of the fame nature, made fince.*

Ome liue with mee, and be my deere,
And we will reuell all the yeere,
In plaines and groaues, on hills and dales:
Where fragrant ayre breeds fweeteft gales.

There fhall you haue the beauteous Pine,
The Cedar, and the fpreading Vine,
And all the woods to be a Skreene:
Leaft *Phœbus* kiffe my Sommers Queene.

The feate for your difport fhall bee
Ouer fome Riuer in a tree,
Where filuer fands, and pebbles fing,
Eternall ditties with the fpring,

There

Figure 2 *England's Helicon* (London, 1600) signature AA1v–AA2v. © The British Library Board. Image published with permission of ProQuest. Image produced by ProQuest as part of *Early English Books Online*. Further reproduction is prohibited without permission.

juxtaposed, the 1599 and 1600 versions of the exchange show that "making a life" was a site of contestation in the Renaissance, and each text is situated differently in that debate by virtue of its individual rhetorical structures. In these rhetorical differences, the poems stage the debate over the nature of intimacy and its relation to temporality, pleasure, and inwardness.

Critics have noted that features specific to the *England's Helicon* pairing have a normalizing effect on the poems' representation of affective relations. In *England's Helicon*, the poems have titles that stabilize the gender of the speaker and addressee and thus decide that the poems depict heterosexual relations, even though the invitation poem has no gendered pronouns in it and the homoerotic was conventional in pastoral literature.[55] Furthermore, this invitation poem creates a vision of intimacy that differs fundamentally from that in *The Passionate Pilgrim* on bases other than gender. In *The Passionate Pilgrim*, the reply weakly challenges the invitation poem's vision of short-term intimacy focused on the pleasures of surfaces. However, *England's Helicon*'s reply rejects this vision and defines intimacy as the experience of interiorized desire within long-term coupledom. While this understanding of intimacy has become standard in Western culture, the existence of these two versions of the exchange suggests that it was possible to think of affective relations in multiple ways in the Renaissance. Indeed, only through elements specific to the *England's Helicon* pairing do the poems line up with modern normative intimacy.

The four-stanza *Passionate Pilgrim* invitation contains much of the same sensual detail as its counterpart in *England's Helicon*, with the exception of the latter's wool gown stanza (stanza 3). Yet this stanza conflicts with the speaker's almost contractual sense that the invitation is to temporally bounded pleasures. Saying that they will make a wool gown and "Fayre lined slippers for the cold" ("Passionate Sheepheard" 15), the *Helicon* speaker suggests that the landscape will turn harsh and unpleasant and their relationship will endure even when there are no more pleasures to prove, which is inconsistent with the logic of the offer in stanza one.[56] Further complicating the *England's Helicon* invitation, the final stanza repeats the request to "live with mee, and be my love" ("Passionate Sheepheard" 24) with which the penultimate stanza ends. This is repetition with a difference, for this stanza introduces a reference to time that seems out of place and that contradicts the wool gown stanza by indicating that the temporality of the relation is specifically bounded: "The Sheepheards Swains shall daunce & sing, / For thy delight each May-morning" ("Passionate Sheepheard" 21–22). Their time together – thirty-one spring mornings if "May" is taken literally or one season if "May" stands in metonymically for spring – will not last until woolen gowns and slippers will be required. The temporal contradictions particular to the *England's Helicon* version of the invitation make its argument seem duplicitous in a way that the speaker cannot fully cover over.

This final stanza of the 1600 version also relocates the pleasures the speaker describes from material surfaces to non-material depths. In both, the invitation's speaker spends most of the poem describing immediate, sensual pleasures – they will listen to harmonious birds while wearing an organic wardrobe of fine wool and flowers, accessorized by gems. The 1600 version, however, concludes with an appeal to interiority, "If these delights thy minde may move, / Then live with mee, and be my love" ("Passionate Sheepheard" 23–24), even though these delights are more corporeal than intellectual. In contrast, the final lines of *The Passionate Pilgrim* version are "And if these pleasures may thee move, / Then live with mee and be my Love" (15–16), a rendering of the line that does not subordinate the body to the disembodied mind. Thus, just as *England's Helicon* invitation introduces a long-range temporality in the wool gown stanza, in the sixth stanza the speaker brings interiority into a situation that had little to do with it.

The elements that are specific to the invitation poem in *England's Helicon* and lacking in *The Passionate Pilgrim* version are exploited in the *Helicon*'s reply to argue that long-term affection grounded in psychic depth is better than immediate, short term, sensual pleasure. While it appears that the *England's Helicon* poems, with the same number of stanzas, are argumentatively on an equal footing, in fact the additional stanzas of the six-stanza invitation make its argument thematically more inconsistent when compared to that of the *Passionate Pilgrim* and consequently rhetorically weaker in the face of the *Helicon* reply. As Douglas Bruster notes, "the Nymph's reply argues against an eternizing conceit never made fully explicit by Marlowe's shepherd."[57] Time corrodes the pleasures depicted in the invitation, insists the reply's speaker, whose mention of the reckoning of "wayward winter" links up with the reference to cold weather in stanza four of the invitation in *England's Helicon* ("Nimphs Reply" 10). Here, the speaker responds to a stanza that is proper to the *England's Helicon* version and that contradicts what the rest of the poem says about the invitation speaker's attitude toward the long-term potential of their life together. *England's Helicon*'s reply claims that the invitation speaker offers an untenable long-term commitment to pleasure, and the speaker castigates the addressee for offering superficial temptations rather than deep, abiding affection. Doubting that there is "truth in every Sheepheards tongue" ("Nimphs Reply" 2), the reply's speaker suggests that the addressee, whom the *England's Helicon* version's titles refer to as a shepherd, knows that time decays pastoral pleasures, but lies by omission to make the vision of their life together more attractive. These pleasures, the speaker concludes, are trifles, "in follie ripe, in reason rotten" ("Nimphs Reply" 16), and they serve as a poor foundation for the kind of relationship the reply speaker desires.

The invitation's speaker offers pleasure in the form of adornments that might be called superficial, in the sense of dealing with surfaces, but the reply also claims these pleasures are superficial in the sense of insubstantial and inconsequential. The reply's speaker prefers psychic depth and inwardness in affective relations. In stanzas three through five of the invitation, the speaker offers the addressee intricately designed clothing, from "a cap of flowers, and a kirtle, / Imbroydred all with leaves of Mirtle" ("Passionate Sheepheard" 11–12) to "a belt of straw, and Ivie buds, / With Corall clasps and Amber studs" ("Passionate Sheepheard" 17–18). These items are visually appealing, and the natural fibers could be construed as pleasurable to wear, especially for the surfaces of the body that touch the clothes. For the reply speaker, however, they are inherently deceptive because they are associated with surfaces and because they can deteriorate over time. Just as a "honny tongue" can hide a "hart of gall" ("Nimphs Reply" 11), the immediacy of these pleasures distracts attention from their eventual deterioration and, consequently, their triviality. The heart, as a material symbol of interiority, contains the truth about a person, and the tongue, using language to bridge the gap between interior and exterior, can never fully communicate that truth. Contaminated by its association with exteriority, the tongue is always potentially deceitful. Thus, according to the reply, true intimacy involves a long-term relation where depths are the sites of connection between the partners.

England's Helicon's presentation of the exchange suggests that the reply merely points out inadequacies in the invitation that any reader would acknowledge. However, the reply actively shapes our understanding of the invitation as inadequate. In the *Passionate Pilgrim* invitation, the limited duration of the life together that the speaker imagines is unqualified, but in *England's Helicon*, this glance at short-range temporality is muddied by features specific to the 1600 version that the reply speaker exploits as the basis for a demand for lifelong commitment. Indeed, these contradictory features allow the reply poem to argue for its version of long-term, profound intimacy without appearing to go outside the bounds set up by the invitation poem. The long-term life trajectory that the reply speaker desires does not figure at all in the *Passionate Pilgrim* version of the invitation and seems out of place when it is implied in the *England's Helicon* version, but this lack of emphasis on futurity does not mean that the invitation speaker should be read as dishonest. In *England's Helicon*, the invitation speaker offers pleasures that are unlikely to deteriorate extensively in the course of a month or season, if we take the "May morning" reference to set up the temporal boundaries of the offer. The reply poem in *England's Helicon* denies that pleasures might be unmoored from futurity and interiority and still produce intimacy. Yet this possibility is precisely what is imagined in the *Passionate Pilgrim* and, at least partially, the *England's Helicon* invitations, and my juxtaposition of these exchanges points to the multiple, even contradictory ways that intimacy could be imagined in the Renaissance.[58]

It may surprise modern readers that such a debate would be staged in printed, publicly consumed literary texts; one might instead expect the key texts to engage questions about intimacy to be journals, letters, and other "private" writings. Even though such "private" texts often involved some form of public circulation or consumption (just as these poems have privately circulated manuscript forms), I focus on literature to trouble more directly the equation of intimacy and privacy. It is tempting to assume that non-literary texts give us clearer access to intimacy as it was actually practiced in the period, but letters and journals provide us no less mediated access to the period's intimate economies. Literature's imaginative dimension also interests me; literary texts function for me as an archive of possibilities, gestures, suggestions, and alternatives that potentially push on the margins of the practices of everyday life and the boundaries of the intimate sphere. Though many of the texts I discuss are plays, I bring together drama, poetry, and prose to examine texts' conflicting and conflicted investments in various forms of affective relations. These generically diverse texts are often not literary in the same way in the period, and they were produced under varying circumstances for different audiences. Their genres inflect without predetermining the particular contests over the nature of intimacy that appear in these texts. Nevertheless, I aim to show that the effects of the narrowing of the intimate sphere were widespread in the period, and equally widespread was the textual circulation of knowledge about alternatives to this narrower version of intimacy. Many Renaissance authors experimented with generic conventions, such that isolating genres from one another seems inapt for thinking about literary production in the period. Further, a rigidly essentialist approach to genre, as opposed to a nuanced dialogue among canonical and non-canonical texts of different genres, can prohibit inquiry from complicating dominant understandings of Renaissance sexuality and culture.

In the discussion that follows, I survey a number of texts that imagine, sometimes seemingly for the purposes of prohibiting, intimate relations outside of long-term monogamous coupling motivated by interiorized desire. The non-marital form of affection that probably is most often imagined in Renaissance texts is male friendship, which has some purchase on normative status during the period in terms of intimacy as long-term coupling grounded in interiorized desire, even though it was increasingly represented at best in an uneasy coexistence with marriage, as I showed above. While many questions remain about Renaissance friendship and other non-normative intimacies, like prostitution and incest, I instead focus on affective relations whose conflict with marriage and coupling were more localized and have not received as much critical attention in the terms of embodiment and narrativity through which I investigate them. I begin in Chapter 1 by articulating a non-teleological reading practice that is calibrated to Renaissance texts that separate narrative closure from textual endorsement in order to contest the dominance of long-term monogamy over the intimate sphere. Drawn from Christopher Marlowe's *Hero and Leander*, this reading practice allows me to recuperate the value such texts ascribe to temporary and situational bonds even when their narrative trajectories ostensibly move toward monogamous coupling. That is, the practice is sensitive to the narrative forms in which it is possible to represent and valorize forms of intimacy that do not pattern themselves on the narrative of the long-term monogamous couple.

The remainder of the book applies this reading practice to a variety of texts – dramatic and non-dramatic – that imagine, however briefly, alternatives to long-term monogamy grounded in interiorized desire. I have chosen texts that, like *Hero and Leander*, have a narrative trajectory toward coupling but also have counternarrative currents that circulate knowledge about ostensible "failures of intimacy." Chapter 2 discusses the challenge to marriage, inwardness, and futurity posed by anal pleasure between men in two Shakespeare plays. In Chapter 3 I examine how masochism in Renaissance drama enables the reimagining of hierarchical social relations and fosters erotic male-male relations unmediated by marriage. Dramatic representations of the communal relations in the convents, especially their potential to interrupt the sexual circulation of women and their threat to emerging notions about the nation, are the subject of Chapter 4. Finally, I analyze in Chapter 5 the ways that cross-racial and same-sex affection combine to differentiate non-standard relational forms from normative heteroerotic bonds in the poetry and prose of Lady Mary Wroth. Though the intimate possibilities that these chapters investigate are often fleetingly entertained in Renaissance texts, they are nevertheless made intelligible to their various readers and audiences. As these representations circulate, they function as potential scripts for the intimate lives of their audiences and readers. Thus, as these texts encode resistance to the increasing dominance of long-term monogamy over the intimate sphere, their circulation also enables such resistance. The "failure" of these forms of relationality to signify as intimate, then, is never entirely the final word.

CHAPTER I

Intimacy and narrative closure in Christopher Marlowe's Hero and Leander

HAPPILY EVER AFTER: NARRATIVE CLOSURE AND AFFECTIVE RELATIONS

To many readers of Renaissance texts, Christopher Marlowe's name serves as a by-word for dissident sexuality in the period. Yet, as Stephen Orgel has recently suggested, though work on Marlowe has made sexual dissidence in the Renaissance visible for modern readers, the assumption that Marlowe himself was a sexual rebel rests on the testimony of his enemies and on a conflation of the author with his characters.[1] A narrow pursuit of the biographical relevance of his texts obscures questions about how those texts are situated within his culture; furthermore, such a dualistic view – either he (or his text) is or is not queer – effaces the complexities of both Marlowe's writing and Renaissance attitudes toward sexuality. Though the intimate sphere was coalescing around long-term monogamy in the period, the modern outcome of this process was by no means inevitable, and neither marginality nor outsider status was a prerequisite for contesting it. Marlowe's *Hero and Leander*, in its representation of short-term, situational intimacy, challenges the centrality of the long-term monogamous couple in terms that were also widely available to his culture and accessible to his readers.

Historical research into intimate life reveals that while texts from the period touted long-term coupledom, practices differed markedly from this ideal because of low life expectancies, the late age of marriage, and the frequency of remarriage in the period. Lawrence Stone argues that "the incessant preaching on the imminence of death must have been a constant reminder of the essential transience of all human relationships. In practice, the probability of a durable marriage was low, since it was likely to be broken before very long by the death of the husband or the wife."[2] According to Stone, the average early modern English first marriage lasted about seventeen years and almost a quarter of all marriages performed during the period were remarriages. While seventeen years is not short-term, it stands to reason that individuals entertained the possibility that for at least one partner, a marital relationship might be temporary and succeeded by another. Stone, controversially, has concluded from this high mortality rate that closeness, between parents and children and between husband and wife, must have been unlikely and imprudent.[3] In contrast, Alan Macfarlane advises caution in deducing from these figures early modern attitudes toward marriage: "If marriages were relatively vulnerable and partners often replaced, does this tell us anything of the depth of the emotion involved? The problem is a complex one, for swift remarriage can be interpreted in two ways: as evidence of lack of affection – or as the opposite."[4] The "opposite" situation, according to Macfarlane, is one wherein a widow or widower finds affection in marriage so plentiful and pleasurable in spite of the possibility of losing a partner, that one is willing to risk marriage again. Macfarlane exposes the equation of longevity and intimacy that operates in Stone's interpretation of these data, and he suggests that relations in the Renaissance, including marriage itself, may not all have been evaluated based on their longevity. Only when marriage attempts to assert itself over the entire relational field does it elevate longevity as a signifier of pleasure and value and, in turn, advance itself, somewhat fantastically and fictitiously, as the definitive long-term relation. One has to remain open to the possible significance of short-term relations in texts from the Renaissance, when this transition had not been fully achieved.

Narrative, interpretive, and intimate practices intersect in *Hero and Leander* in ways that can also help us understand the competing forms of relationality represented in Renaissance literature more generally. The poem is an erotic text preoccupied with the way erotic texts are read. Erotic texts circulate everywhere within the poem: from Hero's gown on whose sleeves Venus and Adonis are portrayed, to portraits of "the gods in sundrie shapes, / Committing headdie ryots, incest, rapes," in the floor of Venus's temple.[5] The poem's commencement during Sestos's annual solemn feast of Adonis implies that a heteroerotic mythic text, incorporated into the Sestian calendar, structures the day-to-day existence of Sestos's citizens. Even the title characters' bodies are erotic texts. When Leander presses his suit to Hero, "at everie word shee turn'd aside" (195) in seeming displeasure; however, Hero's love seems to be transparent to all who know how to read her body's signals. She trembles after Leander touches her hand, prompting the narrator to remark "Love deeply grounded, hardly is dissembled" (184).

For Leander, as Gregory Woods observes, "only those who desire him can read him."[6] The narrator becomes one such reader when he remarks of Leander's first verbal attempts at seduction, "Now begins Leander to display / Loves holy fire, with words, with sighs and teares" (192–193). Eventually, according to the narrator, "Even as an Index to a booke, / So to his mind was yoong Leanders looke" (613–614). His status as a lover is legible to anyone who can properly read his face.

This pervasive concern with the reading of erotic texts results from a sense that texts circulating within a culture act as scripts for intimate life, but the textual scripting of intimate life that *Hero and Leander* recognizes is not as straightforward as it might appear. The historical relationship, or lack thereof, of Renaissance narrative texts, including prose, poetry, and drama, to more recent narrative practices mandates a different approach to reading representations of intimacy insofar as current approaches are thoroughly bound up with novelistic teleology. Lorna Hutson has compellingly argued for the revision of the history of narrative forms that casts English Renaissance prose fiction as a precursor to the novel. In her words, "sixteenth-century developments in prose fiction are not part of a teleological evolution of historical consciousness."[7] Readers with "modern expectations of narrative coherence" may be disappointed by Renaissance prose, where "competing interpretations of the same set of narrative circumstances are offered to the reader without one being privileged or authorized over another."[8] I would expand Hutson's argument beyond Elizabethan prose to suggest that many Renaissance poetic and dramatic narratives also resemble what Roland Barthes calls "texts of pleasure" that resist closure by being "outside any imaginable finality."[9] Renaissance writers employed a variety of narrative strategies, some of which bear no relation to the teleologies to which later narratological reading strategies are calibrated. Many Renaissance texts leave significant room for doubt about whether what is achieved in their moments of closure is what the texts endorse, and this space of doubt makes room for the potential valorization of intimacies not guaranteed futurity by narrative. What follows, then, is a critique of the dominance of closure-based reading strategies in the form of a demonstration of those practices' impoverishing effects upon representations of intimate life and pleasure. Where these reading strategies are unable to index these possibilities in Renaissance narrative texts, the non-teleological approach that I shall advance by way of *Hero and Leander* can attend to the alternative forms of relationality that various Renaissance texts imagine, experiment with, and make available to their readers or audiences.

"LET IT SUFFISE": NON-PENETRATIVE SEXUAL PRACTICES,
NARRATIVE, AND SITUATIONAL INTIMACY IN *HERO AND LEANDER*

Implicit in *Hero and Leander*'s advocacy of non-teleological reading is
the argument that a different way of reading an erotic text will result in
changes in intimate life and sexual practice. From a teleological perspective,
it does appear, as Bruce R. Smith argues, that the poem is entirely "about
desire's frustration" and that "we never get to see sexual activity."[10] Yet,
unlike modern mainstream romantic comedies and some pornographic
films, Marlowe's poem undoes the equation of narrative and sexual consummation; here, sexual penetration neither signifies the *sine qua non* of
sexual activity nor does it carry the privilege that "consummation" would
potentially confer upon it. In Judith Haber's words, the poem is characterized by a "disruption of end-directed sexuality."[11] The story of the title
characters not only seems to be without a stable closural moment, but
the text also calls into question the very desirability or possibility of stable
closural moments in narratives. Seemingly setting up a typical structure of
deferred consummation, both narrative and sexual, the poem makes clear
that on his first visit to Hero's tower, Leander does not sexually penetrate
Hero. The narrator remarks of Leander, "dallying with Hero, nothing saw
/ That might delight him more, yet he suspected / Some amorous rites or
others were neglected" (546–548). In a teleological reading of the scene, the
humor of this episode is that Leander does not know what to do with Hero
now that he has won her. Yet the poem makes a space for the pleasures
of aimless "dallying" even if Leander's suspicions of lack move the reader
away from such pleasures. His attempt to perform these "amorous rites or
others" mixes humor at Leander's expense with non-penetrative pleasure:

> Therefore unto his bodie, hirs he clung,
> She, fearing on the rushes to be flung,
> Striv'd with redoubled strength, the more she strived,
> The more a gentle pleasing heat revived,
> Which taught him all that elder lovers know,
> And now that same gan so to scorch and glow,
> As in plaine terms (yet cunningly) he crav'd it,
> Love always makes those eloquent that have it.
> (549–556)

As he rubs his body against Hero's, Leander is met with terror as she thinks
he is going to throw her down. Her struggle provides more non-penetrative
stimulation for Leander's body, but his arousal is recast teleologically, possibly through the reference to "all that elder lovers know," such that Leander

figures out that penetration is the amorous rite he neglected. "Cunningly" is available as a pun on the female genitals, and thus he turns his energies toward the pursuit of genital intercourse. Leander's eventually exclusive desire for Hero's maidenhead through sexual penetration recasts all the pleasures of this encounter as foreplay, lack, and insignificance in a way that makes him seem even more ridiculous and oblivious.

This encounter is just part of the poem's investigation of privileging both penetration in sex and outcomes in narrative when abstracting interpersonal relationships from sexual practice. These effects are further examined during the scene that holds the place of the consummation of the narrative: when Leander returns to Hero's tower and they have sex. The narrative ends not with the lovers' mutual afterglow, but in Hero's post-coital shame as she trips out of bed:

> So Heroes ruddie cheeke, Hero betrayd,
> And her all naked to [Leander's] sight displayd.
> Whence his admiring eyes more pleasure tooke,
> Than Dis, on heapes of gold fixing his looke.
> (807–810)

Instead of "boy meets girl, boy gets girl," we have something more like "boy meets girl, boy gets girl, boy trips girl when she runs out of bed trying to hide her nudity and shame the next morning." Sexual consummation is associated with shame for Hero and, for Leander, a possessiveness that degrades the other.

The poem ends with profound ambivalence about this relationship, and there have been attempts in its textual history to correct for this ambivalence. For instance, the printer Edward Blunt in 1598 placed at the end of his edition of the poem "*Desunt nonnulla*" – some things are lacking – seeking to stabilize an unstable ending by recasting it as the middle of the narrative.[12] Similarly, George Chapman organized the poem into sestiads and continued the story to its tragic end. Near the beginning, however, Marlowe differentiates his poem from the "tragedie divine *Musaeus* soong" (52), which follows the lovers to their deaths, and he thereby opens up the possibility that his way of ending the poem has other purposes, one of which, I contend, is to challenge the expectation that narrative and sexual consummation must coexist. The assumptions about narrative and eroticism that may have guided Chapman and Blunt are part of a set of critical commonplaces wherein the focus on narrative outcomes in making meaning out of texts contributes to the normative sense that long-term, monogamous relations are the only valuable forms of intimate contact and that penetration alone signifies meaningful sexual contact.[13]

I do not wish to position Blunt and Chapman as the spokesmen for an Elizabethan culture against which Marlowe rebels, because I would not argue that what Marlowe does in *Hero and Leander* was out of step with his own times, and, as I suggest at the end of this chapter, because more complexity than we currently appreciate governs Chapman's continuation. It is to me more accurate to view Marlowe's poem and its afterlife as a site of contention over erotic meanings in the Renaissance. In an essay that I discussed in the introduction, Henry Abelove hypothesized that a diverse array of non-reproductive sexual practices were recast as foreplay during the eighteenth century and lost their cultural value independent of penetrative and ejaculatory sexual practices.[14] Thus, the narrative, familiar from Freud, of "the union of the genitals in the act known as copulation, which leads to a release of the sexual tension and a temporary extinction of the sexual instinct," is a historical development rather than a transhistorical psychic phenomenon.[15] In keeping with Michel Foucault's refutation of the repressive hypothesis, we might say these practices were not so much repressed by society so much as their relative value was socially redistributed.[16] Modern queers often find themselves demonized and criminalized by this sexual teleology because, as Lauren Berlant and Michael Warner point out, they have cultivated "relations and narratives only recognized as intimate in queer culture."[17] One form of queer politics, then, looks forward to the development and safeguarding of spaces in which what Berlant elsewhere calls "minor intimacies" might be practiced as a form of ongoing resistance to the historical reorganization of sexual activity.[18] However, the shift that Abelove locates enables us to rethink the boundaries we have drawn around sexual activity when it comes to representations from pre- and early modernity; by doing so, we avoid marginalizing and misrecognizing relations and narratives that were considered erotic or intimate in the past but that may not be widely recognized as such currently.

Some voices in Renaissance culture did argue that either penetration or ejaculation were definitionally central to certain kinds of sexual activity, but this was part of a historical process whose outcome was contingent and whose impact was unevenly felt across Renaissance discourses. Discussing Henry VIII's sodomy law from 1534, which was renewed under Elizabeth in 1563, Edward Coke argued that the law defined sodomy in terms of penetration: "the least penetration," Coke writes, "maketh it carnall knowledge."[19] Even if there is ejaculation, without penetration, then, an act is not sodomy; ejaculation is at most "evidence in the case of buggery of penetration."[20] Thus, in 1631, when the Earl of Castlehaven was tried for assisting his servants in the rape of Lady Castlehaven and for committing buggery with his servants, Castlehaven and his servants testified that there was no penetration, hoping to make use of the penetration requirement as a loophole. The Lord High Steward, the King's Counsel, however, argued that lack of penetration should not afford the "least mitigation to such abominable sins," especially in light of Castlehaven's other crimes, such as religious prevarication.[21] The Lord Chief Justice agreed that "the Law of this Land makes no distinction of Buggery, if there be *emissio seminis.*" What Coke understood as supporting evidence, ejaculation, the Lord Chief Justice saw as proof positive, insisting on a teleological understanding of sodomy.[22] The Castlehaven trial record betrays a concern that sodomy itself is not coextensive with the range of sexual practices that we might, from a modern perspective, deem non-normative. Yet even in light of the Lord Chief Justice's expansion of sodomy, the law is still inattentive to a variety of non-penetrative acts that may have been considered sexual, as Bruce Smith notes in his own discussion of interpretations of sodomy laws from the period.[23] Just as, according to Abelove, non-penetrative sexual practices do not signify in straightforward ways in demography, non-penetrative and non-ejaculatory acts that escape censure are unlikely to be recorded in legal discourse. Their marginality in this discourse, however, does not mean that they were rarely practiced or culturally unimportant.[24]

Literary discourse offers a different archive: because it is not primarily interested in keeping track of populations, literature can cast a wide imaginative net when representing non-reproductive sexual practices; because it is not always motivated by censure, literature can give voice to what an author believes are desirable, pleasurable, and valuable sexual practices when he or she constructs attendant narratives of intimacy in which they might flourish; and because of a greater flexibility with regard to narrative teleology in the Renaissance, an author can sustain such representations and a reader can identify with them even in narrative contexts whose outcomes appear unsupportive of these practices. In general, then, despite the existence of condemnations of non-penetrative and non-reproductive practices in religious and legal discourses, sexual activity was not always organized around penetration and ejaculation in other discourses, and a reader in the Renaissance might not have seen representations of kissing, fondling, and mutual masturbation as incomplete in relation to penetrative sex. Instead, these practices might have functioned representationally as part of a broad landscape of available sexual practices. By implication, readers might have evaluated these practices and their intimate contexts, or the relationships in which they occur – whether long-term or situational, monogamous or not – independently of penetration. Thus, in our own reading, if we broaden "sex" as a category, we might expand the current canon of Renaissance sexual representations as well to include more forms of pleasure and different narratives of intimate life. Instead of taking the modern privileging of long-term monogamy and penetrative sexuality as a *fait accompli* in the Elizabethan period and assuming that *Hero and Leander* participates in a debate whose outcome was already decided, I seek to attend to the terms the poem establishes for itself that construct a reader's experience of the poem's erotic representations. Moreover, because the poem encourages its readers both to think of erotic texts as scripts and to think differently about their narrative structures, it makes itself available as an intimate script for its readers' own erotic lives.

Consummation is problematic both in terms of *Hero and Leander*'s narrative structure and sexual economy, which makes it unusual from the perspective of modern erotic texts that often rely on sexual consummation to precipitate narrative closure. For instance, the narrative structure of many modern pornographic films – both heterosexual and male homosexual – involves penetration – whether oral, anal, vaginal, or some combination – followed by a concluding cumshot; such scenes combine the narrative and sexual sense of the term "climax" in all its phallocentric glory. Nevertheless, they frequently encounter logistical difficulties in making simultaneously visible penetration and ejaculation and the solutions to these difficulties – the removal of prophylactics if in use, masturbation, withdrawal and reinsertion, among others – often require interruption, disconnecting the climax from the narrative and physical movement that supposedly generates it. Though Ian Frederick Moulton has reminded us that the early modern texts are "before pornography," and thus should be treated with a historical specificity, we assume early modern erotic texts conform to an idealized narrative structure that is problematic even in modern erotic texts.[25] Furthermore, we use a sexual vocabulary that reinforces an unhistoricized view of erotic narrative. Consummation has inscribed within it a value judgment: according to the *Oxford English Dictionary* it derives directly from the Latin *consummare*, or "to finish" and indirectly from *summus*, or "highest." Thus, our sexual vocabulary, insofar as consummation is equated with penetration, conveys a teleological sense that penetration is the highest form of sexual activity, and our narrative vocabulary conveys a teleological sense that narrative ends are a privileged location for a text's meaning.

In *Hero and Leander*, Marlowe depends on the possibility that there are readers who would be willing to suspend a connection between consummation and the value of intimate relations. That is, in order to advance the pleasure and ethics of situational, non-monogamous affective relations, the poem offers a reading practice that, by avoiding a deterministic reliance on narrative outcomes, helps a reader ascribe value to representations of non-normative intimate contact, such as non-penetrative sexual acts. Even before we get to the final encounter between Hero and Leander, the digression recounting the story of Mercury and the country maid has already cued the reader to mistrust moments of closure that proclaim their own definitiveness for the sake of valorizing consummated affective relations. Clark Hulse situates the digression on Mercury as "just one of a series of false aetiologies in the poem, explaining why Cupid is blind, why half the world is black, or why the moon is pale."[26] Etiologies, by definition, cast a retrospective meaning on previous events; thus, they structurally resemble traditional narratives in terms of closure. Emphasizing this commonality, Marlowe offers an etiology at the end of this narrative-within-a-narrative. The Mercury digression begins by attempting to explain an aspect of the narrative itself, specifically, the reason the Destinies refuse Cupid's request that Hero and Leander "might enjoy ech other, and be blest" (380). For the next 105 lines, the narrator recounts what happened when Mercury fell in love with a shepherdess who will only have sex with him if he steals some nectar from the gods for her, in consequence of which Jupiter banishes him from the heavens. The Destinies, after Cupid makes them fall in love with Mercury, dethrone Jupiter and restore the Golden Age. After he has no need of the Destinies, Mercury spurns them, and they restore Jupiter to his former power. However, the narrator does not end the digression with a comment on the pitfalls of sexual desire, as one might expect from the way sexual desire motivates so much of the digression's plot. Such expectation was fostered in the reading practice suggested by Sir Thomas Elyot in *The Boke Named the Governour* (1531), where he writes that if a reader "do rede wanton mater mixte with wisedome, he putteth the warst vnder foote and sorteth out the beste, or if his courage be stered or provoked, he remembreth the litel pleasure and gret detriment that shuld ensue of it, and withdrawynge his minde to some other studie or exercise shortly forgetteth it."[27] It could be possible that Marlowe is trying to help the reader "forget" what he or she has just read when he ends with the trite etiology, "to this day is everie scholler poore, / Grosse gold, from them runs headlong to the boore" (471–472). However, Marlowe's use of *sententiae* makes a mockery of moralizing reading practices that involve heeding "wisdom" or "forgetting" vice, such as those advocated by Elyot. Exceeding the digression's originary purpose of explaining the fraught relationship of Cupid and the Destinies, the end of the digression connects the financial fate of scholars to their association with Mercury. Bringing the narrative to a screeching halt, the narrator's sententiousness sharply contrasts with the digression's riveting, fast-paced catalogue of various types of sexual intrigue. The digression's ending is thoroughly inadequate as a sexual moral or as a closural moment, but this disappointment helps instruct the reader in how to interpret the digression. The poem insists that the reader look to other parts of the digression for its meaning and relevance and paves the way for a third way of reading "wanton mater," beyond the two reactions Elyot lays out: identification with alternate scripts of intimacy.

Within the digression itself, a link is made between narrative structures and the erotic. A. R. Braunmuller reminds us that the Destinies were "sometimes themselves considered to embody origin, development, and telos" – principles of narrativity.[28] Their inclusion in a digression that ultimately interrupts a narrative is therefore paradoxical in a way that signals the poem's challenge to traditional understandings of narrativity. Furthermore, by having personifications of narrativity succumb to Cupid's machinations, the poem insists on a connection between affective relations and narrative, but in this instance, the connection serves to call into question the rigidity of these narrative principles, for, as Gordon Braden notes, "what [the Destinies] are primarily observed doing is changing their minds."[29] The Destinies expect to consummate the love induced by Cupid's arrows and translate it into a permanent arrangement, in keeping with their status as the embodiment of traditional principles of narrative structure – as those principles in general and *telos* in particular – which construct the value of a relationship according to the bond's duration and consummation. The digression, then, allegorizes the catastrophic consequences of applying such a rubric to intimacy. When Mercury does not return their love, the Destinies take vengeance upon him by restoring Jupiter to power. Though it allows Jupiter to punish Mercury, the restoration also involves the return of "Murder, rape, warre, lust, and trecherie" (457) to the world. Therefore, these worldwide consequences of the Destinies' vengeance – that is, the end of a restored Golden Age – can be traced to narrative's role in a sexual ideology that valorizes long-term intimate relations.

The poem does not stop at situating itself against certain erotic and reading practices. *Hero and Leander* offers a poetics of non-consummation that places non-penetrative sexual acts and non-ejaculatory pleasures, especially same-sex ones, at the center of the poem's sexual economy, the ethics of which seem to be governed by the possibility of a sexual practice that is pleasurable but that does not seek to take possession of the other. To borrow the words of Leo Bersani and Adam Phillips, Marlowe's poem is relationally innovative insofar as it begins to imagine the intimate possibilities of not being "interested in penetrating – invading and possessing – anyone else's desire."[30] In the narrator's well-known blazon of Leander, we first find cues for this alternate narrative and sexual ideology:

> His bodie was as straight as Circes wand,
> Jove might have sipt out Nectar from his hand.
> Even as delicious meat is to the tast,
> So was his necke in touching, and surpast
> The white of Pelops shoulder, I could tell ye,
> How smooth his brest was, & how white his bellie,
> And whose immortall fingers did imprint,
> That heavenly path, with many a curious dint,
> That runs along his backe, but my rude pen,
> Can hardly blazon foorth the loves of men.
> Much lesse of powerfull gods, let it suffise,
> That my slacke muse, sings of Leanders eies.
>   (61–72)

Though he suggests his inability to blazon Leander, the narrator covers an extensive amount of corporeal territory as he turns Leander's body into an erotic text by drawing on the language of printing. Tracing Leander's body vertically, the narrator's "backside" gaze follows curious dints along the heavenly path of Leander's back, but the narrator stops, complaining of his "slacke muse." Though it represents a figurative encounter, this blazon is itself an erotic narrative in miniature; its trajectory seems to be the penetration of Leander's body, but it stops before reaching that culmination. The narrator's indication that he has trouble blazoning forth "the loves of men" has suggested to readers an anatomical deficiency on the narrator's part because masculine sexuality is frequently, if falsely, associated with penetrative teleology. Yet it may not be necessary or even historically accurate to look at the blazon as figuring a failed sexual encounter, for the narrator separates male pleasure from the ejaculatory blazoning forth and articulates, in the terminology of writing, a non-teleological narrative of pleasure that can "suffise" both him and the reader. As the *Oxford English Dictionary* tells us, "suffise" or in the modern spelling "suffice" draws etymologically on the Latin prefix *sub* or under, which contrasts with the vertical position of consummation's *summus* as "highest," and *facere*, "to do." By insisting on the pleasure of "underdoing," the narrator calls into question the hierarchy of consummation and its control over sexual meaning that would cast "to suffise" as a compromise covering over absence or lack. Furthermore, extending Abelove's hypothesis about changes in sexual practices to same-sex relations might help explain why, despite the narrator's invocation of the humility topos, his experience is ultimately not unpleasurable for stopping where it does. Readers might assume that the narrator is gearing up to anally penetrate Leander in the blazon, for the urge to resolve the indeterminacy the narrator leaves about his trajectory and cross the metonymic gap between Leander's back and his anus is palpable, but that is exactly the kind of reading strategy – equating penetration, consummation, closure, and value – that the poem asks its readers to resist. Perhaps the anus does not arouse the narrator's curiosity as much as Leander's other "dints," which he traces, but does not enter. The narrator focuses on the outside edges of orifices and concavities rather than the spaces inside the body to which they might lead. Although the narrator says he will discuss Leander's eyes, which could metaphorically signify an interest in penetration – the eyes being the windows to the inner space of the soul – he quickly moves to Leander's "orient cheekes and lippes" (73). By returning to more pleasurable surface terrain and not going beyond the lips into the mouth, the narrator resists thinking of Leander's body in terms of what would later be called "erotogenic zones" – the genitals, the mouth, the anus – and "non-erotogenic zones." This form of embodiment is necessary in order to organize sexual activity around penetration, but the narrator, to borrow a phrase from Freud, turns the skin into "the erotogenic zone *par excellence*."[31]

Marlowe depicts Neptune similarly cultivating the pleasures of the body's surfaces when he seduces Leander. Indeed, Neptune and the narrator's shared proclivity for surface pleasures suggests that the narrator's sympathies, if not the text's, may lie with the unconsummated relationship between the god and the fair young man.[32] Leander's encounter with Neptune begins as a case of mistaken identity, as Neptune thinks the naked Leander is Ganymede come down from the heavens. When Neptune "imbrast him, cald him love, / And swore he never should returne to Jove" (651–652), he has rivalry with Jove in mind along with whatever interest he may have in the naked youth. Neptune here not only fantasizes about possessing something because it is valued by another, but also about satisfying the "displeas'd" Ganymede in a way that Jove has not satisfied him (641). Much in the way Leander thinks possessively about Hero after they consummate their relationship, Neptune, in Marlowe's depiction, is interested in possessing Ganymede in a power struggle with Jupiter, and since

Neptune imagines him never returning to Jupiter, he desires a long-term relationship.

The narrative shifts away from Neptune's desire for abiding possession to something more ethical on Neptune's part. This detour through mistaken identity serves to underscore how Neptune attempts to maximize the pleasure of the encounter, given how thoroughly eroticism is saturated by power relations in the culture and how tempting it is to substitute power for pleasure in sexual relations. Neptune is thus ethical in the way Foucault develops the ethics of the care of the self, which is not about abandoning power because power is not something that one has; instead it "is exercised . . . in the interplay of nonegalitarian and mobile relations."[33] Care of the self, then, "enables one to occupy his rightful position" in those relations and thereby avoid "the risk of dominating others and exercising a tyrannical power over them."[34] Even though Neptune's relation to Leander is age-graded and could fall prey to the power dynamic that allows the older to claim dominance over the younger, Neptune nurtures Leander without being domineering. Though he protects Leander out of self-interest – the advancement of his own pleasure – he does not lay a claim such that Leander cannot experience other kinds of pleasure. Upon recognizing his error in thinking Leander is Ganymede, Neptune treats Leander with protective care and gives him Helle's bracelet, Helle being the drowned Theban princess for whom the Hellespont is named. With the bracelet to safeguard Leander against Helle's tragic fate, they can enjoy their encounter. Yet the bracelet also enables Leander to swim to Hero more easily, for his cry, "O let me visite Hero ere I die" (662), prompts Neptune to give Leander the bracelet. With this gift, then, Neptune seeks his own pleasure but does not treat the sexual availability of his would-be lover as his exclusive possession.

Possession, penetration, and consummation eventually are linked in Hero and Leander's encounter, and what differentiates Neptune's seduction of Leander is its insistence on pleasure without possession, penetration, or even consummation. Neptune pursues the pleasures that the surfaces of Leander's body can afford him:

> He clapt his plumpe cheekes, with his tresses playd,
> And smiling wantonly, his love bewrayd.
> He watcht his armes, and as they opend wide,
> At every stroke, betwixt them he would slide,
> And steale a kisse, and then run out and daunce,
> And as he turnd, cast many a lustfull glaunce,
> And threw him gawdie toies to please his eie,

> And dive into the water, and there prie
> Upon his brest, his thighs, and everie lim,
> And up againe, and close beside him swim.
> (665–674)

Touching Leander's cheeks, playing with his hair, and sliding between his arms, Neptune traces the erotic topography of Leander's body much as the narrator does in the blazon. Elizabeth Harvey has argued that the skin functions as both border and interface in Renaissance anatomical and allegorical representations, thereby undermining any easy equation of the skin with surface over and against depth. In a reading of Edmund Spenser's representation of the Castle of Alma in Book II of *The Faerie Queene*, Harvey argues "the skin or flesh is at once a figure of covering and protection and a sign of the body's vulnerability to erotic or painful stimulation."[35] Marlowe too describes the skin as a site of stimulation, but he avoids reducing eroticism to penetration and challenges the idea that stimulation is a form of corporeal vulnerability by refusing to locate such stimuli – and refusing to direct the reader's gaze along with Neptune's – anywhere but at the surface. The text does not indicate that Neptune is interested in penetrating Leander sexually at this moment. Neptune specifically does not "pry into" Leander's breast, thighs, and limbs; he pries *upon* them. The phrase "pry into," to mean to investigate the inner or true nature of something, would have been available to Marlowe, according to the *OED*. In contrast, Marlowe's phrasing precisely indicates that Neptune pores over these body parts with a gaze that is attuned to surfaces. Both the narrator's blazon and Abelove's historicization of sexual acts should caution us against assuming that erotic pleasure for Neptune is reducible or equivalent to penetration.

At the level of the individual sexual act, Neptune imagines a way around the cultural nexus of eroticism and possession in a way that Leander cannot with Hero. More broadly, an affective practice of ethical, situational non-monogamy can be abstracted from the non-penetrative pleasures of Neptune's seduction.[36] Neptune tells Leander a tale about

> How that a sheepheard sitting in a vale,
> Played with a boy so faire and kind,
> As for his love, both earth and heaven pyn'd;
> That of the cooling river durst not drinke,
> Least water-nymphs should pull him from the brinke.
> And when hee sported in the fragrant lawnes,
> Gote-footed Satyrs, and up-staring Fawnes,
> Would steale him thence.   (678–685)

The critical assumption that the tale teaches Leander about homoerotic pleasure casts the relationship of the shepherd and the boy in the tale as expressive of Neptune's desire to begin a similar kind of relationship with Leander.[37] Though the homoerotic content of the tale cannot be denied, the pathways of identification the tale opens up may be more complicated. There is no mention of any reluctance on the boy's part to play with the shepherd, as there is on Leander's part to play with Neptune. Such absence would seem to interrupt Neptune's project of aligning himself with the shepherd and Leander with the boy. On the other hand, the nymphs, satyrs, and fawns' zealous and somewhat unintentionally life-threatening pursuit of the reluctant boy suggests a parallel between Neptune and these mythological figures. Indeed, the tale need not include these other figures if all Marlowe wants Neptune to do is introduce Leander to pastoral, age-graded homoeroticism. In Neptune's tale, the shepherd's ability to "play" with the boy remains unhampered by the boy's occasional relations with "Gote-footed satyrs, and up-staring Fawnes" (684). Whenever the boy is in the satyrs and fawns' vicinity, he can be erotically available to them too. Thus, with the story, Neptune invites Leander, whenever he happens to be in the Hellespont, even if he is on his way to visit Hero, to experience the pleasure of situational intimacy, like that between the boy and the satyrs and fawns. Granted, the satyrs and fawns "steal" him, emphasizing that the boy may be a reluctant participant in these pleasures, but this reluctance is a feature of the story that should encourage us to identify Leander with the boy and position Neptune in line with the aggressive mythological figures. Neptune's story certainly relies on the nexus of eroticism and power pervasive in Marlowe's England, but howsoever inescapable that nexus may be in such a hierarchical culture, the poem's larger point is that Neptune and Leander's relation of power need not be abusive and can yield alternate forms of pleasure and intimacy.

I contend, then, that Marlowe indicates that Neptune is not telling his story to make Leander love him instead of Hero. Neptune's attempted dalliance with Leander need not affect Leander's relationship with her at all. His offer is governed by a "what happens in the Hellespont stays in the Hellespont" logic. Leander does not seem to agree, for he interrupts Neptune's tale not because it is unappealing, but because he worries about his "tardie armes" (689) making him late to reach Hero's tower. However, Leander's previous encounter with Hero did not end with a specific promise that he would come back in the evening; she does not even expect his second visit when it occurs. Before Leander's first visit to her tower, Hero had prepared her abode, but, the second time, she is first delightfully surprised to hear him knocking and then terrified because he has shown up without any clothes on. Thus, the proposed dalliance with Neptune does not threaten to make Leander late to meet Hero. In his offer of situational intimacy, Neptune substitutes pleasure for possession to indicate that homo- and heteroerotic relations need not be mutually exclusive.

Although Leander is unreceptive to the situational possibilities in the Hellespont and refuses to be cast as the boy to Neptune's satyr, this poem is decidedly not about outcomes, and Neptune's alternate way of thinking about relationality, embodiment, possession, and pleasure is nevertheless made available to the poem's readers. Even when Neptune injures himself, the narrator attempts to shape the reader's attitude to the erotic alternative voiced in the encounter:

> In gentle brests,
> Relenting thoughts, remorse and pittie rests.
> And who have hard hearts, and obdurat minds,
> But vicious, harebraind, and illit'rat hinds?
>
> (699–702)

The narrator's question refers to the refinement and sensitivity that Leander demonstrates by reacting sympathetically to Neptune's injuries, but the question extends to the reader's response to the poem. The narrator compels the reader to react, as Leander has, with pity, as opposed to the derision he often solicits from the reader in his representations of Hero and Leander. In fact, he calls into question the reader's very literacy if he or she does not sympathize with Neptune. Although Neptune misinterprets Leander's pity as love and leaves him to scour the ocean for gifts, the text has trained the reader not to equate consummation with narrative endorsement. Leander's pity, then, is evidence of only a partial literacy, as the text extends literacy to include sensitivity to the opportunities of situational intimacy that Leander fails to fully apprehend. Neptune offers Leander an alternate way to think about relationality, embodiment, pleasure, and narrative, and, historically, this and other alternatives come under increasing pressure during the early modern period. Marlowe inscribes within his poem cues for reading it in a way not predetermined by moments of closure, for the ethics of Neptune's offer are only fully locatable by following the cues the text provides for the reader to cast doubt on closure as a means of endorsing a relationship. This reading practice does not efface, ignore, or otherwise subordinate those intimacies whose representation runs contrary to a narrative's trajectory.

The absence of penetration, ejaculation, and/or consummation of this relationship is not figured at all as a lack in the poem; instead, Neptune's approach to sexual pleasure opens up the additional possibility of non-monogamous intimacy. There are both textual and historical details that support a reading wherein this unconsummated homoerotic seduction, with its detachment of eroticism from a tyrannical form of possession, is placed at the ethical center of the erotic economy of the poem. That is, the poem instructs its readers that by not assessing erotic representations in terms of penetration and consummation, it is possible to derive an alternate, more ethical approach to intimate life. Judith Haber is correct that the poem questions "the equation of conventional masculinity and coherence" by being so insistently non-teleological, but I would not position Marlowe's poem in the margins of his culture fighting against an already-dominant ideology.[38] Instead, I would argue that such questions sought to inhibit the ascendance of teleological thinking about intimacy, the dominance of which was not a given in Marlowe's time. A glance at George Chapman's continuation of Marlowe's poem can help to illustrate the difficulty one encounters when assuming a monolithic Renaissance understanding of relationality, or even of narrative, which Marlowe stands fully outside in his oppositionality. Chapman's extension seems partly to privilege narrative teleology and the affective relations that conform to it, thereby offering itself as a corrective to the non-teleological elements within Marlowe's poem. On the other hand, Chapman, cued by the resistance to teleology in Marlowe's poem, may have crafted his part of *Hero and Leander* to be relentlessly teleological in order to offer an ironic commentary on such a narrative technique.

Chapman's continuation concerns itself with two alternative possible endings, the nuptials that Leander plans and the deaths of the lovers that the Destinies plan. Thus, Chapman attempts to give the poem a clearer tone predicated on its outcome – first by establishing the possible outcomes as either comic or tragic and then by following Musaeus in choosing the tragic. Chapman's narrator feels compelled to finish the story:

> O sweet Leander, thy large worth I hide
> In a short grave; ill-favoured storms must chide
> Thy sacred favour: I in floods of ink
> Must drown thy graces, which white papers drink,
> Even as thy beauties did the foul black seas.[39]

This compulsion reveals a narrator who may have internalized the value placed on moments of closure in narratives, and, in describing his compulsion, the narrator foreshadows the liquid form of Leander's death. Even when another storyteller enters and briefly takes over the narrative, this subordination to moments of closure through foreshadowing does not cease. When Hero attends a wedding feast, Teras, a nymph, tells the tale of Hymen's joyful nuptials. "Teras" means "portent" and her narrative style fits her teleological name. Chapman writes of her: "never slight tale flew / From her charmed lips without important sense, / Shown in some grave succeeding consequence" (5.74–76). Chapman's poem is relentlessly sententious as the narrator attempts to interpret and condense events into after-the-fact aphorisms. Some of these maxims even have temporality as their subject. The first one in Chapman's continuation moralizes about Leander's defloration of Hero: "Joy graven in sense, like snow in water, wastes; / Without the preserve of virtue nothing lasts" (3.35–36). Here, the preservation of virtue through marriage promises pleasures in perpetuity, in contrast to the always already decaying premarital bodily pleasures that Hero and Leander have experienced. The maxim also, then, foreshadows the end of the lovers' pleasure because they have not been careful to preserve their virtue.

On the other hand, Chapman so persistently foreshadows the deaths of the lovers that suspense is not much of a factor in the narrative. The narrator's constant sententiousness mocks his own gnomic narrative strategy, for, even as the *sententiae* comment on what has happened just prior, they connect the morality they propound with the fate of the lovers. The poem's early and repeated blatantness about the events at its ending undermines teleological progression. These foreshadowings consistently cast the Destinies as the enemies of Hero and Leander's love:

> The gods, the Graces, and the Muses came
> Down to the Destinies, to stay the frame
> Of the true lovers' deaths, and all world's tears:
> But Death before had stopped their cruel ears.
>
> (5.21–24)

The Destinies are a mythological embodiment of teleological narrativity applied to an individual's life story, but this story even subverts their role in effecting the fate the reader has been expecting for Leander. After all, the Destinies do not cut the thread of Leander's life; Neptune does in his attempt to save Leander:

And (burst with ruth) [Neptune] hurled his marble mace
At the stern Fates; it wounded Lachesis
That drew Leander's thread, and could not miss
The thread itself, as it her hand did hit,
But smote it full and quite did sunder it.   (6.225–229)

That Neptune cuts the thread testifies to his role, as god of the sea, in Leander's drowning; thus, he could be understood as a tool employed by the Destinies to further their goal of ending Leander's life. However, we might read the episode as subverting the control of the Destinies. As Lachesis is wounded too, Chapman may intend to show the Destinies as unready for Leander's death when Neptune hurled his mace at them. Indeed, the Destiny in charge of cutting the thread, Atropos, is not even mentioned here. Lachesis, whose role is to determine the length of the thread before her sister cuts it, has only just drawn the thread.

Chapman's continuation may operate according to a teleological narrative strategy, or it may be resisting it. By implication, Chapman's narrative may embody the increasingly standard view that intimacy is predicated on futurity, or Chapman's extension may resist, along with Marlowe's poem, the increased dominance of that view. Chapman does attempt to iconicize Hero and Leander as lovers, a process that equates the cultural value of their relationship to the lessons that their relationship can teach future generations. At the same time, their story culminates in an ornithological etiology. Neptune turns Hero and Leander into goldfinches after their deaths, and the narrator, rather anticlimactically, explains how various aspects of their story or character attributes translate into different colors observable on a goldfinch's body. Their iconicity, then, may be more relevant to birdwatchers than to lovers. The couple's bawdy appearance in the puppet show in Ben Jonson's *Bartholomew Fair* at the very least indicates that they were not universally sentimentalized, not that one would expect such sentimentality in Jonsonian comedy. We can assert, however, that Marlowe and Chapman's texts provide for their Renaissance and modern readers a way into understanding the complex relationship among the kinds of stories we tell, the methods we use to read them, and the availability of knowledge about non-standard forms of intimacy.

In the chapters that follow, I will extend this discussion to a generically diverse set of Renaissance texts for which a non-teleological reading strategy, such as the one suggested by Marlowe's *Hero and Leander*, can both expose the ways that these texts may have functioned as scripts for alternative forms of intimacy for Renaissance readers and audiences and make those alternatives intelligible to modern readers and audiences. Current approaches to these texts tend to privilege representations of long-term heterosexual monogamy abstracted from penetrative sexual practices. Severing the link between intimacy and futurity, a non-teleological reading practice can attend to the variety of affective relations that are represented as satisfying and pleasurable in Renaissance texts. While these texts are situated in a historical moment when heterogeneity is giving way to the centralization of intimate life around the long-term, monogamous couple, they also challenge the culture in which they were produced to maintain a more inclusive understanding of affective relations.

CHAPTER 2

A funny thing happened on the way to the altar: The anus, marriage, and narrative in Shakespeare

INTRODUCTION: THE INTIMATE ANUS

Though affective relations were increasingly valued in the early modern period according to whether they were grounded in interiorized desire and provided access to futurity through reproduction, this was by no means an instantaneous cultural transformation. In *Hero and Leander*, narrative forms avoid the teleology of monogamous coupling and critique the consolidation of intimacy. Resistance to this transformation of affective relations is even encoded in texts that more assertively assume a narrower definition of intimate life. William Shakespeare's *All's Well That Ends Well* (1604) and *Cymbeline* (1610) stage the reorganization of characters' relations with their bodies, seeking to endow them with inwardness and, concomitantly, amenability to marriage and the promise of reproduction. The plays also make available certain penetrative pleasures for men that conflict with the bodily habitation that marriage requires, and they gesture toward the alternate life narratives that might be abstracted from those pleasures. Insofar as psychic depth promotes marriage and heterosexual reproduction by way of a specific relationship of a man to his body, the anus plays a pivotal role in the socialization that leads to marriage. Its function in the expulsion of matter enacts the difference between interiority and exteriority; when it functions as a receptacle, such pleasurable penetration suggests that interiority is fictive, has no content, but is instead waiting to be filled. Both of these Shakespeare plays predicate their male characters' compliance with marriage upon the repudiation of the anus as a site of receptive pleasure. Typically, readers of Renaissance texts approach such pleasures through the theological-juridical category of sodomy, but by approaching anal eroticism through its relation to the process of socialization, I can give a fuller account of the alternate intimacies imagined in these texts and their interactions with marriage. While demystifying the bodily and psychological violence that often inheres in the process of equating intimacy

49

with marriage, the plays temporarily posit alternate forms of embodiment, pleasure, and affection in order to show their characters choosing marriage. Making those alternatives intelligible for readers and audience members, Shakespeare, perhaps inadvertently, also makes them potentially desirable and their loss an occasion for mourning even within an ostensibly hostile narrative context. This chapter, then, looks at the interaction of narrative strains that reorganize the body and the intimate sphere and that imagine resistance to that reorganization in these plays.

"A VESSEL OF TOO GREAT A BURDEN": THE ANUS AND MARRIAGE IN *ALL'S WELL THAT ENDS WELL*

In *All's Well That Ends Well*, Bertram's reluctant acceptance of his marriage follows the resolution of his internal conflicts among masculinity, sexual desire, reproduction, and marriage that, left unresolved, would prevent him from functioning in society. Yet this socialization is not only psychological and does not solely involve Bertram; other characters' bodies function as pedagogic spectacles for him and the play's audience. He witnesses the King and Parolles undergoing a reorganization of their relationships to their bodies that produces the King's advocacy for marriage and that eliminates Parolles as an impediment to it.[1] This reorganization focuses on the anus, and the play articulates connections between and among the disavowal of the anus, the production of proper inwardness, and the achievement of marriage in comic narrative closure. Bertram's socialization involves learning that the anus is a site of illness, shame, and backwardness, instead of a site of history, status, and pleasure. According to the play's narrative logic, the disavowal of the anus fosters a phallic, forward-looking reproductive economy. Bertram's persistent reluctance to marry creates skepticism about the value and success of this lesson, and Parolles briefly offers a counternarrative when he is at least partially able to resist the organization of the body around inwardness and its concomitant and persistent association of the anus with shame.

Providing one opportunity for Bertram's education, Helen's cure of the King's illness reorients the play toward marital closure and reproductive futurity. The narrative supplants a past, characterized by relations between men, with a future, characterized by cross-gender affective relations. In corporeal terms, the posterior is exchanged for the promise of posterity. Mentioned early in the play, the King's illness is described as a fistula that has achieved notoriety. The King himself locates his disease in his heart (2.1.8–10), but Susan Snyder reminds us that the reference to the heart is part of the play's general displacement upward of the sexual resonances circulating in it.[2] Though the location of the fistula on the King's body is not certain, the alternate forms of intimacy circulating in the play emerge from these obscured references when we make inferences from other contemporary texts. Sujata Iyengar points out that Renaissance medical texts locate fistulae most commonly in the anus, or fundament.[3] In *Treatises of Fistula in Ano*, a 1588 print of a fourteenth-century surgical manual about the repair of anal fistulae, John Arderne describes the surgical procedure to correct this condition.[4] The treatise begins with an investigation into the interior spaces of the body so that they can signify the condition of the patient: "The first Instrument is called *Sequere me*, which is the first Instrument pertaining to the worke: for with the same wee doe both search and prove everye hollowe fore which way the cavitie or holownesse runneth."[5] If the play draws to some extent on this treatise, it does so in a way that conflates conceptions of bodily and psychic health. The physical examination of the body's cavities in the manual becomes in the play an occasion for the interiorization of the self, and the probing Arderne describes becomes self-examination. Furthermore, as Michael Schoenfeldt has argued, "the inner self is constructed by regulating carefully the substances that enter and exit the physical body."[6] Purgation symbolically testifies to the existence of interiority, and each occurrence of evacuation implies the purification of inwardness through the release of that which might disturb it, a process that Gail Kern Paster reminds us could be associated with pleasure: "In medical literature sexual release was regarded functionally as a form of evacuation, as an emission of bodily fluids necessary for health but requiring regulation and moderation."[7] Yet Paster draws on the phallic terms of release and emission that Freud also uses when he discusses an anal erotic economy.[8] According to Jonathan Goldberg, anal sublimation occurs "through associating the anus entirely with its excremental functions, so that lack of control . . . comes to be seen as an unruly insistence of that which should be kept hidden and private."[9] This mode of embodiment organized around the more socially tolerable phallic pleasure subordinates anal pleasure.

The anus, then, connects to psychic health insofar as it remains an expulsive organ, and Renaissance anatomy texts carefully note the body ensures that waste cannot reverse its course because such a reversal gestures toward the anus as penetrated – a presumed exit is used as an entrance to the body. In his *Mikrokosmographia*, Helkiah Crooke discusses the structure of the midsection of the body in terms of layers that suggest depth. The first layer includes the abdominal muscles, under which is the peritoneum, a membrane that "enwrappeth all the inward parts" and that helps to maintain "the free deposition and avoidance of the excrements."[10] Layers organize the inward spaces of the body and keep excrement moving downward and outward. Nature, "being ever more diligent to expel that which is noctious or hurtfull, then to attract that which is profitable or behoovefull," is behind this design, and Crooke concludes that "the expulsive vertue therefore of the guttes, is stronger then the rest."[11] When blocked, this natural, virtuous expulsion is reversed "with such violence, that (alas the while) the Chylus & the excrements are thrown out by the mouth: so diligent and circumspect is Nature to unburden it selfe of that which is noisome or offensive."[12] The motion that culminates in vomiting serves nature's purposes too, for it maintains, in an upwardly displaced form, the evacuative function of the body's orifices. Though this reversal accomplishes a goal of nature, Crooke insists that it is nevertheless a function of disease and cannot be reproduced from below by man's interference, as Crooke goes on to dismiss the rumor that "If a Clister [i.e. an enema] bee with great force and violence shot up, it will arive at the stomacke" by arguing that "in the end of the blind gut there is a valve, which Nature in great Wisedome hath set to hinder the refluence or returne of the excrements and unprofitable humors."[13] In the absence of disease, waste maintains one teleologically expulsive course. Describing the administration of an enema, Crooke finds it important to note that when an external source penetrates the body anally, nature maintains the health of the inner spaces of the body by obstructing the unauthorized reversal such penetration would effect, though penetration is not entirely prohibited.[14]

Whereas Crooke's medical text personifies Nature to discuss the design of the gastrointestinal tract, Phineas Fletcher's poem *The Purple Island* (1633) figures the structure of the body in geographic terms. Fletcher metaphorizes the midsection as a province which has "a fence from forrain enmitie, / With five strong-builded walls encompast round."[15] This emphasis on protecting the entrails points to an investment in keeping this interiorized space free from exterior disturbances, or penetration, so that it can perform its evacuative functions. Fletcher describes the rectum's voluntary control over evacuation as a form of political authority:

> The last down-right falls to port *Esquiline*,
> More strait above, beneath still broader growing;
> Soon as the gate opes by the Kings assigne,
> Empties it self, farre thence the filth out-throwing:
> This gate endow'd with many properties,
> Yet for his office sight and naming flies;
> Therefore between two hills, in darkest valley lies.[16]

In a modern psychoanalytic framework, as Guy Hocquenghem notes, "the ability to 'hold back' or to evacuate the faeces is the necessary moment of the constitution of the self."[17] In *The Purple Island*, absolutist discourse, applied to excretion, figures a person's relationship to his or her body in terms of domination. Yet, even as Fletcher figures such selfhood rectally, the rectum disappears from the space of signification and representation into the unnameable. Despite the broader antisodomitical context of the poem, hinted at in the stanza's treatment of the unrepresentable rectum, *The Purple Island* keeps open the representational possibilities of anal pleasure that the rectum's location "in darkest valleys" would deny.[18] Governing the lower regions of the body, including the rectum, is the liver, which Fletcher, in line with a Renaissance commonplace, also notes is the seat of love.[19] That the seat of love governs the province wherein the anus lies, then, opens up a conditional space for imagining the anus as a site of intimate possibility; it is this way of thinking that *All's Well*, in its obscure references to the anus, liberates and incompletely neutralizes.

Helen's cure of the King orients his interior space toward marriage, reproduction, and the phallus, and away from the anus and male-male bonds, both cast as sterile. Bertram's arrival at court precipitates a flurry of praise for Bertram's father, as the King concludes that the now-deceased count "Might be a copy to these younger times, / Which followed well would demonstrate them now / But goers-backward" (1.2.46–48). In these lines' temporal conflict, the progeny of heterosexual reproduction represented by "these younger times" embodies regress instead of progress. Yet the youth are "goers-backward," and therefore deviant, only by way of contrast, so what the King laments is a present lack of structural or institutional condemnation of backwardness that the old Count's example would provide, and it is telling that the King himself has to go backward in history to make his critique. Absent this condemnation, a non-phallic, non-reproductive economy of embodiment reigns. Instead of fertility, the King wishes for death, itself figured as propulsion, through which he will reunite with Bertram's father: "I after him do after him wish too" (1.2.64). The King then welcomes the Count in the place of his own son, whom he says is "no dearer" (1.2.76) to him than Bertram is. This sentiment, wherein an absent son is replaceable in a father's affections, distances the King from the reproductive order.

Helen provides the pathologization of backwardness the King requests by drawing on knowledge derived from a cross-gender lineage whose representation is steeped in fertility imagery. On his deathbed, Gerard de Narbonne had given his daughter the medical knowledge that she uses to garner the King's assent to a project that she describes as her "low and humble name to propagate" (2.1.197). Although this knowledge displaces her as her father's "issue," it also gives Helen the leverage to initiate the legitimate production of her own offspring. She admits that the past contains death and displacement of the self, but, unlike the King, she disregards it to look toward a reproductive future. Representationally, the King's offstage cure is surrounded with the same darkness that surrounds the fundament in Fletcher's *Purple Island*. Helen's initiative transgresses early modern gender roles, but she seeks a conservative end, marriage; thus, in keeping with the play's teleological focus, we see only the outcome of the cure, establishing something of a pattern whereby the ends, which will be her own pregnancy, not only justify the means, but attempt to obscure the means too. When the King is restored to health, phallic associations accrue around him, replacing the references to death and backwardness. The King, "able to lead [Helen] in a coranto" (2.3.44), as Lafeu observes, says that Helen "has raised me from my sickly bed" (2.3.112). The erectile quality of these references to rising and dancing recall Lafeu's description, from Act 2, scene 1, of another medicine that could "make you dance canary" and "whose simple touch / Is powerful to araise King Pépin" (2.1.74–75). "Lead" also suggests a new forward motion for the King that mimics the proper expulsive motion in the intestines of which Crooke wrote. With Helen's assistance, he has exchanged the backward anus for the forward phallus. His relation to the dorsal and ventral sides of his body reorganized and his relation to past and future reset, he becomes a virtual marriage machine kicked into overdrive, marrying Helen to Bertram, attempting to marry Bertram to Lafeu's daughter Maudlin, and even offering to finance Diana's dowry.

Insofar as reestablishing his anal health allows the King to exert increased political authority over his subjects, his behavior anticipates Phineas Fletcher's metaphorical rendering of rectal control as "the Kings assigne" in *The Purple Island*. To justify Bertram's enforced marriage to Helen, the King allows the claims of reproduction to trump those of ancestry, thereby revealing that, because his corporeal orientation is anterior, or frontal, rather than posterior, or behind, his temporal orientation is toward the future rather than the past. When Bertram objects that Helen's admission by marriage to the aristocratic classes would debase the purity and honor of the aristocracy, the King marshals the resources of reproductive discourse to assert his absolutist authority, rooted in his new phallic vitality, and to advance marriage:

> From lowest place when virtuous things proceed,
> The place is dignified by th'doers deed.
> Where great additions swell's, and virtue none,
> It is a dropsied honour. Good alone
> Is good without a name, vileness is so:
> The property by what it is should go,
> Not by the title. She is young, wise, fair.
> In these to nature she's immediate heir,
> And these breed honour. That is honour's scorn
> Which challenges itself as honour's born
> And is not like the sire; honours thrive
> When rather from our acts we them derive
> Than our foregoers.   (2.3.126–138)

Defending Helen, the King subordinates the claims of patrimony and title to the reproductive union of virtue and deed. The masculine descent of title here is figured as "dropsied," a diseased, hollow copy of the reproductively swelling honor.[20] The King looks forward to the offspring of Helen's youth, wisdom, and fairness, rather than backward to the title of "foregoers." Combining the reproductive and phallic imagery that emerges from Helen's cure, the King says "It is in us to plant thine honour where / We please to have it grow" (2.3.157–158). Paradoxically, the very hereditary system based on "foregoers" rather than acts gives the King his authority as well as the only name by which he is known in the play, and it is undermined in the execution of that authority for the sake of reproduction and marriage.

Though Bertram defers to the King's authority at this moment in the play, does not fully adopt for himself the King's new reproductive outlook. His parting letter to Helen sets up the trajectory of the second part of the play: "'When thou canst get the ring upon my finger, which never shall come off, and show me a child begotten of thy body that I am father to, then call me husband; but in such a 'then' I write a 'never'"" (3.2.57–60). These two tasks are related to Bertram's resistance to undergoing the changes in his relationship to his body that the King experiences. With his "never" he seeks to obliterate the teleology that structures this "when . . . then" proposition. As long as he adheres to a corporeality figured in terms of looking backward to his male line of descent rather than in terms of looking forward to a phallic reproductive future, Bertram will be able to hold on to the ring and he will not reproduce. By assigning these tasks to Helen, however, Bertram inadvertently specifies material ways through which she can impose a reproductive logic on him. When planning the bedtrick, she remarks upon the significance of the ring in terms of male ancestry. It "downward hath succeeded in his house / From son to son some four or five descents / Since the first father wore it" (3.7.23–25). For Janet Adelman, the ring symbolizes a male line of descent that Helen figures in parthenogenetic terms, but in addition to its downward movement, this ring points backwards to ancestry rather than looking forward to a reproductive future, and its backwardness associates it with the network of references to the anus in the play.[21] Until Helen manages to obtain it, its reproductive associations all remain firmly shrouded in the past. The ring's descent "from son to son" secures bonds between men, and the fate of the ring relates to the King's illness and lament over Bertram's dead father, who was the embodiment of honor.

Similarly, Bertram's trade of his ring for what he thinks is Diana's chastity unwittingly exchanges a backward-looking anality for a forward-looking reproductivity with Helen. Though wordplay on the ring as vagina was common, there is a linguistic connection between rings and anuses in the period as well. English derives the word "anus" from a Latin word that could mean either the body part or a ring. Indeed, Crooke refers to the sphincter as "the *Ringe*" in *Mikrokosmographia*.[22] Although the rectum was most commonly referred to as "the fundament" and the earliest citation of *anus* in the *OED* dates from 1658, the rings-rectums connection homonymically encoded in the Latin *anus* would have been available to Renaissance readers. For example, Joseph Webbe, in his 1620 translation of Cicero's *Epistolae ad familiares*, leaves *anus* untranslated in reference to the body part.[23] Shakespeare himself, in *Hamlet*, simultaneously exploits the discursive connection between rings and vaginas and between rings and anuses when Hamlet tells the boy player: "Pray God your voice, like a piece of uncurrent gold, be not cracked within the ring" (2.2.430–431). While Hamlet literally refers to the throat, the erotic resonances of Hamlet's phrase are complicated by the boy actor's participation in the transvestite theater. For the female characters the boy plays, the "cracked ring" refers to the penetrated vagina; "cracking the ring" of the boy himself, however, suggests anal penetration. The transvestism of the Renaissance theatre allows the boy player's body to be open to this layering of erotic signification.

In *All's Well*, Shakespeare attempts to revise the ring's meaning by supplanting an ancestral ring-anus connection with a marital ring-vagina connection. After Bertram notes the honor attached to his ring and the price of giving it to Diana in exchange for sex, she replies, "Mine honour's such a ring / My chastity's the jewel of our house, / Bequeathèd down from many ancestors" (4.2.46–48). She applies to her chastity the same terms of descent that Bertram uses to describe his ring. In the bedtrick, his ring and its backward, anal orientation will be supplanted by Helen's vagina, itself a substitute for Diana's, in order to enable cross-gendered, reproductive relations that look toward the future. Diana's metaphoric ring materializes as an actual one too – that which the King gave Helen for curing him. Diana calls it "that, what in time proceeds, / May token to the future our past deeds" (4.2.63–64). Bridging past and future, this ring brings Bertram back to the scene of the King's cure and installation in a reproductive, teleological narrative. As gifts to Helen, then, Bertram and this ring are allied ontologically. This ring's exchanges are all cross-gendered, in contrast to Bertram's ring's descent. Moreover, this history of exchanges is marshaled to testify to the consummation of Bertram and Helen's marriage, just as Diana predicts. Along with the baby conceived in the bedtrick, the replacement of Bertram's ring with Helen's has temporally and corporeally turned Bertram around, creating the need for such acceptance. The propriety of futurity is a construction of the narrative.

Helen's achievement embodies and problematizes the way that traditional comic closure relies on an organization of the body and bodily pleasures that corresponds to the reproductive logic of the marriage effected or promised at the resolution of the comic plot. In Renaissance theories of comedy, according to Marvin Herrick, the Aristotelian notion of a tragedy's catastrophe was adapted to account for comic closure: "almost always the sixteenth-century critics identified the catastrophe with Discovery or recognition which is usually attended by Peripety or reversal of fortune."[24] Though the new social order created in comic closure is forward-looking, social innovation is justified by casting that new order as a perfected form of the old order rather than the abandonment of it. By appearing to incorporate all that has come before it, comic closure obscures the need to leave something behind so that the new social order that the narrative imagines – for which the marriages that often precipitate comic closure stand in synecdochically – can take shape.

The discourses of the body and the paradigms for interpreting narrative exert a mutual influence over each other, as peripatetic reversal and "recognition," or the discovery of identity, resonate at the corporeal level. Daniel Punday contends that "narrative . . . always first and foremost depends upon a corporeal hermeneutics," but this is too unidirectional, for the body is explained and explored through narrative discourse too.[25] The available ways of thinking about narrative inform our attitudes toward and constrain our thinking about the body. What is left behind corporeally in comic closure is precisely the behind, as Patricia Parker's work on the "preposterous" has demonstrated.[26] As Helen's cure of the King and her substitution of rings demonstrate, closure achieves a new primacy of the phallus that is then rewritten as that which has always existed but which has been temporarily inhibited by looking backward, toward the anus as a potential site of social, libidinal, and narratological investment. When such a corporeal teleology governs texts and our readings of them, the anus and anal pleasure are ultimately cast beyond the scope of representation. *All's Well* is not entirely successful at inhibiting investment in backwardness, however. David Hillman has written that this type of conflict between narrative and counternarrative is common in the treatment of embodiment in plays of the period: "the vitality of much early modern drama relies crucially upon both a re-enactment and a resistance to the sealing of the body."[27] I would suggest that *All's Well* localizes this struggle as a contest between the phallus and the anus, which, in addition to its associations with backwardness, also represents a troubling site of male bodily dilation. As the play seeks to shore up the male body from anal penetration, it only incompletely effaces the alternate pleasures and life narratives of the anus that Parolles embodies. When the Lords Dumaine capture him, the play makes efficient use of Parolles, for, through the confessions they extract, they seek to sever his ties to Bertram and force Parolles to understand his relation to his body in terms of interiority. Although the bond between Parolles and Bertram is successfully severed, Parolles never fully inhabits his body in accordance with the psychic depth model. His plight need not be understood in terms of failed socialization, for as Hocquenghem notes, "to fail at one's sublimation is in fact merely to conceive social relations in a different way."[28] Denaturalizing the reproductive social order, Parolles insists that his abjection only creates another role for him to play.

Initially, Parolles praises the virtues of reproduction that go along with losing virginity, but the same reproductive logic he advocates for Helen exacts its punitive violence on him, as the play ultimately emphasizes Parolles's role in preventing Helen from losing that virginity. Parolles provides a spirited, misogynist defense of Bertram's decision to embrace the masculine space of the battlefield:

> He wears his honour in a box unseen
> That hugs his kicky-wicky here at home,
> Spending his manly marrow in her arms,
> Which should sustain the bound and high curvet
> Of Mars' fiery steed.   (2.3.276–280)

Parolles sees the honor that the King associates with reproduction as the waste of a man's energy and bodily fluids, or "marrow." The "box unseen" casts the vagina, not the anus, as that which is beyond representation. Lafeu – unhesitatingly and, arguably, unreasonably disdainful of Parolles – rewrites Parolles's reactive role as an influence that threatens to spread seductively through the young male population when he tells the Countess, "your son was misled with a snipped-taffeta fellow there, whose villainous saffron would have made all the unbaked and doughy youth of a nation in his colour. Else your daughter-in-law had been alive at this hour, and your son here at home, more advanced by the King than by that red-tailed humble-bee that I speak of" (4.5.1–7). Presumed to be a response to her abandonment, Helen's faked death becomes Parolles's responsibility rather than Bertram's. To Lafeu, Bertram cannot advance in the King's favor because Parolles, whose "red-tail" also connects his flashy clothes to his backwardness, holds him back. The reference to the "red-tailed humble-bee" also manages to extend this image of the harmful effects of penetration with reference to a stinging insect. Lafeu's entomology suggests cowardice, as the bumblebee is generally not quick to sting, and this cowardice is connected to the behind through the mention of the "red tail." Many years ago, seemingly following Lafeu, H. B. Charlton condemned Parolles as a "shapeless clump of cloacine excrement," a negativity that, whether or not it is expressed in scatological terms, is frequently taken for granted in discussions of Parolles.[29] Recasting this persistent interplay of anal references that surround Parolles, I contend that he points to an alternative to the dominant understandings of embodiment and pleasure that the King's cure effects and that Bertram is forcibly socialized to inhabit. Through the nexus of these two strands of his characterization – anality and resistance to inwardness – he deflates the phallic, reproductive economy that the play privileges and suggests, if only fleetingly, a system of relations between men that involves corporeal openness but that is not grounded in interiority.

Parolles offers instruction in such relations to Bertram when he tells him to "use a more spacious ceremony to the noble lords [Dumaine]" (2.1.49), and these lessons compete with other attempts to socialize the young Count. Teaching Bertram a ceremoniousness that Lavatch later satirizes, Parolles instructs Bertram to go "after them, and take a more dilated farewell" (2.1.55–56) because their social importance mandates a special courtesy. Parolles admiringly adds that the Dumaines are "like to prove most sinewy sword-men" (2.1.58–59). These lessons involve leave-taking behavior and language, but they have a corporeal resonance as well, for first the instructions imagine a verbally open or dilated Bertram and then Parolles points to their martial skillfulness at the penetration of bodies. In Fletcher's *Purple Island*, the dilation of the backside – where "the gate opes by the Kings assigne" – allows for expulsion, but here dilation as a part of socialization makes the body vulnerable to penetration. Parolles instructs Bertram not only to say more at parting, then, but also to open up his body to receive favor from the Lords Dumaine. While Bertram's utterances at parting might be considered expulsive, Parolles is also interested in incorporation and vulnerability as aspects of the self. In this sense, some content of the self comes in from the outside when the body is dilated. The corporeal openness through which Parolles figures social relations is problematic, however, given the anal imagery circulating around him; it threatens to collapse the difference between what is kept inside and what is expelled from the self, that which Crooke calls "noisome and offensive."[30] One is left to imagine Bertram following the advice by dilating himself verbally to the Lords Dumaine, and then turning to leave with his penetrable backside facing them. Though Bertram agrees to follow Parolles's instruction in this scene, his dilated farewell remains as unstaged as the King's cure.

As part of the play's deauthorization of Parolles's lessons, Lavatch parodically replicates this scene of instruction with the Countess in Act 2, scene 2, where he offers her some pointed barbs about courtiers with a reference to the posterior. Lavatch claims the phrase "O Lord Sir" responds to all questions by mingling courtly pretension and cowardice. In a particularly interesting simile, Lavatch describes the phrase's endless usefulness: "It is like a barber's chair that fits all buttocks: the pin-buttock, the quatch-buttock, the brawn-buttock, or any buttock" (2.2.16–18). It is, as Phineas Fletcher might say, "endowed with many properties." Testing the phrase's applicability, she asks him if he is truly a courtier and whether he has been recently punished by whipping. As Lavatch employs it, the phrase allows one to resist telling the truth about oneself and specifically involves a reference to the posterior. While Hocquenghem argues that "only the phallus dispenses identity; any social use of the anus, apart from its sublimated use, creates the risk of a loss of identity," Lavatch casts anal selfhood slightly differently: deceptive, without real content that can be expressed.[31]

In the next scene, Lafeu threateningly directs the content of Lavatch's parody at Parolles, and his attack is the culmination of the different representations of courtiership in the preceding two scenes. Lafeu thereby illustrates Hocquenghem's contention that "the phallocratic competitive society is based on the repression of desires directed at the anus," even as the two characters are competing over a potentially homoeroticized dominance of Bertram.[32] Lafeu hypothesizes that Parolles "wast created for men to breathe themselves upon" (2.3.253–254), thereby reliteralizing the physical violence that was put to a more metaphorical use in the context of Parolles's lesson to Bertram about leave-taking at court. Paralleling the questions that the Countess asks Lavatch in the more humorous setting of Act 2, scene 2, Lafeu accuses Parolles of having been recently punished for theft and faking his identity as a courtier: "You were beaten in Italy for picking a kernel out of a pomegranate, you are a vagabond and no true traveller, you are more saucy with lords and honourable personages than the commission of your birth and virtue gives you heraldry" (2.3.258–260). In response to these accusations, he could certainly use a phrase such as the one Lavatch develops. In fact, Parolles eventually uses the phrase "O Lord, Sir!" (4.3.311).

Especially in the speeches that further his characterization as a *miles gloriosus*, Parolles pays lip service to the definition of masculine honor that Lafeu and others in the play advance at his expense. In Act 2, scene 1, Parolles tells the Lords Dumaine a likely fabricated story of how he wounded an enemy captain, and his bragging threatens to reveal by association all such phallic aggression as potentially inauthentic. For this reason, the play distances and differentiates Parolles from authentic phallic masculinity. After he is exposed to Bertram, Parolles says that "every braggart shall be found an ass" (4.3.337), a category that potentially includes anyone attempting to authenticate masculinity verbally.[33] While this prediction has anal resonances in modern English, Renaissance English did not necessarily equate "ass" and arse," an issue that has emerged in readings of Bottom from *A Midsummer Night's Dream*.[34] Whereas Bottom's onomastic, if not zoologic, anality furthers the phallic order in disciplining the unruly Titania, Parolles more directly threatens that order and is himself disciplined. Braggart and ass line up with phallic masculinity and its anal other, and the success of Parolles's masquerade would blur the distinctions between the two. To maintain that distinction for Bertram's socialization, the text uses Parolles, in Jonathan Dollimore's words, to "project and construct an inauthentic other against whom the authentic self is defined."[35] Inauthenticity, in Parolles's case, lies primarily in his resistance to interiority, a resistance that threatens to expose inwardness as emptiness. Lafeu targets Parolles's clothes as signifiers of inauthentic selfhood: "the scarves and the bannerets about thee did manifoldly dissuade me from believing thee a vessel of too great a burden" (2.3.204–206). Lafeu does not view Parolles's clothes as participating in an alternate economy of corporeality not organized around depth. Instead, he hopes his foreknowledge of Parolles's true character will further shame him when Parolles is exposed.

The Dumaine brothers will go even further than Lafeu in constituting for Parolles a shamefully inauthentic self when they orchestrate Parolles's confession of the truth about himself while Bertram watches. The First Lord Dumaine tells his brother, "I would gladly have [Bertram] see his company anatomized, that he might take a measure of his own judgements, wherein so curiously he had set this counterfeit" (4.3.32–35). They function in the same way as the *sequere me* tool for fistula surgery that Arderne describes: they are probing him to see which way his hollowness runs, albeit not for his own sake but for Bertram's. In a general way, their project also echoes Sir Philip Sidney's assertion in *The Defence of Poesy* that comedy is ultimately moral because it uses "the filthiness of evil" as "a great foil to perceive the beauty of virtue."[36] Though the drum the brothers send Parolles to recover could be relatively substantial in size and sound, the Lords Dumaine emphasize its emptiness in order to link Parolles with its hollow noisiness. As the First Lord Dumaine says to Bertram, "when your Lordship sees the bottom of his success in't, and to what metal this counterfeit lump of ore will be melted, if you give him not John Drum's entertainment, your inclining cannot be removed" (3.6.37–40). With passing reference to the posterior, he is sure that Bertram will cast Parolles away when the "bottom," in this case an absence, of Parolles's "success" signifies his truly empty nature. Anticipating Fletcher's description of the way the rectum "Empties it self, farre thence the filth out-throwing" (2.43.4), Bertram will expel Parolles from himself and restore health to his inner life. Their recasting of Parolles's resistance to inwardness as emptiness is not assured, however, and when they entertain the possibility that Bertram's "inclining cannot be removed," they also suggest that the audience might not "learn" what the Lords Dumaine are trying to teach either.

Though Bertram severs his bond with Parolles, the staged capture and interrogation is not entirely effective in forcing Parolles to understand his relationship to his body in terms of inwardness. Shakespeare draws more generally on medical discourse in his representation of the production of inwardness here. Using the term "anatomized," the Lords Dumaine invoke what Jonathan Sawday calls the Renaissance "culture of dissection." The practice of anatomization – whether of the body, through dissection, or of concepts, as in Robert Burton's *Anatomy of Melancholy* – fragments something into a state in which it can be mastered or managed, but it is, as Sawday points out, "an act whereby something can also be constructed, or given a concrete presence."[37] The health of other bodies and a coherent sense of interiority were among anatomization's products, and both processes are represented in *All's Well*. For the sake of the health of Bertram's "judgement," the Lords Dumaine seek to render Parolles powerless over Bertram through fragmentation. By staging a confession, the Lords Dumaine construct for Parolles the inner truth of his character in order to inauthenticate the claims to status and bravery that he has made with his clothes and words. The brothers encounter serious limits when undertaking this quest for Parolles's truth, in part because most of the questions they ask are not about Parolles at all, but about their own reputations, the strength of the Florentine army, and Bertram's character. Though the so-called Interpreter asks Parolles if he will faithfully give up the secrets of the Florentine army, later he reports that "the general says that you have so traitorously discovered the secrets of your army, and made such pestiferous reports of men very nobly held" (4.3.306–308). He decides that Parolles is disloyal by telling the truth about the army and by lying about his friends. Yet such a simplistic, overarching conclusion does not adequately resolve all the problems that arise from Parolles's confession. Parolles says that the Florentine army is "very weak and unserviceable . . . and the commanders [are] very poor rogues" (4.3.135–137). If Parolles's report about the army is as true as the Interpreter concludes, then his confession reflects with shame upon the Lords Dumaine and Bertram who are, after all, part of that army. There is evidence that Parolles is honest about the weakness of the army, for Parolles lost the drum in the first place because, as he sarcastically notes, "there was excellent command: to charge in with horse upon our own wings and to rend our own soldiers" (3.6.49–51). Mirroring the way that these men have captured one of their fellow combatants, the army charged on itself in battle, and it is a wonder they were even victorious. On the other hand, if, contrary to the Interpreter's conclusion, Parolles is lying about the condition of the army, there is a sense in which lying to the opposing army, whom Parolles thinks he is addressing, so that they underestimate their adversaries, could be viewed as a kind of loyalty; though such a lie may provoke another attack, the attackers would be surprised to their detriment to find an army stronger than expected. Further, in his confession, he reveals Bertram's dishonesty with women, a judgment Helen and Diana could validate. Thus, Parolles may be, by extension, telling the truth about the Lords Dumaine, whom he powerfully berates as scoundrels. His confession reveals more about them than it does about himself. While the scene the Lords Dumaine stage has its intended effect on Bertram, a more skeptical spectator might see Parolles using language to both resist the forced reorganization of his relationship with his body and indicate that the Lords Dumaine project onto and into him their own shameful inauthenticity.

The shame associated with inauthenticity arises from a dissonance between inner and outer selves where the inner self is supposed to be the true one. Parolles refuses to abide by this organization of embodiment in the play. Within this confession scene, the Lords Dumaine attempt to wrest control of the truth-value of Parolles's speech away from Parolles so that he will conform to this understanding of embodiment and feel shame. They even try to install him into an economy of heterosexual reproduction: "If you could find out a country where but women were that had received so much shame, you might begin an impudent nation" (4.3.327–329). The truth and the ethical import of the Lords Dumaine's project remains unclear. In the play as a whole, Parolles loses authority in determining the truth about himself and must instead reproduce a truth whose origins are external to him but which he must exhibit as if internal to him. Since the play silences him near its end, it is never quite clear what it means when he says "simply the thing I am / Shall make me live" (4.3.334–335). The thing he has been associated with is the anus, but how he will "live / Safest in shame" (4.3.338–339) by it remains beyond the scope of this play's representational field. Insofar as he persists in his anality, his silence indicates further that the narrative leaves this mode of embodiment behind as it looks toward reproduction.

A shameless cathexis of the anus, such as is implicit in his lesson to Bertram on taking a "dilated farewell," seems unspeakable for him at the end of a play whose narrative fosters the disavowal of anality and transforms characters into proper, phallically oriented subjects. Even if the play forecloses on the alternate form of embodiment that Parolles might offer, he nevertheless de-authenticates the psychic depth model that the play's narrative authorizes. Parolles's silence at the end of the play, when he seems to accept the identity that other characters have forced him to inhabit, suggests that interiorized subjectivity is enforced, unrepresentable, and utterly empty. Parolles accedes superficially to the division between inner and outer selfhood, but he treats living as "the thing that I am" as just another role, which, in this case, requires a change of costume so as to have less "familiarity with fresher clothes" (5.2.3). Both spectacularly campy courtier and shamed supplicant are exchangeable roles for Parolles, and the violence that has been performed to make him a spectacle of anal shame for Bertram has failed to produce adherence to a regime of authentic subjecthood. When a phallic, reproductive economy co-opts the play's representational space, silence thus remains his only alternative to the constant confession of the shame associated with the anus. Seeing him so violently and spectacularly reduced, our "inclining" to him and his lessons about the dilated male body may resist removal more so than Bertram's does.

"RATHER FATHER THEE THAN MASTER THEE": THE EROTICS OF MALE SUBMISSION, MARRIAGE, AND THE WOMAN'S PART IN *CYMBELINE*

In *All's Well*, Shakespeare closes the narrative on a note of ambivalence after having exposed the force inherent in the offstage and onstage manipulations through which Bertram's marriage was achieved. His astonishment at Helen's success is not exactly unequivocal acceptance and love. In *Cymbeline*, Posthumus is not initially resistant to marriage in the way Bertram is, but he is subjected to a similar process that is both displaced onto other characters and internalized: Posthumus's relation to his body is altered to bring him back into the marital fold. With these two plays juxtaposed, the absence of reluctance to marry on the part of Posthumus renders this corporeal interference gratuitous when it affects other characters, and when he rejects a connection to the anus, he takes part in the play's general redirection of the potential eroticism of male bonds characterized by submission. It would be incorrect to assume that the generic distance between comedy and tragicomic romance would leave uncontested in *Cymbeline* the spaces for alternate forms of embodiment and pleasure that are partly foreclosed in *All's Well*, as there is a surplus of investment in the anus and submission that Shakespeare attempts to neutralize and reroute in *Cymbeline*. Though Jupiter himself proclaims the tragicomic truism "the more delayed, delighted" (5.5.196), this delay leads less to delight in the reunification of the married couple and more to delight in the other intimate possibilities already liberated when he appears.

   Posthumus's internalization of the cultural dictate to disavow anal pleasure and the erotics of the penetrated, submissive male body sets the stage for him to be incorporated into a marital, patriarchal, reproductive order at the end of the play. This process of internalization reaches a heightened state of intensity during what has come to be known as his "woman's part" soliloquy, in which Posthumus wishes to disavow the role of women in reproduction generally and in his own conception specifically.[38] This role is not limited to women's biological participation in generation, however; it also involves psychological formation. In the speech, female adultery is made to bear all the faults of patriarchal masculinity. The woman's part thus signifies women's (vulner)ability to be(ing) penetrated by men other than their husbands; it is, according to Posthumus, what "she / Should from encounter guard" (2.5.18–19). Through this vaginal reference, he articulates a belief that legitimate reproduction and uncontaminated masculinity are only possible parthenogenetically, but eventually Posthumus, reunited with Innogen, comes to reaccept the woman's part, albeit in a more subordinate place, in the reproduction of masculinity. Here, I will suggest that we bracket off this standard interpretation of the play in order to show that another layer of meaning is operative in the speech that nevertheless works toward similar narrative and marital ends. If, as Posthumus suggests, there is a "woman's part" in him, should he "from encounter guard" it too? In this speech, he opens up a conditional space of possibility where, if he "could . . . find out the woman's part" in him, he might find there the possibility of pleasure in the sexual penetration of his body.

Male and female bodies have anuses in common, so, in corporeal terms, one "woman's part" in man is the anus. According to Crooke, the perineum, the space between the anus and the scrotum, is also called the *interfoeminium*, a term that indicates the space between the thighs, or *femora*, but that nevertheless evokes "feminine" in reference to the parts of the body behind the genitals .[39] Furthermore, via the anus a man can experience the pleasures of penetration usually accorded to women in patriarchy, but such experience is detached from the reproductive logic of heterosexual coitus. The "woman's part" reference exceeds its role in this genital-centered economy that only accounts for the ventral side of the body.[40] That is, though Posthumus begins to imagine anal penetration by referring to the female body, these are only the initial terms. Insofar as the play goes beyond them, it imagines a dissident economy of male-male pleasure that conflicts with the play's association of anal pleasure with abject effeminacy. By focusing on the moments of resistance to the way the play surrounds male submission with opprobrium, we might demystify and interrupt the play's narrative logic to recuperate a conditional space for anal eroticism and submissive pleasure in the play.

Situating the "woman's part" soliloquy in a discursive network of eroticized male submission, this approach shifts the critical emphasis from gender identity to the forms of embodiment, pleasure, and relationality that are permissible in the play once Posthumus has entered into marriage. This speech's structure microcosmically replicates the play's larger structure wherein Posthumus's relations with men that depend on a potentially eroticized submission conflict with and are supplanted by the prior claims of his reproductive relation with Innogen. He first asks if reproduction can be unhinged from its heterosexual context: "Is there no way for men to be, but women / Must be half workers?" (2.5.1–2). Implicit here is the sentiment that a secure form of descent, in contrast to the current situation in which "we are bastards all" (2.5.2), would necessitate that relations between male ancestors be unmediated by women. Though his fantasy encodes a biological impossibility, the "half-work" that women do in copulation might just as legitimately, in Posthumus's invective, be taken over by other men to establish a secure male line of descent. However, because he begins this line of thinking entirely from within a matrix of reproduction, the triangulating female figure always returns to intrude upon his fantasy of unobstructed relations with other men. He imagines two sex scenes in the speech, the first involving his mother:

> And that most venerable man which I
> Did call my father was I know not where
> When I was stamped. Some coiner with his tools
> Made me a counterfeit; yet my mother seemed
> The Dian of that time.   (2.5.3–7)

The second, with his new bride:

> This yellow Iachimo in an hour – was't not? –
> Or less – at first? Perchance he spoke not, but
> Like a full-acorned boar, a German one,
> Cried 'O!' and mounted; found no opposition
> But what he looked for should oppose and she
> Should from encounter guard.   (2.5.14–19)

The triangulated relationship among his father, mentioned in line 4, the illegitimate 'coiner' he posits as his biological father in line 5, and his mother parallels his relationship with Iachimo and Innogen. Though the comparison between Innogen and his mother as false versions of the chaste Diana (2.5.7) allows him to connect the two fantasmatic scenes of adultery, when he describes each scene he introduces the male figures in the speech (2.5.4–6; 2.5.14–16), then the sexual acts they perform (2.5.6; 2.5.17), and finally the women with whom they perform those acts (2.5.6; 2.5.18). Posthumus points to a relation between a man and the husband he cuckolds, the eroticism of which is routed through the wife. If the "woman's part" refers explicitly to the female presence in reproduction that always already contaminates male descent, then expurgating it leaves men to direct their erotic energy to each other. However, the establishment of these direct relations does not accord with the play's marital and reproductive logic. The "woman's part" in Posthumus may be what enables him to desire relations between men that, according to the play's logic, interfere with marriage. Insofar as he identifies this "woman's part" with sexual pleasure, he can understand his body in terms of the sexual penetration women experience, yet without reference to reproduction. Since he acknowledges the necessity of reproduction in the speech's first lines, I would argue that he is trying to think through the triangulation that reproduction entails so that it does not result in submission to another man. Then, reproduction will not carry the illegitimacy the false "coiner" represents.[41]

If we juxtapose this speech with Sonnet 20, in which Shakespeare engages the same issues of illegitimate economic activity, reproduction, and triangulation, this current of homoerotic meaning becomes clearer. Referring to "false women's fashion," Sonnet 20 anticipates Posthumus's concern about female infidelity, but more directly posits a male substitute – the addressee – as an erotic object who allows the speaker to exclude all the problems incumbent upon desire for women from their relationship.[42] The play and poem erect different hierarchies of reproduction and pleasure, however. Coming to a different conclusion than Posthumus, the speaker of Sonnet 20 allows male homoerotic relations and submission to coexist with marriage in the poem's sestet:

> And for a woman wert thou first created,
> Till nature as she wrought thee fell a-doting,
> And by addition me of thee defeated,
> By adding one thing to my purpose nothing.
> But since she pricked thee out for women's pleasure,
> Mine be thy love, and thy love's use their treasure.[43]

The sonnet speaker highlights the conflict between male-male relations and marriage that Posthumus experiences in *Cymbeline*. In the poem's examination of same-gender bonds over and against cross-gender ones, "woman's pleasure" occupies a place analogous to that of the "woman's part" from Posthumus's soliloquy. Even as the phrases echo each other partially, the speaker's focus on an economy of pleasure marginalizes the economy of reproduction that Posthumus cannot think around. The speaker imagines what Posthumus cannot: the coexistence of male-male erotic relations and marriage.

Just as in the "woman's part" speech, the sonnet speaker's discussion of anatomy is thinly veiled in euphemism, but even when its corporeal meanings are rendered explicit, ambiguity still couches the speaker's positioning of himself, the addressee, and the women with whom the addressee might procreate.[44] In one reading, the final lines of the sonnet recount how Nature, hoping to consummate her love for the addressee, gave him a penis, the "thing" whose "addition" defeats the speaker. Though the addressee is "pricked out" with a penis, the speaker does not relinquish his love, but only the erotic availability of the addressee's body, which will instead be used for heterosexual reproduction. In a contrasting reading of the sestet, the speaker may have the ingenuity to recognize that Nature has not defeated him at all by giving the addressee a penis. While "thing" may still refer to the penis, "pricked thee out" need not follow from the phallic implications of that line, which turn out not to be as clear cut. If "one thing to his purpose nothing" relies on the equation of holes with "nothing," then the anus could be the "thing" itself. Even if these lines are phallocentric, the couplet might enact a break from them, as it starts with a "but" that suggests a shift in rhetorical strategy on the speaker's part. Just as it is possible that nature gave him a prick, Nature also pricked out his body, as the anatomical treatises of the period credit her with doing, indenting it for excretion and making it penetrable sexually and pleasurably.[45] Uninterested in the front side of the addressee's body, the speaker makes use of other available indentations to create pleasure and to give his love to the addressee.

In this reading of the poem, their sexual activity does not need to inhibit the addressee from engaging in the reproductive economy that the speaker, in the sonnets that precede this one, has been encouraging the addressee to enter. Mario DiGangi notes that "for men at least, patriarchal privilege meant that marriage did not necessarily curtail homoerotic desire," and, indeed, the speaker's engagement with the back side of the addressee's body does not preclude women from making use of the generational capacities located on the front side of the addressee's body.[46] Thus, the final line's "and" encodes a non-exclusivity of homoerotic and heteroerotic acts. However, the speaker prioritizes relations between men when he reverses a traditional connection between illegitimate sexuality and usury, thereby casting heterosexual reproduction – "love's use," where "use" refers to the interest generated from usury – as an illegitimate though tolerable appropriation of the love the speaker and the addressee share. Female submission to male patriarchal power in generative acts of copulation takes its form from and becomes an imperfect copy of the submission of men to penetration by other men, because instead of producing pleasure heterosexual sex produces offspring. In the contest between pleasure and reproductive treasure encoded in the rhyme of the final couplet, pleasure is victorious, but the production of pleasure between two men does not, for the speaker, exclude the possibility of the reproductive generation of "treasure."

In contrast to Sonnet 20's non-exclusionary privileging of homoeroticism, Posthumus's soliloquy in *Cymbeline* starts from within a reproductive
logic that requires exclusivity. "Woman's part" and "woman's pleasure,"
though similarly located on the body, ultimately involve a different understanding of the reproductive labor of the body. In the play, the man who
wishes to enter the procreative marital order must not find pleasure in submission to other men because submission might also involve the usurpation
of his place in sexual generation. It is a relation he should "guard against,"
again anticipating the description of the heavily guarded and gated entrails
in Crooke's *Mikrokosmographia* and Fletcher's *Purple Island*. The activation
of the threat to the heterosexual reproductive order posed by male-male
relations arises from Posthumus's rivalry with Iachimo and Cloten for the
sexual possession of Innogen. Both rivals wish to make use of Innogen's
sexuality to secure Posthumus's submission.

Innogen becomes the focal point of Iachimo's rivalry with Posthumus
because Iachimo believes she "words him . . . a great deal from the matter"
(1.4.15–16). Posthumus's reputation derives from her worth rather than
his actions, and it is his subordinate position in relation to Innogen that
Iachimo, through the wager, uses as a model for the relationship he desires
with Posthumus. His machinations resemble the circulation of jewelry
steeped in corporeal symbolism that occurs in *All's Well*. Innogen's ring
signifies the endurance of their love in the face of his exile, as she tells
Posthumus to "keep it till you woo another wife, / When Innogen is
dead" (1.1.114–115). The bracelet's inferiority, for Posthumus, resembles his
social inferiority to Innogen: "as I my poor self did exchange for you, /
To your so infinite loss, so in our trifles / I still win of you" (1.1.120–
122). Posthumus's gift of the bracelet, or "manacle" as Posthumus calls it
(1.1.123), attempts to fetter Innogen to his masculine authority, but the
bracelet's lesser worth nevertheless retains for it a symbolic relationship
with Posthumus's submission to Innogen, as Valerie Wayne points out.[47]
Obtaining the bracelet and the ring, Iachimo reunites these tokens to
bring about Posthumus's submission to him. When it changes hands from
Innogen to Posthumus to Iachimo, the ring encodes the double meanings
of the woman's part as both masculinity's dependence on women and the
erotics of male submission to other men. When Posthumus receives the
ring from Innogen, it symbolizes his submission to a wife of higher birth.
When he subsequently gives the ring to Iachimo after "losing" the wager, it
becomes a material sign of his submission to Iachimo. First in relation to a
woman and then in relation to a man, Posthumus occupies the subordinate

position of woman in patriarchy, and the play suggests and defends against the erotics of Posthumus's occupation of this position.

Twice, Innogen unwittingly refers to the erotics of the wager, though she does so in heteroerotic terms. When she first gives him the ring, she imagines that Posthumus will give the ring to another someday. Iachimo positions himself as precisely that superordinate substitute. Second, when she finds out that Posthumus thinks she has committed adultery, she suspects that "some jay of Italy / . . . hath betrayed him" (3.4.49–50) into thinking that she has been unfaithful so as to seduce him, thereby reversing the charge. Again, she inadvertently positions Iachimo as sexually dominant over Posthumus. Following the substitutive logic suggested by Innogen, Posthumus opens up his "woman's part" to the Italian when he gives him the ring because it is a "part" given to him by a woman and it places him in the submissive position traditionally occupied by women in Renaissance culture. This exchange is, figuratively, almost the opposite of the ring exchange in *All's Well*, for the vaginally-coded ring Innogen gives Posthumus becomes an anally-coded one when he gives it to Iachimo. Furthermore, his incredible eagerness, impeded only by Filario's counsel, to believe in Iachimo's report of Innogen's infidelity produces a scene in which Posthumus repeatedly, almost coquettishly, gives and takes back his ring from Iachimo, only to finally capitulate: "If you will swear you have not done't, you lie, / And I will kill thee if thou dost deny / Thou'st made me a cuckold" (2.4.144–146). So invested is he in this bond between cuckold and cuckolder, Posthumus would kill Iachimo rather than break free from his dominance. Posthumus's submission is only reversed when Iachimo, after being disarmed by him, admits "the heaviness and guilt within my bosom / Takes off my manhood" (5.2.1–2). The specter of his eroticized submission to another man exorcised, Posthumus can reunite with his wife.

With a similar eroticism, though with far less success, Cloten attempts to secure Posthumus's submission through the violation of Innogen. After an offstage swordfight, the First Lord flatteringly assures Cloten that he has penetrated Posthumus with his sword: "His body's a passable carcass if he be not hurt. It is a thoroughfare for steel if he be not hurt" (1.2.8–10). Here, the First Lord imagines that Posthumus's body must either be full of holes put there by Cloten's sword or naturally full of holes that Cloten's sword fills without harm. Either way, Posthumus's body is penetrable, and it is this penetrability that Cloten hopes to take advantage of through his rivalry over Innogen. Continuing the imagery of Posthumus's body as a city, the Second Lord tells us that Cloten's sword did not penetrate Posthumus, but "went o'th'backside the town" (1.2.11–12). Around the swordfight, a contest motivated by rivalry over the sexual penetration of Innogen, the play circulates a series of phallic and anal images that casts male rivalry in similarly penetrative terms.

Cloten's carefully constructed scheme to rape Innogen for insulting him emphasizes the twinned erotic and violent elements of the submission of Posthumus that Cloten desires. Innogen compares Cloten unfavorably to Posthumus's "meanest garment" (2.3.130), insulting Cloten so much that he focuses on the comparison for the rest of his life. These clothes become instrumental in Cloten's plan to take Posthumus's place with Innogen, but the fact that they belong to Posthumus increasingly generates his arousal and taste for violence. After demanding one of Posthumus's suits from Pisanio, Cloten sketches out his plan:

With that suit upon my back will I ravish her – first kill him, and in her eyes; there shall she see my valour, which will then be a torment to her contempt. He on the ground, my speech of insultment ended on his dead body, and when my lust hath dined – which, as I say, to vex her I will execute in the clothes that she so praised – to the court I'll knock her back, foot her home again. (3.5.137–144)

In a spiral of eroticism and violence, Cloten takes special care to plan that he will kill Posthumus first and then, building upon the violence of Posthumus's fatal submission, rape Innogen, with the corpse of the man whose clothes he wears nearby.

For Cloten, both forms of violence, murder and rape, have their erotic components even as they are ultimately about power within the kingdom. The object of this eroticized violence is blurred, aimed as it is at both Innogen and Posthumus. Thinking that he has arrived where he will meet Posthumus, Cloten reflects upon his relative attractiveness and denies the validity of Innogen's insulting comparison to Posthumus. Catching up on his mirror-time, he tells himself:

I dare speak it to myself, for it is not vainglory for a man and his glass to confer in his own chamber. I mean the lines of my body are as well drawn as his: no less young, more strong, not beneath him in fortunes, beyond him in the advantage of the time, above him in birth, alike conversant in general services, and more remarkable in single oppositions. (4.1.7–13)

Cloten positions himself as Innogen in order to understand her attraction to Posthumus. Appreciating his own body while wearing Posthumus's clothes, Cloten admits to an appreciation of Posthumus's body as well, for the comparison specifies that their bodies are equally attractive. The similarity of their bodies is later confirmed when Innogen herself mistakes Cloten's headless corpse for Posthumus, and both scenes pivot on a character's sense of intimate knowledge of Posthumus's body. Cloten's vainglorious response to his own reflection gestures toward an attraction to Posthumus, whom he is attempting to resemble and subordinate for the purpose of raping Innogen. Though Cloten never attains a modicum of the success that Iachimo temporarily enjoys, Cloten's plot as he envisions it is a more intensely violent version of Iachimo's rivalry with Posthumus, and both explore the erotics of male submission as a threat to the play's central married couple.

Shakespeare recasts the play's other representations of male same-sex bonds in familial terms that are safely, though controvertibly, non-erotic, and this reinscription ultimately seeks to prevent the threat of eroticized male submission from metastasizing. The play's treatment of cross-dressing illustrates this representational strategy because it creates further opportunities to stage male submission for the sake of rejecting it as a basis for erotic investment. As Fidele, Innogen is unable to replace "fear and niceness" with "a waggish courage" (3.4.156,158) as Pisanio instructs her to do. Unlike Viola in *Twelfth Night*, Rosalind in *As You Like It*, and Portia in *The Merchant of Venice*, who each achieve an arguable measure of temporary empowerment when in male disguise, Innogen is severely physically weakened in her cross-dressed state to the point of nearly dying. In disguise, then, Innogen stages a version of the male submission the play rejects. What is more, though the extent to which any of Shakespeare's cross-dressed heroines mount a radical critique of gender norms and heteronormativity is debatable, in *Cymbeline* Shakespeare stifles the homoerotic responses generated by the cross-dressed heroine instead of playfully exploiting the dramatic irony surrounding the identity of the cross-dressed heroine to create non-standard erotic pairings. Innogen's major interactions while disguised involve characters who – as Belarius repeatedly reminds the audience in his asides identifying Guiderius and Arviragus as the stolen princes – are members of her own family rather than potential love interests. The brothers nevertheless greet the frail, sickly Innogen in erotic terms that are immediately redefined as familial feelings. When Guiderius says that, if Fidele "were . . . a woman," he "should woo hard" (3.6.66, 67), Arviragus responds that since "he is a man, I'll love him as my brother" (3.6.69). A little thing like the presence of a penis, inferred from the male costume, certainly does not stop Orlando from wooing "Ganymede" in place of Rosalind in this way in *As You Like It*. As Michael Shapiro notes, the defusing of the brothers' sexual response in *Cymbeline* raises and guards against both incest and homoeroticism, but the fact that Innogen, in her weakened condition, elicits such a sexualized response aligns this scene with the threatening erotics of male submission in the play's portrayal of Posthumus.[48] Her weakness and youth doubly subordinate her to these men. The erotic response that necessarily follows from what, in the brothers' perspectives, is an encounter with a subordinate male is supposed to be reshaped and contained by the family feeling that operates on the level of the audience's knowledge. Voicing what the audience already knows, the characters collapse the cognitive differences that had been the source of so much erotic play with his other cross-dressed heroines.

As these levels of knowledge that differ among the characters and between the characters and the audience become more complicated, Shakespeare reroutes into familial terms the erotic content of what, on some level within the action of the play, appears as a male-male bond involving submission. Even though Shakespeare explores incestuous eroticism in other plays, this play seems to operate under the assumption, however false, that the presence of the familial effectively or safely removes the erotic component of the relation. When Innogen awakens from the Queen's potion, she misrecognizes Cloten's recently decapitated corpse as Posthumus, given his clothing and "the shape of 's leg . . . his hand, / His foot Mercurial, his Martial thigh, / [and] The brawns of Hercules" (4.2.311–313). Without a face from which she could determine his real identity, she mourns the man she believes to be her husband because of his body's resemblance to Posthumus's body. Her description hearkens back to two earlier instances of deflected homoeroticism in the play. First, she echoes Cloten's eroticized description of the similarities between his and Posthumus's body. Second, her misrecognition parallels the unwittingly incestuous response of Guiderius and Arviragus to the disguised Innogen, for the man she thinks is her husband is actually her stepbrother. Since she imagines this to be the body of the man she loves, there is presumably an erotic component to the affect that guides her interaction with this corpse. Spreading Cloten's blood on her face, Innogen explains that she wishes to reroute the scene's erotics "that we the horrider may seem to those / Which chance to find us" (4.2.333–334). The imagined passer-by would see two bodies, one headless but both wearing male costume, in a necrophilial embrace and react, Innogen hopes, with horror at the spectacle. However, when Lucius notices them, he does not horrifically associate male-male bonds with violence and death, as the play's construction of Cloten's rivalry with Posthumus has done to this point. Quickly disavowing the necrophilial aspects of the scene, Lucius says "nature doth abhor to make his bed, / With the defunct, or sleep upon the dead" (4.2.359–360). Yet this disavowal does not dislodge the scene's erotics. Innogen recasts her erotic response to this body in terms of service by telling Lucius that she is a page and the body is that of her master. This master-page relation is built on the same eroticized submission that is so threatening in this play, so Lucius rewrites it too. For a moment, Shakespeare seems unable to escape representing eroticized male submission. Ready to turn Fidele, whose loyalty to her master "hath taught [the Roman soldiers] manly duties" (4.2.398), into his page, Lucius redefines Fidele's service to him as a father-son relationship, saying to Fidele that he would "rather father thee than master thee" (4.2.397). Submission characterizes the relation, but its residual eroticism is reshaped into a supposedly more palatable paternal affection.

Through this relationship, Shakespeare addresses the dangers of erotic submission that face the dominant partner, thereby complementing the play's primary focus on dangers that await the submissive male. After the battle, when the disguised Innogen garners favor from Cymbeline, she does not ask for Lucius to be pardoned as he expects, and Lucius comments, "The boy disdains me. / He leaves me, scorns me. Briefly die their joys / That place them on the truth of girls and boys" (5.6.105–107). Instead, Innogen asks Cymbeline to force Iachimo to tell her of the origin of the ring he wears, precipitating the revelations that bring Innogen and Posthumus back together. Innogen and Posthumus embrace while she is still dressed in male disguise, but she also attempts to embrace him earlier, before he knows who she is. With that first attempt, Posthumus strikes her, an action that further develops the association of violence and male-male relations in this play. The submission this violence effects is rerouted into proper heterosexual relations when Innogen's identity is revealed, and, more importantly for the resolution of the play, Innogen's displacement from the succession and her request for Posthumus to "throw me again" (5.6.263) seem to guarantee female submission and masculine dominance in perpetuity, though this is complicated by Innogen remaining dressed as Fidele.

Male dominance is cast as male corporeal impenetrability in the play's staging of the Roman invasion of Britain as well. Posthumus describes the tide turning in the battle with the Romans at a narrow lane that the Romans tried to penetrate. Their rout prevents them from further penetrating Britain, however. The possible, but ultimately averted, British loss is described with reference to the posterior. In retreat, only "the backs of Britons [were] seen, all flying / Through a strait lane" (5.5.6–7). This description of the lane as "strait" recalls the emphasis that Fletcher, in *The Purple Island*, placed on the narrowness of the anus in his poetic description.[49] Eventually, the retreat is even blocked because "the strait pass was dammed / With dead men hurt behind" (5.5.11–12). Though the narrow lane is often understood as symbolic of the vagina in order to identify Britain with the female body, male backsides and male wounds populate the lane and serve as Roman targets. As one of the places where the play exceeds its initial association of the anus with the "woman's part," the emphasis on the maleness of these bodies reminds us, as Richard Rambuss recently has done, that "the ass [can be] a site... of an erotic cathexis that is indicatively male."[50] In this martial setting, this erotic energy undergoes a reversal without becoming unmoored from masculinity. Defending the lane almost miraculously closes off these male bodies to penetration by and submission to the Roman invaders. Fueled with courage, the Britons penetrate the now cowardly Romans: "Having found the back door open, / Of the unguarded hearts, heavens, how they wound" (5.5.45–46). The Roman "hearts" are unguarded, but the Britons restore the "guardedness" of their own country by defending a lane around which anal resonances accrue in the play. Reiterating the individual transformations that occur in *All's Well* on the level of a national army, the Britons in *Cymbeline* collectively exchange exposed behinds for guarded ones, but then become invested in the Roman "back door" which is displaced up to the heart.

There remains a surplus of male submission that the play carefully displaces onto the second-in-line to Cymbeline's throne, Arviragus, and onto the King of the Britons himself, in a manner that seeks to render it benign in relation to the erotic economy of the play, which works toward the reunion of Posthumus and Innogen and looks forward to the marriage's consummation. Cymbeline experiences what in other parts of the play was so dangerous: male submission and parthenogenesis. "Although the victor, we submit to Caesar" (5.6.461), Cymbeline tells Lucius, and he explains that "We were dissuaded by our wicked queen" (5.6.464) from paying the tribute that represented that submission to Rome. Male submission and marriage still oppose each other, but, with the wicked Queen dying offstage, the play does not demand that Cymbeline be married at its conclusion. When his sons and Innogen are restored to him, he becomes "mother to the birth of three" (5.6.370). No partner, male or female, is required in this parthenogenetic fantasy, though Belarius, delivering two of the children, potentially fills such a role. Insofar as the three children symbolize the future of Britain, it is far more important in the play that Guiderius and Arviragus not be submissive and that Innogen submit to a now-dominant Posthumus because Cymbeline represents a past that will be left behind eventually. His present economic and political submission to Caesar takes its form from the past, as Cymbeline remembers, "Caesar knighted me; my youth I spent / Much under him; of him I gathered honour" (3.1.69–70). This description resembles, albeit with a martial, submissive inflection, the way *The Winter's Tale* locates the friendship of Leontes and Polixenes in an idealized past. Marriage has twice intervened for Cymbeline, however, such that the corporeal element of his submission to Caesar is stowed away in the past, and the tribute ensures that Roman bodies will not march on toward British backsides again. The double identity the play gives Rome – it is both the ancient empire and Renaissance Italy – also makes Cymbeline's submission permissible. Although he submits to ancient Rome, Iachimo and Renaissance Italy submit to Posthumus in what Patricia Parker labels a "chiastic exchange."[51] At the level of narrative, the backward-looking plot of Cymbeline unravels a marriage that is no longer expedient and submits to the forward-looking plot of Posthumus and Innogen, whose marriage depends on the restored succession of Guiderius and promises a future population to govern.

The threat of male submission cannot be eradicated from the next generation, though. As younger brother, Arviragus submits to Guiderius even before they know they are heirs: he joins Belarius as cook and servant after Guiderius kills a deer (3.6.30), and his envy is piqued when Guiderius kills Cloten (4.2.157–162). His name evokes the gender-bending *virago*, usually reserved for war-like women, and his domesticity is yoked to Innogen's cross-dressed performance of masculine submission when Belarius tells him to cook with Fidele, effectively becoming the housewife that Belarius insists Fidele become to them (4.2.165). Later, when Arviragus discovers what he thinks is Fidele's body, Guiderius warns him not to "play in wench-like words" (4.2.231). In the world of the play, there is safety in associating Arviragus with the feminine and the abjection of male submission because he is the spare to Guiderius's heir. However, what the play does not say, but Geoffrey of Monmouth and Raphael Holinshed report, is that Arviragus does succeed his brother and returns Britain to Roman submission. The sources reveal what the play prevents us from thinking: that the future inhabitants of the throne will be associated with submission. Whether or not Shakespeare intended to gesture toward these later events, the play associates the future inhabitants of the throne with submission. Because Cymbeline remains alive at the end of the play, the advancement of the next generation is deferred, much as it is at the beginning of *All's Well*. The young men and women at the end of *Cymbeline* submit to an older generation that the play has characterized as submissive.

The two plays discussed in this chapter show that the increasing conflict between non-marital and marital relations manifests itself in competing understandings of embodiment and pleasure as marriage comes to dominate the representational space reserved for the intimate sphere. In *All's Well that Ends Well*, intervention at the level of the body reorients characters in accordance with the narrative's marital trajectories. Even in the absence of explicit enforcement to marry, as *Cymbeline* shows, marriage nevertheless produces a forward-looking embodiment in men that embraces reproduction while rejecting and leaving behind the potential pleasures of submission, pleasures related to, though not completely congruent with, anal penetration. *Cymbeline*, in which Posthumus and Innogen actually desire marriage, nevertheless thematically parallels the enforced marriage plot of *All's Well*. Furthermore, the continual reiteration of marital closure in the comedies and romances on the early modern stage never fully covers over the violent appropriation of the body's powers of signification that are required to bring about such closure. Instead, the dissident strains in these plays show that the force enacted on the body, whether such force is external or internal in origin, contravenes any attempt to naturalize marriage and reproduction as the necessary outcome of a narrative. While the plays suggest that, instead of being a benign historical process, the organization of intimacy around marriage involves the forced disavowal of other forms of pleasure and relationality, they also nevertheless briefly make these alternatives intelligible as modes of living that might be recuperated when the plays are read against the grain of their narratives.

CHAPTER 3

Social status and the intimacy of masochistic sexual practice in Beaumont and Fletcher and Middleton

THE STROKE OF DEATH, THE LOVER'S PINCH: MASOCHISM AND AMBIVALENCE IN RENAISSANCE TEXTS

In the 1599 collection of epigrams by John Davies and elegies by Christopher Marlowe, a reader can find one of the frankest descriptions of masochistic sexual practices in Renaissance England: Davies's Epigram 33. "In Francum" depicts a scene of pleasure through pain and then concludes with the speaker's wish to be a part of it:

> When Francus comes to sollace with his whoore
> He sends for rods and strips himselfe stark naked:
> For his lust sleepes, and will not rise before,
> By whipping of the wench it be awaked.
> I envie'him not, but wish I had the powre,
> To make my selfe his wench but one halfe houre.[1]

The concluding moment of identification is less straightforward than it might appear, for, as Ian Frederick Moulton argues, the phrase "whipping of the wench" could refer either to Francus's whipping the wench or the wench's whipping of Francus in order to arouse him.[2] Since the epigram's speaker wants to be the wench, it is unclear whether he wants to be beaten by or to beat Francus himself. The ambiguous relationship of Renaissance satire to dominant culture further complicates the meaning of these lines. That the Davies-Marlowe collection and other verse satire would be thought subversive enough for the Bishops to ban them in 1599 may seem curious because epigrams and satire usually reserve their scorn for departures from a social norm. In the act of imagining such departures only to critique them, the Bishops worried, epigrams would provide scripts for readers to discover and act on their own potentially transgressive sexual tastes.[3]

Like the other "failures of intimacy" I discuss in this book, Renaissance texts' representations of masochism are suffused with this tension between making pleasures available and calling into question whether such pleasures ought to be desired. For example, in Shakespeare's *Antony and Cleopatra* (1606–1607), Cleopatra eroticizes death when she tells Charmian, "The stroke of death is as a lover's pinch / Which hurts and is desired."[4] For the audience, her imminent suicide shrouds the masochistic pleasure of the lover's pinch that she imagines. What is briefly referenced in *Antony and Cleopatra* becomes in other Renaissance plays a fuller exploration of the politics of alternate forms of sexual practice, and in this chapter, I hope both to map the ideological terrain surrounding these dramatic representations and to complicate our understanding of early modern intimacy by turning to non-Shakespearean drama. Through a transgressive re-enactment of hierarchical relations, between and within classes and genders, masochistic pleasures offered Renaissance readers and audiences an opportunity to reimagine social relations. Bringing same-sex and opposite-sex relations together in this chapter, I seek to expand the scope of queer inquiry to shed light on what Jonathan Goldberg has called "the open secret of the imbrication of alternative possibilities within normative sexualities."[5] In the Renaissance, certain types of same-sex and cross-sex relations were cast as potentially disruptive to sexual normalcy, and such disruption is especially illuminated by focusing not on nascent forms of identity but instead by attending to the history of sexual practices, especially those where the gender of object choice does not play the same role as it does in modern parsings of sexuality, though it may still be influential in shaping a practice's form and meaning.

In relation to this book's larger argument about the contest over intimacy, masochism locates pleasures at the body's surface, uncoupling inwardness from affective relations. Though masochism seems on first glance to appropriate the body much in the same way that differences in class and gender register through surface indicators such as clothing or hairstyle, these latter stabilizing appropriations of the body rely on surface markers to point to a presumably deeper truth about identity and in this way subordinate surfaces to depths. By locating subjectivity on the surface of the body, masochism does not invoke the surface for the sake of signifying depth, but instead interrupts this economy of signification. Moreover, because the masochist enacts his or her submission for the sake of pleasure rather than punishment, the masochist's willful submission challenges the idea that agency can only derive from dominance. By diverting coercive intents into pleasurable effects, masochistic sexual practices call into question the efficacy of social control.

Among the many Renaissance texts that struggle to contain the masochist's disturbances of status hierarchy, patriarchy, and homosocial masculinity, Francis Beaumont and John Fletcher's *Philaster* (1609) and *The Maid's Tragedy* (1610–1611) implicate masochistic eroticism in their ambivalent treatment of gender and absolutism. Thomas Middleton's *The Nice Valour* (1622), however, offers probably the lengthiest dramatic treatment of the ambivalence surrounding masochism and status hierarchy in Elizabethan and Jacobean drama.[6] In Middleton's play, Lapet, who finds pleasure in willingly submitting to beatings, publishes a book on how to optimize the experience of being beaten, a book that suggests that status is a performance that may be imitable by those born outside the aristocracy. Through masochism, he also articulates a mode of erotic relations between men that is unmediated by the exchange of women. Working against Lapet's disturbing potential, the marriages at the end of the play both mediate relations between men and bolster the status hierarchy at court. Nevertheless, as I will argue, *The Nice Valour* allows space for the representation of masochistic pleasures, and through print, those pleasures can still circulate – just as Lapet's book does within the world of the play – made available to audiences who may not know what they would enjoy erotically until they see it represented.

"WHAT PRETTY NEW DEVICE IS THIS?" MASOCHISM'S AMBIVALENT ALLURE IN BEAUMONT AND FLETCHER

Ever since Richard von Krafft-Ebing first referred to the experience of pleasure in pain as "masochism" in *Psychopathia Sexualis* (1886), the origin, nature, and effects of such pleasure have been debated in psychological and philosophical contexts. Most recently, masochism has played a role in debates within feminist and queer theory about the political implications of sexual practices, especially regarding whether masochism replicates and extends forms of domination. I would argue that, since masochism insists that submission be geared toward the production of pleasure, masochistic sexual practice endows the simulated position of powerlessness with a degree of control over the terms of the simulation. Freud, in *Beyond the Pleasure Principle* (1920), recognized an implicit form of agency in repeated unpleasure when he described the child playing the *fort-da* game: "at the outset he was in a *passive* situation – he was overpowered by the experience; but, by repeating it, unpleasurable though it was, as a game, he took on an *active* part. These efforts might be put down to an instinct for mastery that was acting independently of whether the memory was in itself pleasurable or not."⁷ This mini-drama positions him as an agent experiencing pleasure. Taking pleasure in excessive submission trains the body to withstand, resist, and respond to domination. Kaja Silverman suggests that even the apparent identification of the masochist with power structures is belied by the masochist's substitution of pleasure for subordination: "although he seems to subordinate himself to the law of the father, that is only because he knows how to transform punishment into pleasure, and severity into bliss."⁸ According to Silverman, the masochist's pleasure is a subversive substitute for the disciplinary effects that the ideologies of oppression presumably seek. Thus, domination in masochism is a repetition with a difference.

In a re-evaluation of the subordinate status of masochism to sadism, especially as they are coupled in Freud's "The Economic Problem of Masochism" (1924), Gilles Deleuze situates the masochistic scene in pedagogy to find the masochist as an agent securing his own pleasure: "the masochistic hero appears to be educated and fashioned by the authoritarian woman whereas basically it is he who forms her, dresses her for the part and prompts the harsh words she addresses to him. It is the victim who speaks through the mouth of his torturer, without sparing himself."⁹ Deleuze's description, involving costumes and scripts, is particularly useful for analyzing dramatic literary representation. Staging pleasure as a performance, the masochist actively sets the conditions of his own submission. Yet, rather than re-enacting domination over his partner, the masochist, who for Deleuze is male and heterosexual, enters into a contractual relation that "presupposes in principle the free consent of the contracting parties and determines between them a system of reciprocal rights and duties."¹⁰ Masochistic sexual relations, despite their apparent replication of oppressive structures within society, can be motivated by a utopian and equitable impulse that could be extrapolated as the basis for a more just rearticulation of social relations.

The pleasures of pain have a history that extends back well before Krafft-Ebing. Among the usual Renaissance contexts for pleasure in pain were Petrarchan love poetry, the routine whipping of schoolchildren, and the submission to God and emulation of Christ's passion in religious devotion. The German Johann Heinrich Meibom's tract "On the Use of Flogging in Medical and Venereal Affairs" (1639) was available in English after 1718. By the late nineteenth century, as Havelock Ellis points out, sexual flagellation was regarded as the most common perversion in England and it was even called "the English vice."¹¹ This notoriety developed prior to the emergence of the modern psychoanalytic apparatus that pathologizes masochism and, arguably, prior to the context of contracts and rights that Deleuze invokes to recuperate it. Although the discursive terrain of modern masochism is different from that which surrounded the experience of pleasure in pain in the Renaissance, "masochism" remains a useful term – and one of the few available terms – for describing the eroticized experience of pain represented in Renaissance texts.[12] More generally, modern work on masochism provides me with a set of tools for recuperating the traces of masochism in these early modern texts. This work provides modern readers with a language for talking about the dissident forms of pleasure that, despite their own narrative tendencies, some Renaissance plays made available to their early modern audiences and continue to make available to the modern reader. Masochism provides a model for renegotiating the experience of domination by radically destabilizing the standard active/passive binaries from which structures of domination take their form. Masochistic sexual practice performs a submission that secures, rather than undermines, agency for the masochist.

Francis Beaumont and John Fletcher's *Philaster* and *The Maid's Tragedy* make masochistic pleasures available on the stage and the page for Renaissance audiences and readers while attempting to defuse these pleasures' destabilizing influence on gender roles, status hierarchy, and absolutist rule. Helping to understand this tension, Walter Cohen has argued that Jacobean tragicomedies often retreat from the radical propositions – about sexuality, gender, and class – raised in the course of their plots, and it is in this retreat that one can find, symptomatically, traces of a subversive politics that might not otherwise register as disturbances to the social order. This movement is especially pronounced in tragicomic closure; as Cohen writes, "the more the conclusion feels like a desperate expedient designed to extricate the dramatist from an impossible situation, the greater the probability of radical or subversive tendencies."[13] The potential destabilization of masochistic pleasure may be more rather than less appealing in the plays.

In the tragicomedy *Philaster*, Princess Arethusa resists her father's patriarchal and absolutist attempts to govern her body and instead pursues her own pleasure and relationship with Philaster. Speaking of Sicily and Calabria, which she will inherit from her usurping father, Arethusa declares to a more than usually flabbergasted Philaster: "then know I must have them, and thee."[14] Arethusa is aware of the transgressiveness of her actions when she asks Philaster to look away from her so that she may make her admission. Nevertheless, her defiance of proscriptions on women's speech and of her father's patriarchal and political authority serves a greater moral purpose: the restoration of Philaster to his rightful inheritance through their union. She contends that their love "Will be the nobler and the better blessed / In that the secret justice of the gods / Is mingled with it" (1.2.102–104). The ethical weight given to Arethusa's active pursuit of affective relations provides an important framework for her later figuration of pleasure in terms of pain. When Philaster becomes jealous of her relationship with Bellario, she imagines herself, in the context of her father's hunting party, receiving the same punishment as Actaeon for discovering the naked Diana bathing. This fantasy of what Jeffrey Masten calls "unsafe hunting practices" is theatrical in that it involves the spectacle of Diana's body and Arethusa's inhabiting the role of Actaeon, and it is textual both because it derives from a classical myth and because she wishes to produce another such text of her own body.[15] When Arethusa experiences this spectacularized, eroticized violence on stage in Act 4, scene 5, the play becomes the script for the audience that the myth was for Arethusa, and Arethusa has shown, by identifying across gender lines with Actaeon, that this script is available to men and women. Stabbing Arethusa, Philaster substitutes violence for consummation, and that violence continues to be eroticized when Arethusa becomes angry at the Country Fellow's attempted intercession. "What ill-bred man art thou to intrude thyself / Upon our private sports, our recreations?" (4.5.90–91), she demands, implying that masochistic sex is an activity that well-bred people would recognize as pleasurable and not requiring intervention. Like a female version of the Deleuzian masochist who instructs the dominant partner in order to achieve pleasure and who "stands guilt on its head by making punishment into a condition that makes possible the forbidden pleasure," Arethusa manages this scene, scripts her own achievement of pleasure, and resists being recast as lacking agency.[16] Whereas Silverman describes masochism as "providing a crucial mechanism for eroticizing lack and subordination" for female subjectivity, Arethusa's masochism helps her make use of the agency that comes with her aristocratic position while temporarily attenuating expectations for subservience based on gender.[17]

Beaumont and Fletcher downplay the possible emergence of such pleasure from Arethusa's defiance of her father and King. Instead, they cast her pursuit of masochistic pleasure as an extension of patriarchy and absolutism's power over her. Specifically, when comedy and tragedy collide in the forest, the play moves to foreclose on masochism as an alternative mode of experiencing pleasure. On the tragic side, Philaster's violent encounter with Arethusa is the result of the King's exercise of his patriarchal and absolutist authority to keep them apart. Replicating that authority, Philaster similarly treats Arethusa's sexuality as his property: "Now you may take that little right I have / To this poor kingdom; give it to your Joy, / For I have no joy in it" (3.2.119–121). The kingdom is literally the Kingdom of Sicily that her father usurps and that she plans to return to Philaster upon their marriage. Symbolically, the "kingdom" refers to her body, and as her future husband he expects to be the absolute monarch of her sexuality. We are reminded that Philaster borrows the King's language when the King demands that his subjects produce Arethusa's body when she goes missing from the hunting party: "I do command you all, as you are subjects, / To show her me! What, am I not your King? / If ay, then am I not to be obeyed?" (4.4.32–34). With these words, the King ties together his absolute authority over his subjects and his authority over his daughter's body, but he soon finds out he controls neither. Dion's retort, "if you command things possible and honest" (4.4.35), exposes the limits of the King's authority as ruler, man, and father just as Philaster's resignation of his claim on Arethusa exposes his limits. The Country Fellow's comic incomprehension and pretension turn the critique of absolutism into anti-court satire. Arethusa's comment about the Country Fellow's ill-breeding associates masochism with the court and sexualized violence with the absolutist political philosophy practiced there. Thus, the pleasure of pain is cast as a symptom of a disorder at once familial and courtly – in the relationship between sovereign and subject, father and daughter, and man and woman – that requires the intervention of the similarly non-aristocratic citizens.[18]

While the King may eventually recognize his dependence on the people, the challenge of his authority over his daughter as property is not resolved in the same way. Indeed, the resolution of the citizens' revolt helps move the play away from the subversive implications of a female character who says of her disobedience to her father, "there's nothing that can stir me from myself" (5.3.68). Inverting her role as custodian of Philaster and Bellario during their imprisonment, Arethusa calls Philaster her "keeper" (5.3.48), and her carceral language not only foreshadows her imprisonment for defying her father, but it also anticipates the simultaneity of the citizens' revolt and her agency's evaporation upon her secret marriage to Philaster. When the King offers his blessing on the marriage in return for Philaster's successful pacification of the revolt, Arethusa's orchestration of the marriage in defiance of her father is rewritten as the male-male exchange of political favors and women that resembles the King's original arrangement with Pharamond. "Take thy right, take her; / She is thy right too" (5.5.15–16), the King says, handing over his daughter and the inheritance of the kingdom of Sicily in one gesture. In Act 1, scene 2, Arethusa plays an active role in determining her erotic fate through that original plan, but here she remains in the background while the men make a deal. The end of the play de-emphasizes her political acumen and her initiative in securing her own pleasure and focuses instead on men negotiating the resolution of their political conflicts. Moreover, she is still suspected of being unchaste and is unable to demonstrate otherwise on her own until Bellario is revealed to be a woman. The prospect of marriage places Arethusa in a far more passive position than she was in when she argued with the Country Fellow. The play ends with ambivalence about the position of women in marriage, for Bellario/Euphrasia rejects the King's offer to find her a husband: "Never, sir, will I / Marry; it is a thing within my vow" (5.5.194–195).[19] Bellario's reply indicates that marriage is no panacea for male or absolutist domination, but is a repackaged form of it. Marriage, not masochism, then, extends patriarchal control over women's bodies and the absolutist sovereign's control over his female subjects.

Bellario/Euphrasia's refusal to marry is a logical extension of several instances where Bellario offers up his own body for masochistic punishment. When Philaster prepares him to serve as Arethusa's page and as a go-between, Bellario believes he is being sent away out of disfavor and pleads, "Let me be corrected / To break my stubbornness if it be so, / Rather than turn me off; and I shall mend" (2.1.37–39). Masochism here is offered as a reparative to the status subordination of servants that dispossesses them of control of their own employment. Later, when Philaster confronts Bellario with his suspicion that the page has had sex with Arethusa, Bellario asks him to

> Hew me asunder, and whilst I can think
> I'll love those pieces you have cut away
> Better than those that grow, and kiss those limbs
> Because you made 'em so.   (3.1.255–258)

The play eroticizes service as masochism and as a threat to the romantic and marital union of Philaster and Arethusa. At the end of the play, when Bellario/Euphrasia is incorporated into Arethusa and Philaster's household, the threat of service to marriage has only seemingly dissipated because Bellario is actually female. In Bellario/Euphrasia's refusal to marry, the play concludes with a woman's expression of her pleasure, which Beaumont and Fletcher have positioned from the start as defiance of masculine political and sexual control of the female body.

Written a year or two after *Philaster*, Beaumont and Fletcher's *The Maid's Tragedy* continues, but in a different generic framework, this reflection on sexual practice, defiant women, and unruly subjects. *The Maid's Tragedy*, with similar ambivalence, locates masochism within Renaissance concerns about the politics of absolutism and gender.[20] Not only does an absolute monarch imagine masochistic pleasures, he places his mistress, Evadne, in a position of power. Such empowerment, however, is ultimately only a temporary necessity that makes it possible to punish the King for abusing his authority. In one of the most remarkable scenes in Renaissance drama, the King, tied up by Evadne, excitedly and ironically believes they are about to engage in erotic play:

> What pretty new device is this, Evadne?
> What, do you tie me to you? By my love,
> This is a quaint one. Come, my dear, and kiss me.
> I'll be thy Mars; to bed, my Queen of Love,
> Let us be caught together, that the gods may see
> And envy our embraces.[21]

Like Arethusa's invocation of Diana and Actaeon, the King hopes to outdo a scene from myth – in this case where Vulcan traps Venus and Mars together. The reference to the gods enviously seeing them together acknowledges the theatricality of masochism and registers a consciousness that the play participates in the circulation of new sexual knowledge by making transgressive sexual pleasures available for identification. With "new device," the play admits to challenging the boundaries of what counts as sex. Although the play's narrative structure strains to undermine the potential of masochistic pleasure to offer alternatives to political absolutism and patriarchy, the representation of royalty indulging in masochism nevertheless prompts a status-conscious audience to desire these pleasures of a king.

Like Deleuze's masochist, the King actively scripts the scene, and though he uses and extends his prerogative as monarch to do so, he nevertheless embraces a form of sexual pleasure that reverses the dynamics of male patriarchal authority that so often underwrite male sexual violence against women, as well as other forms of male regulation of female sexuality encoded in patriarchal marriage. Beaumont and Fletcher's representation of the King's sexualized response departs from their source in Thomas Acheley's translation of Matteo Bandello's *A Most Lamentable and Tragicall Historie Conteyning the Outragious and Horrible Tyrannie which a Spanish Gentlewoman named Violenta Executed Upon Her Lover Didaco*, where Didaco does not misinterpret Violenta's intentions in the way the King does with Evadne. Instead, in the masochistic scene that Beaumont and Fletcher have the King imagine, he puts Evadne in a position that could extend the sexual autonomy upon which she has already drawn in the play.

She has admitted to flouting proscriptions against unchaste behavior when she disabuses the duped Amintor of his assumption that her resistance to consummating their marriage is based on virginal modesty. "Unapt for such a vow [of chastity]" (2.1.289), she has sought erotic pleasure on her own terms. According to Kathleen McLuskie, Evadne's refusal, which brings Amintor's naïve preconceptions about women and marriage crashing down upon him, undermines "the narrative and the social conventions which assume that marriage will achieve the happy and automatic conjunction of social form and sexual pleasure."[22] Evadne also unabashedly admits that she has been strategic rather than conventional with her sexuality: "I do enjoy the best, and in that height / Have sworn to stand, or die" (2.1.296–297). Frank about her sexuality's utility, Evadne is fortified against the male expectation of exclusive access to her in marriage. Evadne's autonomy remains independent of the King's specific authority because, motivated by ambition rather than a desire for long-term monogamy, she will "forsake [him] and would bend to him / That won [his] throne" if the King were ever deposed (3.1.173–174). With no direct avenue to power on her own, she will use her sexuality to shape patriarchy to her own ends from within.

Melantius produces in Evadne a coercive and disciplinary shame for even entertaining such thoughts. Instead of constituting a moment of pleasure that subverts marital regulations of sexuality, binding the King challenges his absolutist authority without representing an extension of Evadne's power and ambition as a woman. That is, while her killing of the King involves a challenge to royal authority, this challenge is based on the reinstitution of normative proscriptions against female sexuality. McLuskie writes that in the play "sexual relations are simply the context in which other stories of honour and power are enacted," and even though Evadne is a tool in this contest, the struggle for power in the King's binding is actually between Melantius as patriarch – in this case a brother who plays the role of father – and the King as absolutist monarch.[23] Specifically, they fight over whether, when the monarch's authority interferes with patriarchal authority, the king's male subjects owe him obedience. Melantius explains to Lysippus, the King's brother, that though he served him dutifully as a soldier in the past, he has "flung him off with my allegiance, / And stand here mine own justice, to revenge / What I have suffered in him" (5.2.49–51). The King's affair with Evadne reflects on him as her nearest kinsman; it "brand[s] my noble actions with his lust" (5.2.42), Melantius says. Thus, Melantius throws off his loyalty to the King for moral reasons almost as easily as Evadne says she could do if the King, through a fall from power, no longer suited her ambitions.

Despite the similarities of the brother and sister, Evadne suffers from Melantius's patriarchal morality, which condemns her subordination of loyalty, sexual and otherwise, to power and ambition, while Melantius seems to escape censure for disloyally instigating a vengeful regicide. It is not so much that Evadne operates under a false sense of her own empowerment when she is with the King, or that she is only empowered once she stands up to his absolutism, for when she resists absolutism she pays heed to Melantius's sexual morality, in which marriage is the only legitimate arena for her sexual experience and female ambition is prohibited. In contrast, as the King's mistress, her mock-marriage to Amintor pays lip service to that morality only to deauthorize it. I would argue that not only does Evadne tap into a discourse of ambition to which women were traditionally denied access, she is far more sexually free when she associates herself with the King's royal authority than she is when she is acting under Melantius's moral authority. When the play associates sexual license with royal authority run amok, it reinstalls patriarchal authority over sexual pleasure to undermine absolutism. As part of its critique of absolutism, then, the play forecloses on the alternate forms of sexual pleasure that it entertains in the course of its plot, including the masochistic sexual practices the King briefly imagines.

Aspatia offers a different challenge to the patriarchal regulation of female sexuality through marriage. She resembles Bellario/Euphrasia from *Philaster* when she imagines her own version of masochistic pleasure. Though powerless to prevent Amintor from casting her off to marry Evadne, she increasingly controls the suffering that results. Thus, even as she confirms Silverman's claim that female masochism is the eroticization of the normal subordinate status of women in patriarchy, Aspatia iconicizes her masochism in a way that affects her place in power relations. On Evadne and Amintor's wedding night, Aspatia offers Evadne a mixed blessing in which she asserts her status as the authority on women's suffering at the hands of men:

> May all the marriage joys
> That longing maids imagine in their beds
> Prove so unto you! May no discontent
> Grow 'twixt your love and you! But if there do,
> Inquire of me and I will guide your moan,
> And teach you an artificial way to grieve,
> To keep your sorrow waking.   (2.1.90–96)

Aspatia here invokes the multiple meanings of "artificial" that the *OED* indicates were available in the seventeenth century. The grief she will teach is a kind of art, human-fashioned as opposed to natural, and it is performed skillfully. Thus, "an artificial way to grieve" will aestheticize the experience in order to prolong it and "keep [her] sorrow waking." Grief may also be "artificial" in the sense of "artful," that is, involving cunning. Through grief, Aspatia articulates a politics of resistance to patriarchal subordination. In his account of modern masochism, Theodore Reik maintains that the masochist's submission rebelliously reroutes oppression: "the purpose to obtain satisfaction *in spite* of all threats develops into the tendency to gain satisfaction *to spite* all threats."[24] For Aspatia, a woman may extend her suffering at the hands of men beyond the original circumstances that generated it in order to define a subject position through which she can control her erotic fate and find such satisfaction.

When her waiting-gentlewoman Antiphila makes a needlework picture of Ariadne, abandoned on Naxos by Theseus, Aspatia expounds upon the role iconicity plays in empowering her in her suffering. Aspatia feels kinship with this forsaken female figure, but ultimately envisions supplanting Ariadne in the pantheon of women cast off by their lovers. Assuming an authoritative tone, she tells Antiphila to "do it again by me, the lost Aspatia" (2.2.66). Eventually the needlework commemorates Aspatia's experience in love with Amintor when Aspatia commands Antiphila, "strive to make *me* look / Like sorrow's monument" (2.2.73–74, emphasis mine). She aestheticizes her dejection and rejection: Aspatia's "miserable life" and Antiphila's "poor picture" (2.2.78) become interchangeable as Aspatia embraces her status as the embodiment of female suffering and abandonment.

Suffering, according to Aspatia, is the inevitable outcome of the clash between "the truth of maids and perjuries of men" (2.1.107). Yet she realizes that if she can extend her experience of suffering so that it transforms her into an icon, that iconic status, even as it makes her the object of the gaze, will turn her powerlessness in determining her erotic fate into a position of authority that can, in turn, empower other women. She instructs her waiting-gentlewomen:

> If you needs must love,
> Forced by ill fate, take to your maiden bosoms
> Two dead-cold aspics, and of them make lovers;
> They cannot flatter nor forswear: One kiss
> Makes a long peace for all.   (2.2.22–26)

Because women are "forced by ill fate" into it, Aspatia indicates, romantic love is inherently a situation of powerlessness for women: men who

promise them marriage can abandon them, and this abandonment dispro-
portionately stigmatizes women. In a reference to phallic aspics that recalls
Cleopatra's eroticization of death in Shakespeare's play, Aspatia advocates
a proactive, eroticized suicide. Through the active pursuit of their own
death, Aspatia argues, women can subvert the intentions of the "ill fate"
that caused them to fall in love in the first place. Moreover, with the experience of suicide figured erotically, women can control their experience of
pleasure in suicide in a way that they cannot in romantic love.

Putting this argument to the test later in the play, Aspatia remains
ever the instructor, modeling masochistic practice for audience members
and making sexual knowledge available to them through performance. Her
cross-dressed dueling scene has the potential to be as comical as the reluctant
fighting between Viola/Cesario and Andrew Aguecheek in *Twelfth Night*.
Unlike Viola, Aspatia is looking for a fight and eventually gets one, hitting
Amintor until he engages her in combat. To his surprise, she positions her
body to maximize the impact, as Amintor observes: "the blows thou mak'st
at me / Are quite besides, and those I offer thee / Thou spreadst thine arms
and tak'st upon thy breast, / Alas defenceless!" (5.3.100–103). The result for
Aspatia is a satisfaction at once juridical, because of the dueling context, and
erotic: "I have got enough, / And my desire" (5.3.103–104). Lee Bliss rightly
notes that the play substitutes the "death" of orgasm with Aspatia's real
death, but the substitutive logic of this scene involves Aspatia's replicating
marital consummation with an empowering difference.[25] Although what
Aspatia desires is her own death, it is significant that she expresses the
content of her desire outside of any marital bond. Jennifer Low argues
that "the combat recontextualizes Aspatia as an exemplar of an extreme
type of feminine virtue, a marked contrast to her unpleasant, morally
confused rival [Evadne]."[26] Yet I would argue that her eroticization of this
combat, through her spread arms and her claim that her desires have been
satisfied, makes her the temporary heir to Evadne, not her opposite. Evadne
demonstrates "unpleasantness" and "moral confusion" only when she is
judged from the patriarchal perspective of Melantius, which eventually she
internalizes, but there is continuity between the determination with which
Evadne begins the play and that with which Aspatia departs from it.

Aspatia actively pursues sexual pleasure on her own terms within circumstances that are incredibly limiting for women. Even though this masochistic scene takes its cues from the marital consummation that she expected
from Amintor and from the male domination encoded in the marital
bond in patriarchy, her masochism is decidedly non-marital and not passive. Indeed, Aspatia's suffering is initially the result of her powerlessness,

but she ultimately asserts some control over her pleasure by experiencing abjection as erotic rather than as shameful. That is, she is in control of an eroticized moment in the play with a man who is not her husband. Moreover, by eroticizing oppression, she both seeks to interrupt the process whereby disciplinary correction produces coercive shame and docile femininity and teaches the audience how to do so.

"HERE'S ALL YOUR BLOWS AND BLOW-MEN WHATSOEVER":
REDEFINING SOCIAL RELATIONS BETWEEN MEN THROUGH
MASOCHISM IN *THE NICE VALOUR*

The Nice Valour has been associated with Beaumont and Fletcher's corpus at least since it was printed in their 1647 First Folio, and it has striking similarities with *Philaster* and *The Maid's Tragedy* when it comes to representations of masochistic pleasures. Now, the attribution of *The Nice Valour* solely to Thomas Middleton and its publication in his collected works situates it in a canon where we can see that, though the play presents material familiar from earlier plays that Middleton authored, such as *A Fair Quarrel* (written with William Rowley, 1616), *The Nice Valour* reworks that material in new contexts. Like the Colonel in *A Fair Quarrel*, *The Nice Valour*'s Chamont, the Duke's favorite, has a precise sense of his own honor, but unlike the Colonel, Chamont is placed specifically within the court setting. Violence interferes with and inheres in male relations in both plays, and marriages, between Chamont and the Duke's sister in *The Nice Valour* and the Colonel's sister and Captain Ager in *A Fair Quarrel*, draw female characters in to repair those relations. These plotlines of *The Nice Valour* and *A Fair Quarrel* tend to replace violence with marriage, differentiating them from *The Maid's Tragedy*, which replaced marriage with violence. In contrast to both patterns, however, the subplot involving Lapet in *The Nice Valour* transforms the violence of subordination, which appears to be the inevitable experience of men at court, into erotic pleasure and intimate relations without much reference to marriage. Commemorating the encounter between bodily surfaces, the bruises Lapet receives testify to his presence at court and his embeddedness in social relations there, and they relocate identity and intimacy to the surface of the body.

The eroticization of violence between men was also a topic Middleton had treated before. In *A Fair Quarrel*, male-male relations are sexualized when there are power differences between the men. For instance, Captain Ager's friend praises him for being uniquely level-headed for his age, calling this quality "a virtue as rare as chastity in youth."[27] When the Colonel dismissively calls him "a boy," Captain Ager extends this comparison: "Virginity and marriage are both worthy."[28] Ager's claim to worthiness seems to rely on an analogy with the standard rubric for female worth, sexual purity. Yet the reference to virginity is not gendered and thus, to paint himself as worthy, he may be drawing on the conventional erotic valences and desirability of boys.[29] After the insulted Colonel offers to go "to pricks when he please," this homoerotic component to their quarrel is redirected through the female figures, Jane, Lady Ager, and the Colonel's sister, who become the subjects of the quarrel or are instrumental in its resolution.[30] By separating Lapet from the marriage plot of *The Nice Valour*, however, Middleton departs from the triangulation framework of *A Fair Quarrel* and explores the possibility of unmediated male-male masochistic intimacy.

This exploration carries radical implications for social relations because, as Mario DiGangi writes, "*The Nice Valour* implies the desirability of a society in which men graciously accept a certain degree of physical and social humiliation."[31] Lapet wishes to replace the jockeying for position at court with the pleasures of eroticized submission. His book, *The Uprising of the Kick and the Downfall of the Duello*, models a submission that interrupts the escalation of violence into duels. His hope "to move most gallants to take kicks in time, / And spurn out the *duelloes* out o'th'kingdom" situates this play within the cultural concern over dueling in Renaissance England.[32] In addition to having treated the subject in *A Fair Quarrel*, Middleton had written against dueling in a pamphlet called "The Peacemaker" in 1618. Many historians argue that early modern anti-dueling campaigns are implicated in the development of absolute monarchy's monopoly on the exercise of punitive violence and justice.[33] James's lengthy *Edict and Severe Censure Against Private Combats and Combatants* (1613) indeed constitutes a defense of such a monopoly. Yet Lapet is not necessarily advocating that the aristocracy stop performing violence altogether in order to reserve such a prerogative for the Duke. Instead, Lapet advocates a change in the way that violence is executed and received. He wants "to see a dissolution of all bloodshed" (3.2.21) because it is potentially fatal to the recipient of the violence, and the performer of the violence may be executed as well. He reasons, "if I kill, I'm hanged; If I be killed myself, / I die for't also" (3.2.27–28). The state need not be involved at all in the inevitable exercise of violence between men at court when blood is not shed and life is not threatened, so Lapet's book does not have the same absolutist aims as other anti-dueling efforts of the period and does not give the monarch proprietary control over violence.

In contrast to what critics of masochism say about its replication of structures of domination, then, Lapet's masochism avoids re-validating the social hierarchy upon whose material and political inequities absolutism and also courtier status are built. Indeed, his work destabilizes aristocratic identity by making it more widely available through performance and reading. In addition to propagating the pleasures of eroticized submission in book form, Lapet teaches others within the world of the play through a dance. Through these actions, he not only redefines courtly hierarchy but also broadcasts the possibility that the status of courtier is imitable. To temper the instability that could result from opening up the court and eroticizing the male relations that occur there, the play mocks and dismisses Lapet as it reinstalls male-male relations within a triangular structure in which women, through marriage, mediate relations between men. These marriages also serve to re-establish the boundaries between degrees within the social hierarchy, boundaries which were in practice somewhat fluid in the period. Nevertheless, within the world of the play, Lapet's book circulates, and, beyond it, so does his story with *The Nice Valour*. Thus, as I will argue, the representations of class-subverting masochism in the text and the text-within-the-text exceed the text's foreclosure and remain available to readers and audiences.

This sort of humiliating violence inflicted on Lapet regularly appeared on the Renaissance stage, exemplified in Dauphine's treatment of the cowardly Sir Amorous La Foole and Jack Daw in Ben Jonson's *Epicoene* (1609) and Arbaces's beating the servile Bessus in Francis Beaumont and John Fletcher's *A King and No King* (1611) among more instances. Lapet does not experience shame from his beatings as other beaten characters on the Renaissance stage do, and his shamelessness is a major source of the play's humor. The audience members are encouraged to laugh at the idea of voluntary masochistic submission as a part of the play's anti-court satire, much in the way that *Philaster* satirizes Arethusa's refiguration of violence as courtly sport in front of the outré Country Fellow. However, the idea that the audience and author are necessarily or automatically aligned through the mockery of a character or character type assumes the very linkage between sadism and masochism that, as Deleuze suggests, is one of the ways of denying agency to the masochist. The play opens other avenues of identification for the audience when aspects of Lapet's representation depart from these satiric purposes. Silverman notes the subversive connection between the masochist and the social order in a way that is useful for understanding the possibilities of identification with Lapet: "he acts out in an insistent and exaggerated way the basic conditions of cultural subjectivity, conditions that are normally disavowed."[34] Lapet frequently seems the voice of reason and demystifies the economy of violence at court. For example, when Chamont tells him not to take any more blows from other men, Lapet retorts rather sensibly, "you should advise them not to strike me then, sir, / For I'll take none, assure you, 'less they are given" (1.1.127–128). Through this commonsensical diagnosis of the causes of courtly violence in those who strike as opposed to those who are struck, Lapet shows he is not entirely meant as a ridiculous figure we might summarily dismiss. We should take seriously his pleasure-based deflection of the humiliating intent of those who beat him.

Somewhat like Aspatia in *The Maid's Tragedy* does when dueling with Amintor, but purposefully avoiding rather than seeking fatality, Lapet has trained himself to maximize the pleasure and to minimize the experience of shame from a blow or kick. His relationship with his body allows him to avoid the conundrum that Chamont finds himself in with the Duke, especially as Chamont's inability to respond to the Duke striking him with a switch is an unpleasant reminder to Chamont of his subordinate status. Once humiliated, Chamont asks Lapet, "what manner of blow / Is held the most disgraceful or distasteful?" (3.2.50–51). Chamont's request for counsel from Lapet testifies to the different ways they understand their relationships to their bodies and to the bodies of other men. Since Lapet "dost only censure [blows] by the hurt, / Not by the shame they do [him]," his answer is not framed in the terms of disgrace raised in Chamont's question (3.2.52–53). Lapet puts a positive spin on "distaste" by answering in terms of pleasure that are totally alien to Chamont, beginning, "I hold so reverently of the bastinado, sir, / That if it were the dearest friend i'th'world, / I'd put it into his hand" (3.2.60–62). Through the discourse of friendship, Lapet conveys his reverence for being bastinadoed, or cudgeled. When Chamont rejects the bastinado as a suitable answer to his query and hastens Lapet to move the discussion past his description of the bastinado to enumerate other forms of injury, Lapet replies, "Would I were past it too! But being accustomed to't, / It is the better carried" (3.2.65–66). As this violence is customary at court, Lapet has trained his body to "better carry" it – not as discipline, but as beneficence. Reminiscent of Quieto's prescription of binding and injury for Tangle's madness in Middleton's *The Phoenix* (1604), Lapet lists remedies for common ailments that different kinds of beatings can effect: a thump "destroys a colic" (3.2.72) by knocking the wind out of a person, and a "twinge by th'nose" (3.2.75) relieves headaches because it "makes your pent powers flush to wholesome sneezes" (3.2.80). To Lapet, the salutary effects of being beaten are clearly many, as indicated by Lapet's response to Chamont's incredulity, "O plenitude sir!" (3.2.82).

Going further than in *The Phoenix*, Middleton here also accounts for the erotic pleasures of pain. For Lapet, beatings intended to subordinate him are both salubriously and erotically advantageous to him. While his protestation echoes Lavatch's use of "O Lord Sir!" to mock courtier behavior in *All's Well That Ends Well*, the orgasmic form of Lapet's utterance indexes his body's sensitivity to masochistic pleasure and opens up a space for identification with those pleasures. Even a verbal recounting of masochistic pleasures provokes a fantasy of identification, and the role of fantasy in masochism is well documented in post-Freudian thought.[35] The significance of this can be seen by contrasting Lapet with Laxton from Middleton and Dekker's *The Roaring Girl* (1611). When Laxton observes Moll trouncing another man, his voyeuristic pleasure is not one of identification with the beaten man; instead he takes Moll's spiritedness as a sign of sexual availability. In contrast, Lapet identifies himself as the recipient of the beatings he is imagining and describing for Chamont.

The surface of the body matters more than the inner psychic space in masochistic fantasy. Michel Foucault observes that practitioners of sadomasochistic sex (S/M) "are inventing new possibilities of pleasure with strange parts of their body – through the eroticization of the body."[36] In a masochistic sexual scene, the body's surfaces are a canvas for pleasure, but masochism's focus on surface pleasure has precluded it from being considered traditional intimacy, in which the corporeal merely extends a primary psychic connection between persons. Furthermore, its at best oblique relation to genitality has at times resulted in S/M being written out of the category of sexual practice altogether. The focus on surface pleasure in masochistic sexual practice sidesteps a model of interiorized subjectivity in a way that has been particularly troubling for psychoanalysis. In *Three Essays on the Theory of Sexuality* (1905), Freud discusses masochism's expansion of the body's erotogenicity beyond the genitals: "in the case of those components of the sexual instinct which involve pain and cruelty the same role [i.e., the role of an erotogenic zone] is assumed by the skin – the skin, which in particular parts of the body has become differentiated into sense organs or modified into mucous membrane, and is thus the erotogenic zone *par excellence*."[37] Here Freud incorporates masochism (and sadism) into the sexual instinct almost as if they represent ultimately benign alternative forms of pleasure rather than pathologies, but in other parts of the *Three Essays*, Freud appears less accepting of the refusal to differentiate between erotic zones. This use of the body becomes misuse or, at the very least, it deviates from a "normal" sexuality that for Freud focuses on the genitals and has the aim of producing orgasm and ejaculation.[38] In masochism, however, erotic pleasures can occur without genital stimulation, as Freud recognized when he mentions childhood corporal punishment – specifically "the painful stimulation of the skin of the buttocks" – as one source for adult manifestations of masochistic desires.[39] Since the pleasures of masochism are not necessarily focused on the excitation of the genitals, if ejaculation even occurs it is no longer the *telos* of the sexual act. Masochistic pleasures are located outside of Freud's ejaculatory model of healthy sexuality. In light of the connection between ejaculation and inwardness that I discussed earlier, masochistic pleasure undermines the notion that erotic activity is dependent upon or signifies an inner psychic state.

The body's surface serves as a transit point for the theatrical audience's identification with Lapet. The kind of pleasure that he imagines is specifically non-penetrative insofar as it is tied to the avoidance of duels, whose substitutive relation to phallic penetration we saw with Aspatia's challenge in *The Maid's Tragedy*. Lapet, however, would prefer to be kicked, cudgeled, and otherwise manipulated such that his body is not penetrated and blood is not spilled. Though there are some resonances of anal penetration that accrue around Lapet, as Celia Daileader has noted, the play emphasizes the effects and pleasures these violent interactions produce on the body's surfaces without penetration.[40] The First Gentleman claims that Lapet's "buttock's all black lead; / He's half a negro backward. He was past a Spaniard / In eighty-eight, and more Egyptian-like" (4.1.219–221). Referring to the botched invasion by the Armada in 1588, Middleton invokes a proverbial connection between foreignness – here represented by a hierarchy of degrees of skin pigmentation from "Spaniard" to "negro" – and the sodomitical male buttock, but Lapet's blackness is a surface feature produced by bruises. Thus the play reminds us of and challenges the centrality of the genitals and penetration in naming a discrete category of acts "sex," much in the same way, as I argued in Chapter 1, that Marlowe's *Hero and Leander* does. Furthermore, the blackness caused by bruising has other valences in relation to Lapet's masochistic courtly practices and the inwardness of intimacy. Discussing the skin's role in mediating "the relation between a body and the animating principle it harbors," Elizabeth Harvey argues that medical texts from the period view the skin as important in the construction of interiority.[41] Middleton's play, however, seems to resist implicating the skin in this way. Though bruises signal internal bleeding, as medical texts from the period acknowledge, they become significant in the play's treatment of corporeality because of their appearance at the surface of the body where the beating occurred. They do not so much signify an inner state as they commemorate the connection of two surfaces, a visible trace of intersubjective contact. Galoshio the Clown insists that "Blows should have marks, or else they are nothing worth" (4.1.310) because the visible surface after-effect matters to him. Here, he is talking about the printing of Lapet's book and the marks on the page, but just as printing marks the surface of a page where the inked typeface touches it, the bruise marks the skin where the stroke lands.[42] Masochism makes proofreading not only stageable but also potentially pleasurable.

This exhibition of the body's bruises may seem to put masochists such as Lapet in a passive position, much in the way that the transformation of Aspatia into an icon of masochism in *The Maid's Tragedy* threatens to subject her to the gaze. Indeed, whether it is the King or Aspatia in *The Maid's Tragedy* or Arethusa in *Philaster*, what unites these masochists is the desire that others look at them or their injuries. Following Freud's "Instincts and Their Vicissitudes," Jean Laplanche argues that masochism and exhibitionism are passive in that these practices involve "an extraneous person substituted for the subject himself" and that person does the looking or the beating.[43] Yet Deleuze's pedagogical model emphasizes the search for and training of that person by the masochist in a way that grants the masochist agency over the experience. Though other courtiers need little provocation, Lapet actively seeks to inhabit and exhibit a position at court that places him in the path of painful and pleasurable experiences. What is more, his agency trains others for masochistic sexual experiences. His body communicates his experience through bruises, just as his book communicates to its readers and the play to its audience. The bruise becomes the site of a masochistic fantasy for the reader of Lapet's book, for other potential courtiers within the world of the play, and for the audience member seeing Lapet onstage.

Lapet's bruises commemorate one man touching another in homoerotic, masochistic, non-interiorized intimacy. Harvey discusses the competing corporeal and emotional meanings of the term "touching" – that is, something can be touching in the sense of physical abutment or in the sense of affectively provocative. She notes that the latter is a metaphor of the former that is central to the psychic depth model: "Although touch is usually associated with the surface of the body, it becomes a metaphor for the conveyance into the interior of the subject, particularly the capacity to arouse emotion (registered in the figurative sense of 'touching' as kindling affect)."[44] I would argue that such metaphoricity subordinates the corporeal to the interior life, making the body only useful as a signifier of inwardness. Lapet interrupts this metaphorization of touch, and insists that kindling affinity and commemorating intersubjective relations occur on the surfaces where bodies come together.

By refiguring these relations as features of the surfaces of bodies, the play's references to bruises reconfigure identity as a surface feature. Galoshio recommends his aptness to serve Lapet by testifying to his endurance of beatings from his previous master, the Passionate Lord. Drawing from the tradition of the beaten servant in Renaissance comedy, Middleton figures Galoshio's body as a text where others might read his character, just like Aspatia and Arethusa had wanted for themselves. Though he has "large commendations" from his friends, the Clown has even greater proof of his endurance. "I've endured as much / As mortal pen and ink can set me down for," he says, "I have it under black and white already; / I need no pen to paint me out" (3.2.134–135; 137–138). Lapet hires him because his bruises, the "black and white" of his body, speak to his character better than any letters of recommendation can.

Chamont, through his scorn of Lapet, explains the status implications of spectacularly reconfiguring identity as a surface feature such as a bruise. Chamont first suggests, insultingly, that Lapet is a tailor, thereby implying that Lapet's excessively fashionable dress hides a lower status. When Lapet insists that he can "show [his] arms and all" (1.1.135), Chamont replies,

> How black and blue they are?
> Is that your manifestation? Upon pain
> Of pounding thee to dust, assume not wrongfully
> The name of gentleman – because I am one,
> That must not let thee live.   (1.1.135–139)

Chamont puns on the corporeal and heraldic resonances of "arms" to delegitimize Lapet's claims to gentry status. Lapet becomes the inauthentic other to Chamont's authentic courtier. Lapet's bruises do mark him, but whereas Chamont would have these marks preclude Lapet's status as a gentleman, Lapet turns them into signs of his identity as a courtier.

We have seen how in *Philaster* and *The Maid's Tragedy* masochism's re-enactment of hierarchy toes the line between confirming and challenging the status quo. Grounding subjectivity in the superficial, Lapet appears to reinforce established aristocratic notions of identity, too. According to Patricia Fumerton, the aristocracy in the Renaissance located their subjectivity in "the fragmentary, the peripheral, and the ornamental."[45] Lapet ornaments his body with bruises to signify his social status in the way an aristocrat might with jewelry and other finery. His *Kick* book also draws on the discourse of civility and conduct that attempted to authenticate and shore up, via proper behavior, a coherent ontology for people of high degree because, as Frank Whigham has noted, "the pressure from below of so many able young men attempting to enter the ruling elite . . . caused the established aristocracy much anxiety."[46] Freud's work on masochistic fantasies even suggests these more conservative underpinnings of masochism. In "A Child is Being Beaten" (1919), Freud connects masochism with fantasies of identification of the sort that might produce Lapet's orgasmic reaction to the description of the benefits of beatings. Fantasies about other children being beaten by a father figure, according to Freud, combine desire for the father figure, whose love is shown as exclusive by beating other children, and guilt for that desire, which casts the other children in the fantasy as substitutes. The result, then, is pleasure in pain: "It is not only the punishment for the forbidden genital relation, but also the regressive substitute for that relation, and from this latter source it derives the libidinal excitation which is from this time forward attached to it, and which finds its outlet in masturbatory acts."[47] In cultural terms, the desire for the father supports the structures of domination that are the source of power.

Lapet's aspirations are not a form of desire for the Duke and for the social order of which he is the head, as the contrast between his courtiership and Chamont's relationship to the Duke show. Helping us to see instead the more radical implications of this play's representation of masochism, Deleuze argues that the fantasy of masochism has a different relationship to the father: "what the subject atones for is his resemblance to the father and the father's likeness in him: the formula of masochism is the humiliated father."[48] It is this patriarchal humiliation that Arethusa and Evadne both threaten. Lapet's actions similarly destabilize the social hierarchy upon which the Duke depends for his own power and even his very name. The *Kick* book shows that aristocratic identity is performative, behavioral, and therefore imitable. Masochism's destabilizing potential in this play comes from its theatricality, which makes it available as a fantasy for others. When the First Gentleman inquires after the title of Lapet's book, he and Lapet discuss the effects the plan will have on the nobility:

First Gentleman: Bring that to pass, you'll prove a happy member,
    And do your country service. Your young bloods
    Will thank you then, when they see fourscore.
Lapet: I hope
    To save my hundred gentlemen a month by't,
    Which will be very good for the private house.   (4.1.329–333)

Lapet will prove a "happy member" because he will have reorganized relations at court to maximize his own pleasure and the pleasures of others. Moreover, there will be more gentlemen around because fewer will be killed by duels or executed for killing another in a duel. While this increase in the courtier demographic is directly the result of the longer life expectancy of men who are already courtiers, indirectly it occurs because Lapet's project enables others to come to court the way Lapet, who bought his way in, did. The audience of Lapet's book is the upwardly mobile man who, like Lapet, is most likely to be the target of challenges from established aristocrats defending their class from infiltration from below.

Lapet's reference to these additional courtiers attending performances at "the private house," or theater, connects these salvaged new courtiers with stage performance. Lapet in fact chooses a stage performance to supplement his book's lessons about pleasure in kicks and the imitability of courtliness. Like Aspatia, who positions herself as teacher and icon, Lapet seeks a wider audience to view and know his masochistic experiences. Lapet's method of instruction – "I'll teach 'em in a dance" (4.1.355) – is particularly apt as a mode of transgression against status hierarchy because of its theatricality. David Scott Kastan argues that because actors traverse the social strata to play a variety of roles, "the constitutive role-playing of the theater demystifies the idealization of the social order that the ideology of degree would produce. The successful counterfeiting of social rank raises the unnerving possibility that social rank is a counterfeit."[49] In the world of *The Nice Valour*, Lapet, as a newly minted gentleman, poses the same threat to the status hierarchy as the actor on the Renaissance stage.

Lapet becomes such an actor in the course of the play when he stages and directs the dance to teach others to take their blows with pleasure. The stage directions recount the dance: "*Enter Lapet and Clown, and four other like fools, dancing, the Cupid leading, and bearing his Table, and holding it up to Lapet at every strain, and acting the postures*" (5.1.79.1–4). Through seven strains, Lapet and his company act out these different "postures," a word that evokes Pietro Aretino's *I Modi*, a collection of pornographic images with sonnets known in English as "The Postures." The actors are cued by the pictures from the *Kick* book, which were derived from Lapet's own experiences of being beaten. Aptly calling the dance the "masque of kicks," DiGangi writes that it "appears to enact the eroticization of a carefully delimited, ritualized form of male aggression."[50] The "twinge" (5.1.80) builds to a "kicksy buttock" (5.1.85), after which the beaten men fall over, in the almost post-coital "down derry" (5.1.86), to enact their full submission and capitulation to the men beating them and the pleasure the beating affords. The violent social relations at court are homoerotically pleasurable rather than punitive, and in this way they become attractive to outsiders. Though the audience for this particular performance is the mentally unstable Passionate Lord, Lapet hopes to have the opportunity to stage the dance repeatedly in order to teach outsiders how to turn shame into pleasure when they come to court and are faced with its violent social relations.

Before the destabilizing potential of ritualized violence can be realized, the actual violence of the Soldier barges in on the production. His vengeance against the Passionate Lord represents the very escalation of violence that Lapet seeks to interrupt, but which interrupts Lapet instead. The Soldier's violence de-authenticates the ritualized violence of Lapet's dance and neutralizes its threat to class stability. Lapet is thus caught up in the play's broader restoration of hierarchy and the ontology of degree through the cure of the Passionate Lord's illness, one manifestation of which was that his sexual desire led him to prefer "the very prentice of a laundress" to an empress "higher spirited / Than Cleopatra" (1.1.54, 57–58). When a text represents masochism, can a reference to Cleopatra be far behind? While the Soldier's wounding of him cures the Passionate Lord of his class-transgressive desires, Lapet is derided for having broken class boundaries in his masochistic ascent to court. Lapet even attempts to give up his new gentry status to be part of the Duke's experiment to fill the court with non-aristocrats after Chamont leaves him, but the Duke refuses to allow Lapet in: "He that disclaims his gentry for mere gains, / That man's too base to make a vassal on" (5.3.72–73). Even as the Duke threatens to undermine the status hierarchy by flirting with opening up the court, his plan relies on the same logic that status cannot be the result of the performance of an action. Lapet's attempted involvement in the replacement of the courtiers threatens this logic by exposing how freely one might move between different and utterly arbitrary social positions when status is recognized as an imitable, performative characteristic.

The play's conservative closure comes when it utterly marginalizes Lapet and obscures his insistent reminder to those within and outside the court that hierarchical male relations at court are corporeal, erotic, and, under the right circumstances, pleasurable. Specifically, the narrative strand that follows the Duke's relationship with Chamont supplants the play's representation of Lapet's project and the implications of his book. Instead of taking pleasure in submission, Chamont experiences his love for the Duke as shame. When Chamont and the Duke are reconciled by the Duke's pardon of the Soldier, the Duke unites Chamont and his sister, the Lady, in marriage to solidify their own repaired bond. This union avoids transgression of degree: the Duke's sister and Chamont are both high aristocrats, so their marriage is essentially class endogamous. Their marriage also positions a woman between the Duke and Chamont, and, though Chamont already loves the Lady when the play begins, Middleton projects onto the marriage the surplus erotic, corporeal, and pleasurable aspects of the bond between the men, so that their relationship will not suffer another similar crisis. The play puts under erasure the same-sex eroticism implicit in the exchange of women and seems to indicate a clear preference for establishing these mediated relations between men over the eroticized direct contact between men that Lapet promotes in his book. Lapet has a wife, but the couple never appears together, and his energy is entirely directed toward his articulation of a generalized theory of male relations at court.

In terms of its narrative structure, the play returns to the pattern that Middleton also drew on in *A Fair Quarrel*, that we saw at the end of *Philaster*, and that we saw violated in the course of *The Maid's Tragedy*: marriage mediates relational and erotic economies between men. Since marriage is cast as an abiding relation, it can precipitate narrative closure. In contrast, the social relations Lapet imagines are situational and temporary, shifting and flexible, with no injunction to monogamy. Lapet imagines them in place-specific terms; tied to court, these relations do not aspire to the transcendence of places that marriage claims for itself. Spontaneously, these relations emerge in the hierarchical male-male environment at court and disappear just as quickly. They last only as long as the violent yet pleasurable encounter lasts between the "givers" and the "takers," Lapet's words for positions that are roughly analogous to "tops" and "bottoms" in contemporary S/M (4.1.337). A beating leaves its traces in a bruise, but it heals eventually and the "giver" and the "taker" are also free to participate in other relations or to renew a previous encounter.

In the plot involving the Passionate Lord and the she-Cupid, masochistic abjection is taken up in the play's trajectory toward marriage, but it troubles marriage's domination of the text's ending. The Cupid is threatened with sexual shame and has had to marry a man who has to be convinced to love her before they can go public with their marriage. Her costume inflicts psychological suffering, as she laments a loss of identity: "I cannot be myself for't" (3.1.32). Also physically painful, her costume is becoming restrictive because of her pregnancy, which, when she breaks through the costume, will unleash a torrent of shame upon her. The Cupid's abjection produces desire for the respectability of marriage. Even the pain of wounding removes the Passionate Lord's aversion to marriage. His choice of a wife without

the Duke's consent threatens the system of exchange of women because of
its independent undertaking, but, at least initially, it also brings back into
the forefront direct male-male erotic relations since the Duke believes that
the Cupid is male. The Duke takes the Passionate Lord's report of his
marriage as a sign of the Lord's continuing madness, for the Lord had, in
Act 1, scene 1, declared his love for the First Gentleman, whom he thought
was a woman in male disguise. Chamont announces "desire is of both
genders" (5.3.180), a truism that helps the Duke accept the Passionate Lord's
marriage, prompts him to unite his favorite with his sister, and broadly
describes the play's movement from same-sex to cross-sex relations. When
the early homoerotic scene is replicated at the end with a disguised female
character played by a boy actor, the homoeroticism is never fully effaced.

Lapet imagines masochism as an alternative to these kinds of exchanges,
and the play only problematically recasts masochism as integral to them
through the She-Cupid's subplot. Nevertheless, her experience of abjection
limits her choices, and her pregnancy produces an urgency that her brothers
stress for the audience. The gendered limits to the radical possibilities of
masochism in this play seem to support the argument for caution about
female masochism in ways that the representation of Bellario/Euphrasia
in *Philaster* and Aspatia in *The Maid's Tragedy* do not. The "givers" and
"takers" are male and to an extent the volitional embrace of the position
of a "taker" is a male prerogative. The play attempts to direct female
identification not toward those positions but toward the Cupid figure.
Lapet has at least the freedom to imagine and publicize a social experiment;
the female Cupid must withdraw into disguise to effect the only positive
outcome the play makes available for her. Yet Middleton destabilizes gender
identity in a way that works against the limits set up for his audience. Lapet's
name blends a masculine French noun with a feminine article, and the she-
Cupid's masculine disguise bulges because of a growing fetus, itself part
of the apparatus that turns the boy actor into the female character in this
case. This philological and sartorial gender indeterminacy complicates the
prohibitions on cross-gender audience identification, much in the same way
the speaker of the Davies epigram with which I began has an ambiguous
attitude toward the masochistic scene with Francus and his whore.

Though the relations that Lapet imagines fail to facilitate narrative
closure on their own, they are available to the reader or audience member.
Silverman notes that "perversion intrudes as the temptation to engage in a
different kind of erotic narrative," and Lapet tempts the reader away from
the main dramatic and erotic trajectories of the play.[51] Lapet inhabits a
more independent representational space in this play than the eroticized

dueling does in *A Fair Quarrel*, where such male-male relations are totally embedded in a marital trajectory. *The Nice Valour* similarly tries to foreclose on them, but these relations still hold attraction for those readers, who, by disassociating textual endorsement from narrative closure in this text, imagine and even put into practice the masochistic pleasures and alternate social relations that Lapet tries to live. Lapet's book continues to circulate in the world of the play, and *The Nice Valour*'s glimpse into an alternate way of organizing social and erotic relations was staged and revived sometime after 1627.[52] What is more, with its publication in the 1647 Beaumont and Fletcher First Folio, *The Nice Valour*'s eroticized violence might have resonated with the previously printed *Philaster* and *Maid's Tragedy*; in 1679, the three plays were printed in the same volume, the Second Folio, affording a reader the opportunity to juxtapose Arethusa's defiant quest for autonomy over her own pleasure, Bellario's resistance to marriage, the King's playful powerlessness, Aspatia's iconicity in abjection, and Lapet's negotiation of social hierarchy at court. With *The Nice Valour* now firmly part of the Middleton canon, its departure from Middleton's earlier treatments of violence between men can now newly underscore the radical potential of Lapet's masochism. When modern readers attend to the circulation of the play within these two canons, it becomes possible to recuperate the political and intimate possibilities encoded in its representations of masochism.

In a discussion of the way current regulations on pornography are harmful to erotic communities, such as the S/M community, for whom pornography is one of the few available modes of transmitting sexual knowledge, Michael Warner acknowledges that printed texts enable "the circulation and accessibility of sexual knowledge, along with the public elaboration of a social world that can make less alienated relations possible."[53] Though Lapet's *Kick* book and *The Nice Valour* are not identical to modern pornography, Warner's statement describes well the furthering of sexual autonomy that Lapet's project makes possible for audiences and readers. While watching the so-called "masque of kicks" to see if it will have the intended effect on the Passionate Lord, the audience receives a demonstration of masochistic sexual practice. The play even shows Lapet and Galoshio the Clown, upon reading the *Kick* book, experiencing new pleasures or reconfirming old ones. The pictures in the book represent "all your blows and blow-men whatsoever, / Set in their lively colours" (4.1.336–337), and Lapet and the Clown offer the audience of the play a model for responding with affection, identification, and pleasure to a book that contains transgressive knowledge about the pleasures of pain:

Lapet: The standing of the takers I admire
  More than the givers: they stand scornfully,
  Most contumeliously. I like not them.
  O here's one cast into a comely figure . . .
  How sweetly does this fellow take his douse?
  Stoops like a camel, that heroic beast,
  At a great load of nutmegs. And how meekly
  This other fellow here receives his wherret!
Clown: O master, here's a fellow stands most gallantly,
  Taking his kick in private behind the hangings,
  And raising up his hips to't. But O, sir,
  How daintily this man lies trampled on?

                              (4.1.339–351)

As a manual of courtly masochism, Lapet's book reconfirms for the author his pleasure in the various positions it depicts. Lapet says the "givers" stand "contumeliously," filled with contempt for the "takers," and he indicates a clear preference for the figures taking the beatings, which, in the context of the play, suggests his identification with them. Lapet imagines himself experiencing their pleasure – indeed he has experienced it. Moreover, Galoshio praises as gallant the man "taking his kick in private behind the hangings"; in modern parlance, he might be called an active or aggressive bottom. Depicted "raising up his hips," he is exercising agency through altering his bodily comportment to maximize pleasure. In fact, Lapet recasts the passivity of "receiving" beatings into the activity of "taking" in his nomenclature and general preference for forms of the verb "to take" in this passage and the rest of the play. Though among the many meanings of "to take" is "to endure," and often characters use the word that way to subordinate Lapet, the comportment of the book's gallant fellow suggests the "takers" acquisitively and actively seek the pleasures of pain.

  In the sense of "taken" that means "enthralled," Lapet and the Clown are taken by the takers' image, and the play occasionally seems to encourage the audience to be similarly taken by the pleasures of "takers." Through the imagined identification with the pictures in the book, the pleasures of submission, and the potential route to agency those pleasures provide, become available to Lapet's readers. Two such readers, Poltrot and Moulebaiser, appear in Act 5, scene 3. Their names, French for "coward" and "mussel-kisser," portend an abject existence at court for them, but Lapet's book offers them the possibility to recast their shame as pleasure. Just as Moulebaiser and Poltrot will be asked by Lapet's book to imagine the pleasures of masochism, *The Nice Valour* asks its audience to do the same when it temporarily opens up representational space for identification with Lapet as a "taker." The more the text circulates, the more likely that an audience or reader might respond to Lapet as the Clown does to one of the men pictured in Lapet's book: "Would I were in thy place, whate'er thou art. / How lovely he endures it!" (4.1.352–353).

Just as in the John Davies epigram with which this chapter began, representations and displays of masochistic pleasures in *The Nice Valour* become the basis for scripts of intimate experience through acts of imagination and identification, thereby resisting any textual foreclosure on the appeal of masochism. Texts are integral in making these pleasures available for identification, as such pleasures are sexually eccentric for their distance from penetration and reproduction and politically eccentric because they create the conditions for traversing status hierarchies and rearranging power relations. In *The Nice Valour*, as in the other Renaissance texts discussed in this chapter, masochistic pleasures are made available in defiance of the texts' larger narrative structures and ideological valences. While the texts attempt to inhibit such acts of identification with masochistic pleasure and instead foster a rejection of or revulsion at those pleasures, they nevertheless concede representational space to them. A reader or audience member can sustain that space as one of possibility rather than let the hostility of the rest of the narrative toward masochistic intimacy overwhelm it.

CHAPTER 4

Nuns and nationhood: Intimacy in convents in Renaissance drama

HOW DO YOU SOLVE A PROBLEM LIKE ISABELLA?

As the previous chapter's discussion showed, violence characterizes relations between men at the court in *The Nice Valour*, and Lapet tried to transform the violence of that space into a form of intimacy. Place similarly exerts a shaping influence over the intimate economy of many early modern texts in which convents play a role because the convent offers a space for non-marital intimacy. For instance, at the end of *Measure for Measure* (1603–1604), the Duke's offer of marriage to Isabella is met with her silence. The text refuses to guarantee a future for the couple, and this textual indeterminacy has prompted critical discussion of the implications of the choice Isabella faces between returning to the convent and marrying a man in whom she has not shown the slightest interest romantically, an act which would involve her reintegration into the city-state of Vienna. While *Measure for Measure* does not stage Isabella's decision, a number of Renaissance dramatic texts do represent a heroine choosing or compelled to choose between a convent and a husband, often in favor of the husband. Frances E. Dolan argues that some early modern texts ridicule nuns for taking themselves out of marital circulation in order to manage concerns that "normative expectations for women institutionalized through marriage and the family are just as excessive and doomed as those institutionalized through the cloister."[1] However, as I will show, Robert Greene's *Friar Bacon and Friar Bungay* (1589), the anonymous *Merry Devil of Edmonton* (c. 1602), and *Measure for Measure* at the very least fail fully to denounce, ridicule, or manage their representations of convents in ways that we might expect in English drama after the Reformation. To the extent that these texts invest in the Catholic cloister as a potentially desirable alternative to Protestant marriage, the nun remains a subversive figure.

The nun's subversion is only partly related to religion, however. Kate Chedgzoy rightly notes that the convent is "a fictive space in which women's ambiguous relation to central institutions of early modern society could be reimagined."² Targeting Chedgzoy's analysis to the nation as a whole, I argue in this chapter that the figure of the nun is a threat because of her simultaneous involvement in a supranational religious organization and a single-sex community; this threat reveals that our assessments of the early modern analogies between the female body and the space of the early modern nation and between the early modern household and the monarchical state are limited insofar as they fail to account for marriage as an intimate economy of mediated circulation. Renaissance dramatic representations of the convent challenge the nationalist uses and implications of the consolidation of intimacy around marriage, interiority, and futurity. When the plays I discuss in this chapter show women desiring to be installed in economies of insufficient circulation with men and unprofitable, non-reproductive circulation with other women, by implication they imagine alternatives to dominant understandings of the nation as a space and the subject's participation in the life of the nation. Advancing this book's rethinking of Renaissance intimacy, my analysis of representations of convents reveals that intimate life was situated along a continuum of sexual and non-sexual relations of care and that forms of affiliation not usually associated with intimate life, such as national identity and political subjection, were in fact tethered to the Renaissance intimate sphere.

"WHAT LOVE IS THERE WHERE WEDDING ENDS NOT LOVE?" THE CONVENT IN *FRIAR BACON AND FRIAR BUNGAY*

In one of the first English romantic comedies, Robert Greene's *Friar Bacon and Friar Bungay*, a romantic plot is woven together with a more overtly nationalist plot. Wendy Wall is certainly right when she claims that through Prince Edward's marriage and the failure of Bacon's wall, the play's position is that "the court-controlled marketplace must remain permeable and free."³ The plots of the play are united in their resistance to isolation and enclosure. Wall goes on to suggest that the play, especially in Margaret and Lacy's marriage, does not fully erase the traces of the "homespun" associated with forms of national insularity and enclosure that conflict with the internationalism of the court. Yet Greene's representation of the convent aligns their eventual marriage with the ideology of national permeability. In the nexus of its plots, the play articulates a national and nationalist justification for the regulation of intimate life. At the national level, the play rejects the isolationism that would result from Bacon's wall and translates this rejection of geographic enclosure into intimate terms in

Margaret's rejection of the convent. Ambivalence surrounds her choice of marriage, and it is the convent, not domestic heterosexuality, which lingers to undermine the nationalist ideology of the play.

When she receives a letter from Lacy informing her that he will marry one of Eleanor of Castile's waiting women, Margaret describes the moral realization that grounds her rejection of a marital future for herself:

> The world contains naught but alluring baits,
> Pride, flattery, and inconstant thoughts.
> To shun the pricks of death I leave this world,
> And vow to meditate on heavenly bliss,
> To live in Framingham a holy nun,
> Holy and pure in conscience and in deed;
> And for to wish all maids to learn of me
> To seek heaven's joy before earth's vanity.
>
> (14.19–26)

Feeling misled about Lacy's love for her, she has reason enough to want to reject married life. Claustration, however, threatens to be a contagious lifestyle, as she wants to evangelize other women to think as she does about an alternative to marriage. In this passage, she imagines a future characterized by female community and solidarity that she portrays as a higher, more desirable calling than marriage. While Margaret only gestures toward relations with the women at Framlingham, she gives voice to the subversive possibility that married life might not be the most desirable script for governing affective life and that "all maids" might learn this truth from her, thereby collapsing the institution of marriage altogether. What is more, she paints the convent's all-female community as more desirable when the audience's sympathy is with her after she resists Prince Edward's temptation, only to be met with Lacy's cruel test of her fidelity.

Critics have acknowledged that representations of cloistered women offer models for resistance to marriage as a patriarchal institution. Theodora Jankowski has argued of such representations that "lives lived in isolation from men provide a space within which traditional notions of gender and gender-marked pleasure can be challenged, redefined, and reinvented."[4] Moreover, as Valerie Traub notes, "the cultural mandate that women remain virginal until married and chaste within marriage does not address, much less exhaust, the possibilities of female bodily conduct if one is willing to consider erotic practices eccentric to phallic definitions of sexuality and the normative patriarchal life cycle."[5] As a form of communal living, claustration involves a specific mode of inhabiting the body and experiencing the bodies of others. A woman entering a convent could expect a considerable portion of her experience – including praying, eating, cleaning, working, and sleeping – to be undertaken in the presence of a community of several other women, even though many of these experiences are currently understood as involving fundamental privacy. In the Rule of Saint Benedict, taking meals alone was a punishment, whereas communal refection typified convent life.[6] While the same rule mandates that each nun have her own bed, they were nevertheless to have common sleeping quarters.[7] Thus, due to the greater communal structure of the convent space, their fundamental experiences of corporeality differed from a wife's experience of her body within the domestic sphere, especially as the architecture of the home changed to cordon off private spaces.[8]

Intimacy in convent life is organized with little reference to the erotic and non-erotic aspects of marriage. Though the appellation "Bride of Christ" borrows the language of marriage, Nicky Hallett points out that some orders forbade "particular friendships," and I would suggest, therefore, that the convent provided a space to resist the dyadic in intimate life.[9] Convent life offered various possibilities for breaking down the distinction between erotic and non-erotic relations, maintaining the possibility of fulfillment in either. Nuns had regular contact with other women's bodies; for instance, Hallett notes such intimacy occurred when nuns nursed each other through illness.[10] Judith Bennett explains this continuum: nuns are "women whose lives might have particularly offered opportunities for same-sex love; woman who resisted norms of feminine behavior based on heterosexual marriage; women who lived in circumstances that allowed them to nurture and support other women."[11] Marriage organizes the intimacy of those inhabiting a space around a heterosexual couple, whereas a cloistered woman can develop multiple non-familial, fulfilling physical and emotional relations of care. According to early modern advice manuals, marriage was supposed to be the locus for the mediated experience of desires whose arousal was both inevitable and manageable. In *A Bride-Bush* (1623), William Whately advises couples facing the inflammation of sexual passion:

The married must not provoke desires for pleasures sake, but allay desires, when they provoke themselves. They must not strive by words and gestures, to enflame their passions, when were it not for such inforcements, they would be coole enough. But when such passions are of themselves moved, then must they take the benefit of their estate to asswage them, that for want of just satisfaction, they may not be troublesome to them in the duties of religion, and of their callings.[12]

Marriage allows the regulated, sinless indulgence in unavoidable passions, which would otherwise be quite dangerous, without letting it interfere with a couple's higher, more spiritual duties. Even within marriage, however, passion can get the best of the couple: "Excessivenesse breeds satiety, and makes them each weary of other, desirous of strangers."[13] The unregulated experience of marital passion undermines the economy of mediated circulation of bodies and can lead to adultery. Extrapolating from Whately's ideas, then, marriage allows women to experience male penetration of their bodies through sexual circulation, but their experience of "passion," to use Whately's term, is limited to one partner, a husband, with whom such indulgence should occur "seldome and sparingly." As Whately notes, the companionship function of marriage can gild a limited amount of erotic desire with propriety, and married persons thus can guiltlessly proceed with the business of procreation.

This opposition of marriage and convent life intersects with a sense that monastic celibacy is threatening to the nation's strength in post-Reformation discussions of monasticism, such as John Bale's two part *Actes of Englysh Votaryes* (1546). Alan Stewart notes that the specter of "a sodomitical monastic past" haunts Bale's Protestant-humanist propaganda, which attempts to equate sodomy with Catholic clerical celibacy as a perversion that the Protestant Reformation corrected.[14] What is more, with clerical celibacy constructed as a threat to the English nation, Bale makes marriage and reproduction pillars of national integrity in the face of foreign threats. For, even if it functions only as a cover for sodomy, clerical celibacy, as an attempt to enclose the body sexually, renders the geographical boundaries of the nation more permeable and exacerbates the situation that allowed it to take hold in the first place, according to Bale. Its arrival in England linked to an invasion in Book I of Bale's text, celibacy increases English susceptibility to foreign incursions. In Book II, Bale writes that Edward the Confessor, under the influence of the celibate clergy, was convinced to forgo the pleasures of marital sexuality. Instead, Edward and his wife practiced "conjugall love wth out conjugall act."[15] Bale claims they understood marriage as "an entraunce into violent whoredome, and a fylthy deflourer of virginite" (II, sig. D2r). Edward's permissiveness about celibacy has dire national consequences: Edward "died without issue to geve place to the Normains our moste grevous enemies in the base bloude of a bastard" (II, sig. D8r). To Bale, the Norman bastard William the Conqueror took advantage of English weakness caused by Edward the Confessor's assumption of the celibate life of the monks under whose spells he fell.

While Bale primarily discusses male celibacy, he established some of the parameters operative when later writers, including dramatists like Greene, were thinking through the national implications of female claustration.[16] We can begin to understand the way that economic and political developments, at both the national and international levels, inflected representations of marriage and alternatives to it, such as convents, by attending to the relationship of the state and the female body as it was articulated in the period. Peter Stallybrass argues that the enclosure of the female body was justified through an analogy between the chaste female body as "the perfect and impermeable container" and "the integrity of the state."[17] However, this familiar *hortus conclusus* model is limited if we look at the post-Reformation state from a global perspective and at the marriageable female body. More useful is the mediated enclosure model that Stallybrass claims for the relationship between social mobility and the female body:

Like the members of the male elite, the class aspirant has an interest in preserving social closure, since without it there would be nothing to aspire *to*. But, at the same time, that closure must be sufficiently flexible to incorporate *him*. His conceptualization of woman will as a result be radically unstable: she will be perceived as oscillating between the enclosed body (the purity of the elite to which he aspires) and the open body (or else how could he attain her?).[18]

This same oscillation becomes apparent in terms of the nation when we discuss England as a state involved in political, religious, and economic affairs outside its borders. England had to negotiate carefully its international involvement so as not to embroil itself in conflicts that did not serve its greater interests or that would undermine its national security. Examining the relationship between representations of convents and representations of state power using this model, we will be able to better understand why Greene takes up the connection between celibacy and moments of national trauma Bale had also articulated.

In a juxtaposition that foreshadows the failure of Margaret's plan to join the convent, her decision to enter the convent is followed by the scene in which the self-destruction of the brazen head signals the failure of Bacon's plot to encircle England with a wall of brass. These enclosure plots comment upon each other through this juxtaposition. The play ultimately indicates that Bacon's plan will lead to unreasonably isolationist consequences and that the nation must resist enclosure for the sake of its own glory. Even when Bacon introduces his plan, especially where he refers to "the market place of Rye", there are hints that this enterprise might be foolish.[19] While Bacon's wall might protect seaside cities from invasion, it would also sever the nation's economic ties with foreign markets. Such a prospect would certainly have been undesirable to London's merchant class, whose traffic in foreign goods – from the continent, from exploration and exploitation of the Americas, and from trade with Russia and Asia – provided them with a livelihood, enriched the English economy, and signaled England's position on the international scene. English overseas trading was gaining momentum in the years leading up to the appearance of *Friar Bacon and Friar Bungay*, and contemporary writers observed these developments with some interest both before and after the Armada's attack. In *The Description of England* (1587), William Harrison notes the increased scope of English merchant activity:

> Whereas in times past their chief trade was into Spain, Portingale, France, Flanders, Dansk, Norway, Scotland and Iceland only, now in these days, as men not contented with these journeys, they have sought out the East and West Indies and made now and then suspicious voyages, not only unto the Canaries and New Spain, but likewise into Cathay, Moscovia, Tartary, and the regions thereabout, from whence (as they say) they bring home great commodities.[20]

While lauding exploratory and commercial ventures, Harrison is also critical of the English merchant fleet's monopoly on the importation of goods, which inflated commodity prices that were already high because of the scarcity created by exports.[21] Harrison calls for increased opportunities for foreign traders to sell their goods in English markets, citing a 1335 statute that allows for such freedom, and Harrison's focus on markets suggests that it is not only the court that benefits from overseas trade.[22] Although he offers guarded praise of English international economic activity, he nevertheless views multidirectional traffic across England's borders as vital to English society broadly.

During the second half of the sixteenth century, England's international involvement – including interference in the Protestant Low Countries' pursuit of independence from Spain, John Hawkins's slaving in violation of the Spanish monopoly, and Francis Drake's piracy and raiding of Spanish ports – increasingly provoked Spanish ire, resulting in their attempt to invade England with the Armada. These overseas ventures would not have been possible under an isolationist foreign policy; they required English involvement in international affairs that had the side effect of angering the Spanish. While the conflict between the two countries was heavily overdetermined, one cannot ignore the role that economic rivalry played in contributing to the hostilities between England and Spain. As the attack by the Spanish Armada occurred in the year before Greene wrote *Friar*

Bacon and Friar Bungay, England's changing role on the international scene provides an important historical context for the play. We might be tempted to dismiss Greene's post-Armada argument against isolationism as a sense of invincibility in the wake of victory, but it is clear that how or if England was to play a role on the international scene had not been fully decided even after 1588. One year after the Armada, when the English might be tempted to isolate themselves politically and economically, Richard Hakluyt argues in *The Principal Navigations* that eschewing national enclosure has led to the glorification and enrichment of the nation and the monarch. In the dedicatory epistle to Francis Walsingham, Hakluyt compares Elizabeth to her predecessors and asks, "for which of the kings of this land before her Majesty, had theyr banners ever seene in the Caspian sea? which of them hath ever dealt with the Emperor of Persia, as her Majesty hath done, and obteined for her merchants large & loving privileges?"[23] With a list of the new voyages and trading routes in Asia, South America, and the South Pacific that Elizabeth's encouragement of exploration have made possible, he ties Elizabeth's glorification to her beneficence toward her merchant adventurers.

Greene too addresses the role the importation and availability of foreign goods plays in signaling English power when, after Bacon's defeat of Vandermast, the monk-mage conjures up an international feast to impress visiting heads of state. Bacon's enumeration of the contents of the feast reads like a bill of lading from a ship that has visited South Asia, the Levant, and Northern Africa before arriving in England filled with goods:

> And for thy cates, rich Alexandria drugs,
> Fetch'd by carvels from Egypt's richest straits,
> Found in the wealthy strond of Africa,
> Shall royalize the table of my king . . .
> Kandy shall yield the richest of her canes;
> Persia, down her Volga by canoes,
> Send down the secrets of her spicery;
> The Afric dates, mirabolans of Spain,
> Conserves and suckets from Tiberias,
> Cates from Judea, choicer than the lamp
> That fired Rome with sparks of gluttony,
> Shall beautify the board for Frederick;
>
> (9.250–264)

This display of luxury goods serves to "royalize" Henry, thereby elevating England and Henry's power and prestige above and beyond that of the King of Castile and Emperor Frederick of Germany, the guests who are to be impressed by a feast which "all the German peers / Could not afford" (9.244–245). Though Bacon here discusses only the presentation of these commodities at court, if he were to immure England in brass, the markets he earlier mentioned, as well as those in London, would be bereft of international commodities and England's international prestige would evaporate. The failure of this enclosure project preserves English glory derived from the country's international economic and diplomatic ties.

Greene clearly is trying to work out what Jonathan Gil Harris has identified as the "paradoxical logic of transnationalism" which "pathologizes foreign bodies [and] ratifies global connectedness as the basis of the healthy nation-state."[24] In this play, it is not the medical discourse that Harris analyzes but marriage that corroborates this resistance to the enclosure of national spaces in Edward's attempted seduction of Margaret. For his audience, Greene demonstrates the need to situate early modern England's political, monetary, and sexual economies in a global system. When Edward has discovered Margaret and Lacy are in love with each other, he presses his own suit more forcefully and fervently:

> In frigates bottom'd with rich Sethin planks,
> Topp'd with the lofty firs of Lebanon,
> Stemm'd and incas'd with burnish'd ivory,
> And overlaid with plates of Persian wealth,
> Like Thetis shalt thou wanton on the waves,
> And draw the dolphins to thy lovely eyes,
> To dance lavoltas in the purple streams.
>
> (8.53–59)

Immediately prior to Bacon's description of the feast, Edward's speech figures male power and authority in terms of the commodities he can amass for her. Edward links and domesticates the commodities out of which both the ships and England's glory are constructed in service to Margaret. Edward's pursuit of Margaret, however, does not secure an international alliance as his marriage to Eleanor of Castile will. The only way to acquire the commodities on these frigates is through involvement in global affairs and trade, exposing a country to competitive, enemy states, such as Spain represented to many Elizabethans. Here it is important to note that Eleanor is from Castile, the medieval ancestor of early modern Spain. The play demonstrates the competitive nature of international power, where one either subdues competitors, as Bacon does with Vandermast, or forges an alliance, as Edward does with Eleanor.

Edward's dalliance with Margaret produces internal dissension; England threatens to "[make] a shameful conquest of itself" as John of Gaunt, in *Richard II* (1595), claims it has become when Richard leases out his right to tax in order to raise money for wars in Ireland.[25] Thematizing the consequences of the unproductive use of England's wealth and the alienation of the nobility, Edward's suit of Margaret projects a future expenditure and waste of English wealth – in this instance, on an English woman – and endangers the loyalty of his aristocrats such as Lacy, rather than imagining the productive use of that capital to forge an international alliance. Only when he remembers that he is "that famous Prince of Wales / Who at Damasco beat the Saracens" (8.112–113) does he abandon his pursuit of Margaret and his death threat against Lacy. Resuming a princely demeanor, Edward couches the mastery of his lust for Margaret in terms of self-conquest, reasoning that "conquering thyself, thou get'st the richest spoil" (8.121), but this self-conquest is productive of wealth and spoils because of its international outlook, as opposed to the unfruitful, domestic conquest of Margaret. Even as it glorifies the Virgin Queen in Bacon's prophecy, the play takes a risky, though perhaps belated, stance on monarchical marriage in light of Elizabeth's self-presentation, dating back to 1559, as married to England.[26] Greene makes the same argument that Parliament repeatedly and unsuccessfully advanced to Elizabeth: foreign alliance through a monarch's marriage is in the best interests of both monarch and country. What is more, the play calls into question assumptions about the unequivocal glorification of England's separateness by water, which, according to Gaunt, "serves it in the office of a wall / Or as a moat defensive to a house, / Against the envy of less happier lands."[27] Greene's play instead recognizes that England needs to supplement the protection that island status gives the country with the economic and political leverage that comes with international engagement. In the absence of war, Bacon foresees "wealthy favors plenty shall enrich / The strond that gladded wand'ring Brute to see" (16.53–54). In his prophecy, wealth is strewn about as though heaped up by the sea onto the nation's geographically liminal zones, the very beaches near which Bacon's wall presumably would have stood. The point of the prophecy is that peace has enabled trade to swell the economic power of England, which further stabilizes the country's political position to ward off threats to that peace. In the shadow of the Armada attack, such a forecast of peace is quite a striking statement of confidence that the English will be able to ward off threats without extreme measures and without changing trade policy. Ironically, this prophesied peace would not come, as conflict with Spain would continue through the rest of Elizabeth's reign.

To bring sexuality in line with other modes of circulation in the play, Greene does more than stage Margaret's abandonment of the convent option to indicate support for marriage. The characters also retrospectively recount the events of the plot somewhat differently than they took place, and the effect is that marriage has greater ethical weight. Margaret's father first suggests this reshuffling of the play's chronology. Implying Margaret acted first, he tells Lacy, "she leaves the world because she left your love" (14.51). These uses of the word "leave" suggest renunciation in a way similar to when Margaret says "I leave the world" (14.21) to enter the ascetic community of the convent. Yet these renunciations are reactive, coming out of a narrative of her own rejection that, in this moment, the play downplays. Margaret reminds Lacy: "Did not my lord resign his interest, / And make divorce 'twixt Margaret and him?" (14.71–72). Lacy, however, deflects culpability for pretending to forsake her by focusing instead on the ethics of her faithfulness. Alleging that Margaret betrays him by entering the convent, Lacy responds with incredulity at the prospect that she might desire another life:

> A nun? What holy father taught you this,
> To task yourself to such a tedious life
> As die a maid? 'Twere injury to me
> To smother up such beauty in a cell.
>
> (14.54–57)

This rhetoric of the enclosure of Margaret's beauty connects Lacy's speech to the failure of Bacon's enclosure of England. Describing celibacy as "tedious," Lacy ties pleasure, desire, and intimacy to male penetration, monogamous heterosexuality, and marriage. Margaret herself subscribes to this equation of intimacy and marriage until Lacy's letter arrives, for she asks Lacy about his own motivations for pursuing her: "What love is there where wedding ends not love?" (6.119). Yet Margaret does not turn to Serlsby or Lambert, who are still alive and willing to marry her when she receives the letter. Instead, Margaret turns to the enclosure of her body within the walls of a community of women rather than subject herself to marriage and its dictates governing intimacy. However, entering the convent is not equivalent to the total abjuration of affiliation as Lacy implies, for Margaret would thereby only reject the company of one man in favor of physical, emotional, and intellectual bonds with several other women.

These other women or the convent they inhabit never appear on stage. Especially in light of Margaret's earlier fantasy of persuading other women to join the convent with her, this exclusion seems to make speaking of the convent possible. The convent is not spoken of as a community or even a place where an alternate social harmony might be possible, but a "cell" in which Margaret will be entirely isolated. Though materially absent, the convent nevertheless is a kind of absent presence because of how carefully Greene manages its representation. When Margaret discusses her plans, she mentions that she will "be shorn a nun" (10.161), and she repeatedly figures her postulancy in this depilatory way that simultaneously and ambiguously points toward and away from the community she will join. First, Margaret's hair is a source of her beauty, as Edward notes that "in her tresses she doth fold the looks / Of such as gaze upon her golden hair" (1.52–53). Her hair is not intrinsically beautiful, but instead is only beautiful insofar as it suggests to the man who wishes to possess her that, if he obtains her, he will have an object that others gaze at with desire but cannot possess. Planning to destroy an aspect of herself that had signaled the sexual competition over her that characterizes the first half of the play, Margaret embraces a new aesthetic – or, from the point of view of the men in the play, a counter-aesthetic. Her hair is part of the vanity of the world, and she would instead inhabit her body in a way specific to the convent, where the sexual competition and male possessiveness characteristic of patriarchal coupledom do not apply. At the same time that she points to a new understanding of embodiment, her use of passive voice, though likely a conventional way of referring to entering a convent, nevertheless denies that Margaret will join other women in the convent who inhabit their bodies in a similar way. Presumably, she will not cut her own hair, but another woman, possibly the abbess of the convent, will cut it. Greene also specifically sets her choice in her father's house in Fressingfield, not at the door of the convent in nearby Framlingham, where the play might potentially develop a sense of urgency about her choice. Without such urgency, the choice is highly asymmetrical. The presence of other nuns or the setting of the scene at the convent would grant the same materiality to the convent that the play seeks to grant to marriage. As far as Margaret's potential intimacy with other women, however, she can only refer to, and subsequently bid farewell to, a fantasmatic "show of holy nuns" (14.91) after she has decided to marry Lacy, supposedly neutralizing the convent's threat to marriage.

The play's commitment to de-authorizing the convent alternative resonates with its nationalist concerns, which connect legitimate heterosexual reproduction through marriage with the continued existence of the state. Just as Margaret does not enclose her body in the convent, Friar Bacon fails to enclose England. Bacon's abandonment of his plan to encircle England, Edward's abandonment of his seduction of Margaret, and his acceptance of an arranged marriage with a Spanish princess allow England to interact with the community of nations. England remains open to the sea and the traffic of goods that occurs there, and Edward's marriage creates an alliance with another powerful nation. The same permeability of its boundaries and involvement in international affairs that expose England to the threat of invasion also enhance England's economic and military power to ward off such threats. Margaret's refusal to be the prince's mistress and her refusal to enclose her body in a convent allow her to circulate sexually, but in a regulated manner through the couple form. England, Edward as Prince of Wales, and Margaret's body are parallel in that all three require a well-regulated balance between enclosure and openness. In this parallelism, the play's nationalist valorization of married life constructs the nation, as a community, as the accretion of several married couples.

Greene aligns the convent with the *hortus conclusus*, whereas marriage represents a seemingly more favorable, though distinctly limited economy of female circulation. It is not unexpected on religious or national grounds that Margaret would ultimately return to Lacy. What is dissident is the failure to efface fully the convent as a viable and desirable alternative in this play. Margaret's nun's habit, dictated by the stage directions at the beginning of scene 14, remains an isolated presence that contrasts markedly with the absence of her wedding clothes, which Lacy says are still at the tailor (14.69). The materiality of the play's costuming neither denies non-marital forms of intimacy access to representation nor grants marriage full representation. Further qualifying the ascendancy of marriage in the play, Greene depicts Warren, one of Prince Edward's friends, as perplexed by Margaret's change of heart, suggesting that the choice of marriage over the convent might not be as automatic as one might assume for a play with a predominantly Protestant audience. He claims that it is natural for women "be they never so near God, yet they love to die in a man's arms" (14.103–104). Even with recourse to an essentialized "nature of women," he cannot fully rationalize the reunion of the two lovers (14.103). Ermsby's remark that Warren is "in a brown study" (14.101–102) points to the presence of mourning in the midst of celebration and to the inadequacy of his "woman's nature" explanation for understanding Margaret's preference for marriage over the convent.

Margaret echoes Warren when she suggests that her actions are implausible without the presence of coercion. She admits, "the flesh is frail. My lord doth know it well, / That when he comes with his enchanting face, / Whatso'er betide, I cannot say him nay" (14.86–88). Margaret admits that her body suffers from a natural weakness to Lacy's charms, but she also maintains that he exploits that weakness to achieve his goals with her. He even dictates the form of her decision, ordering that her "answer must be short" (14.85) when she is to announce her choice between the convent and him. While the questions the play raises about the couple's reunion have a formal and generic impact, Greene's execution of narrative closure points to the political failure of the play's ideology to mask its own coerciveness. The sexual ideology underwriting the dominance of marriage over the intimate sphere cannot completely efface the mechanisms by which marriage achieves control over the circulation of bodies in intimate relations. Marriage fosters an affective bond, but just as Lacy places limits on Margaret's speech but still allows her to speak her desire, the married couple form of intimacy invokes a complex set of tacit norms governing sexuality, pleasure, the body, and the interaction of bodies in the same space. Margaret surrenders herself to the role of "a wife in name, but servant in obedience" (6.124) that her culture dictates for her gender. Yet she also commits herself to living out a particular form of intimate life that involves the controlled sexual circulation of her body, an aspect of the couple form referred to as "constancy." As it is advanced as a principle of the couple form, constancy, however, regulates the circulation of bodies by prohibiting or devaluing the bonds of either of the partners with persons not part of the couple. Although only temporarily, *Friar Bacon and Friar Bungay* imagines an alternative to this regulation of the circulation of bodies. Though the convent wall remains as fantasmatic as Bacon's wall, the play's flirtation with this alternative to marriage nevertheless remains to trouble the play's religious, sexual, and nationalist ideology.

"ILE MAKE THE ABBAS WEARE THE CANNONS HOSE": APPROPRIATING THE INTIMACY OF THE CONVENT FOR MARRIAGE IN *THE MERRY DEVIL OF EDMONTON*

More than a dozen years after Greene offers the mediated permeability of the nation and the mediated circulation of bodies through marriage to resolve conflicts between national defense and economic interests, the topographical comedy of *The Merry Devil of Edmonton* rethematizes in semi-pastoral terms the connection between national enclosure and the convent. With six editions between 1608 and 1658, a court performance in 1613, and a mention of its popularity in the prologue to Ben Jonson's *The Devil Is an Ass* (1616), *The Merry Devil of Edmonton* was not a marginal play in the early seventeenth century, and although the textual problems that classify its seventeenth-century printing as "bad quartos" make a better text neither available nor reconstructible, the play sheds important light on late Elizabethan understandings of nuns, the nation, and marriage.[28] In the two plot lines of *The Merry Devil of Edmonton*, both convent spaces and national spaces are penetrated for different, but related purposes. While the play represents the eventual enclosure of national space, the convent and the women who live there are not granted such security. The convent conforms to Traub's description of female-female bonds more generally in the period as "figurable in terms not only of the always already lost, but the always about to be *betrayed*."[29] There is, however, an implicit recognition of the cost of this displacement, for the same characters who penetrate the enclosed spaces of the convent also imagine that they interrupt the intimate life therein, and their fantasies resist the inevitability of the play's marital trajectory.

The romantic plot of the play is standard New Comedy: the younger generation outwits the older when Milliscent Clare asserts her choice to marry Raymond Mountchesney over her parents' objections to his family's fallen financial status. Much as in *A Midsummer Night's Dream*, a daughter asserting her choice over her marital options ends up in the woods; however, instead of invoking the convent as a threat, as Egeus does with Hermia in Shakespeare's play, Arthur Clare integrates his daughter's potential postulancy into his plan to marry his daughter to Frank Jerningham. The play's representation of the convent is caught up in anti-Catholic sentiment couched in a New Comedy narrative convention. The choice between different kinds of marriage – coerced and freely chosen – distracts attention from the lack of choice between marriage and non-marriage. When Sir Ralph, Frank's father, says that Frank will eventually become "the husband to this pretty Nun," Frank feigns a defense of the sanctity and inviolability of the cloister: "To draw a virgin, thus devour'd with zeale, / Backe to the world: O impious deede."[30] Frank is not interested here in respecting the cloister because he is already committed to Raymond's plan to rescue and elope with Milliscent. He merely uses the sanctity of the cloister to deceive Sir Ralph. In case we are tempted to believe Frank's statement that Milliscent is so averse to marriage that "sheele even shreeke to heare a husband namde" (3.1.90), Bilbo the servant reminds us that Frank's scruples are part of Raymond's plan: "I, a poore innocent shee! Well, heres no knavery; hee flowts the old fooles to their teeth" (3.1.91–93). Almost as if defensively, the play repeatedly tells the audience that taking the convent option seriously is pretense, and such repetition suggests to me that the audience could not be assumed to support the disavowal of the convent option on their own.

Unlike in *Friar Bacon and Friar Bungay*, the female protagonist in *The Merry Devil of Edmonton* actually arrives at the convent, but her arrival occasions further anti-Catholic sentiment and the reiteration of the inevitability of marriage. The first words the Prioress addresses to Milliscent associate the convent with witchcraft, that repository of cultural fantasies and anxieties about female sexuality: "Then, faire virgin, heare my spell, / For I must your duty tell" (3.1.26–27). Her rhymed couplets in trochaic tetrameter resemble an incantation and perhaps anticipate the metrically similar chant of the witches in *Macbeth* (1606). In the Prioress's enumeration of the practices of convent life, there is no overt recognition that Milliscent will live in a community with other women. The practices she mentions – prayer and fasting, for example – could be performed alone as well as in the company of the other nuns. The Prioress instructs Milliscent that "when your blood shall kindle pleasure, / Scourge your selfe in plenteous measure" (3.1.46–47), and this pleasure may derive from living in the company of other women, but the text is silent regarding the stimulus. If this scourging is sadomasochistic eroticism, it is decidedly autoerotic. Bringing this point into relief, Philips van Marnix van St. Aldegonde writes in his polemic, translated by George Gylpen as *The Beehive of the Romish Church* (1579), that in the convents throughout Holland, "everie day, betweene Michaelmasse and All Saints... goeth the Mother or Prioresse of the Cloister into a darke chamber, with a great rodde in her hande, and then come the Nonnes in thither one after another starke naked, everie one alone & turne up their bare buttockes: yea, some of them as naked as my naile, & so lie downe before the Prioresse, and there receive holie discipline for the soules in Purgatorie."[31] In contrast, the pleasures mentioned by the Prioress from *The Merry Devil of Edmonton* emerge *ex nihilo* and the scourging is done *sola*, casting the convent as a space of isolation rather than intimacy.

Harry Clare's asides to the other young men that break up the Prioress's tetrameter couplets further emphasize that we are not to take this option seriously. Harry reminds the audience that Milliscent's stay in the convent is necessarily temporary: "She may be a Nun; but if ever shee proove an Anchoresse, Ile dig her grave with my nailes" (3.1.52–54). If Milliscent were to take up permanent residence in the convent, Harry's reference to the anchoress implies, she might as well be dead because she is unavailable for marriage. We are told that Milliscent "had rather have a man in her bed" (3.1.61) than a "haire cloth," so the play's repetition that the convent is not an option for her is striking. The representation of the convent threatens to introduce a non-marital third term in the binary between the coercive, arranged marriage and the freely chosen partner marriage, and the reminders about the convent attempt to manage this threat by keeping the convent and Milliscent's body open to penetration.

The romantic plot meets the poaching plot in the Royal Forest of Enfield Chase, where assurances are made that the national space will remain secure while the convent space will remain violable. The play's poaching adventures, since their aim is to expropriate royal deer and violate the law, are figurative assaults on monarchical sovereignty and national integrity, and, as such, take the form of penetrating a space associated with the nation.[32] Unlike in *Friar Bacon and Friar Bungay* where the king is part of the dramatis personae, *The Merry Devil of Edmonton* refers only metonymically to royal authority. While the play does not refer to any specific monarch, Blague does recognize that they are going "to steale some of the kings Deere" (2.1.65–66) even as they identify the region of the forest they are targeting as "Brian's Walk" after the forest keeper.[33] Requiring preservation for the monarch and protection from invasion by poachers, Enfield Chase is a distillation of England itself, a national space infused with the same boundary issues facing the nation at large. Poaching seems less threatening than an attack by the Spanish Armada in terms of national defense, but its dangerous resemblance to invasion is exacerbated by its violation of the role of hunting regulation in the maintenance of a hierarchical social structure that is ultimately the source of royal authority as well. That is, transgressions against this system, including the poaching represented in *The Merry Devil of Edmonton*, are implicitly politicized transgressions against the social order. Upon his accession, James took a keen interest in curtailing the practice of poaching, which, according to an edict of 1603, had surged out of control due to the lack of enforcement of Forest Law under his predecessor. Monarchs meted out benefices, such as Royal Forest keeperships, to keep the nobility vying with each other for favor rather than uniting against royal power. Poaching, then, emerges from the imbrication of hunting, social status, and privilege, according to Roger B. Manning: "a considerable part of the unlawful hunting engaged in by the aristocracy and gentry reflected the perennial factionalism among courtiers or the more localized feuding within county and local communities."[34] For example, an aristocrat might challenge the position of another by poaching his deer or the royal deer in his charge. Spatially, poaching then represents threats emerging simultaneously inside and outside the unstable nation.

While Manning argues that poachers "remained on the safe side of the laws of treason," the play's poachers trespass in a royal space, thereby creating an analogic relationship between poaching and treasonous threats to the monarch for an audience in whose recent memory the Earl of Essex had sought to destabilize the government.[35] The play looks further into the English past, to the infamous Dukes of Norfolk, to evoke more generally the similarities between poaching and treason. Blague, also called the Host, repeatedly and proudly utters: "I serve the good Duke of Norfolke" (1.1.8–9). Blague's characterization phrase exceeds its conventional function by evoking English political history, but it is vague as a historical allusion. Among the most powerful of dukes in England, the Dukes of Norfolk were major players in English royal politics in the fifteenth and sixteenth centuries, but they achieved notoriety by frequently opposing sitting monarchs. Due to the indeterminable date of the action of the play, there are various candidates for the specific Duke of Norfolk, all of whom opposed English monarchs at moments of national crisis in ways that could be interpreted as treasonous. The play insists that Peter Fabell – the title character of the play – is a real historical personage whose "monument remayneth to be seene" (Prologue 19). Thomas Brewer's chapbook, based on the play, says that Peter Fabell "lived and died in the raigne of King H. the 7."[36] W. W. Greg, drawing on Fuller's Worthies, suggests that the historical Fabell may instead have lived during the reign of Henry VI (1422–1461).[37] If Fabell lived and the action of the play takes place during the reign of Henry VI, the Duke of Norfolk in question would be John Mowbray, Third Duke of Norfolk, who fought against Henry on the Yorkist side. On the other hand, if Fabell lived during the reign of Henry VII, Blague would then refer to John Howard, the first of the Howard Dukes of Norfolk, who died at Bosworth Field fighting against Henry Tudor. Because another man was not invested as Duke of Norfolk until 1514, Blague would in this instance be reminiscing about service done a man who opposed Henry VII. If an audience were prompted to connect the action to an Elizabethan context, perhaps by Blague's anachronistic reference to the 1557 battle of St. Quentin (1.2.32), the reference would hearken back to Thomas Howard, Fourth Duke of Norfolk, who, in 1572, was found guilty of treason and executed for conspiring against Elizabeth with Mary Queen of Scots.[38] No man had been created Duke of Norfolk between 1572 and the writing of the play, but the memory of such a national crisis could certainly be provoked to provide a context for the play's examination of national spaces. It is impossible to adjudicate among the candidates, and the play does not ask the audience to do so. All are conspicuously associated with opposition to the monarch such that the reference would have been enough for early seventeenth-century audiences to grasp the way it connects the poaching to threats to the sovereign's authority to preserve the integrity of royal, and consequently national, spaces.

As the play's plots commingle, Fabell's conjurations, intended to aid in rescuing Milliscent and raiding the convent, ultimately have their greatest impact on the poachers who make off with one deer. Sir John claims to have seen spirits in Enfield Churchyard, and the Sexton of Enfield Church corroborates this report, while other characters offer different accounts. Though the content of the apparition remains unclear, the significance of the timing and the form of the apparition is not. Frightened by the spirits, Blague vows, "Ile nere serve the duke of Norfolk in this fashion againe whilst I breath" (4.2.88–89). Here, his poaching is named explicitly as part of his service to the Duke of Norfolk. As such, his service involves breaking the law in a way that metonymically violates the sanctity of a national space and royal authority. Because Fabell's conjurations create a cross-reference between the marriage and poaching plots at the moment of Blague's renunciation, the play shows the violation of the convent securing sovereign authority over spaces associated with the nation. As for the form of the apparition, its description as "the devill with a mans body upon his backe in a white sheet" (4.2.69–71) is reminiscent of the play's induction, where a devil has come to carry away Peter Fabell, who then tricks his way out of his Faustian obligation to surrender his soul. While the play does not support the reading that what these men see is the fulfillment of Fabell's deal with the devil, the description reminds one of Fabell's conjuring abilities, which are a product of this deal and which he promised to contribute to Raymond's rescue effort. If this apparition is part of Fabell's conjurations, or even if Banks the Miller, dressed in white, is being carried off by another devil conjured by Fabell, then the marriage plot that seeks to violate a convent space has inadvertently secured the obedience of men who would violate a national space. Moreover, the Sexton's suggestion that the body in the white sheet may be a woman's body (4.1.72) is further reminiscent of the aim of Fabell's conjurations – that is, Raymond's retrieval of Milliscent from the convent. When Milliscent escapes, she could be clad in white as a newly admitted postulant.

In a way, Raymond poaches Milliscent from the protected space of the nunnery, thereby making her the 'deer' – or, punningly, 'dear' – of the romantic plot. When the fathers arrive in the forest, Brian uses his authority to detain them, allowing the young couple to escape. Whereas in *A Midsummer Night's Dream*, the forest is outside the law of Athens, the royal forest in *The Merry Devil of Edmonton* is a space created by the law of England as embodied in the monarch. As an extension of the king's sovereignty and a protector of national spaces, Brian lends tacit legal justification and royal approbation to the invasion of the convent space and suggests that an enforced marriage is equivalent to poaching a daughter from the man she loves. Appealing to the laws of the nation, Sir Ralph complains to Richard Mountchesney about Raymond's elopement with Milliscent, "Ile hang thy son, if there be law in England. / A man's child ravisht from a Nunry" (5.1.15–16). Though he claims that the law is not being respectful of the sanctity of religious spaces, he too has appropriated that religious space for the purposes of arranging a marriage. Ralph appeals to a law that has changed priorities, for, having been marshaled in service of marriage – and, more precisely, of a companionate-style marriage – the law now opposes the arranged marriage.

This apparent shift becomes less dramatic if one examines the play in light of the early modern intersection of religion, politics, and sexuality, all of which, in the two decades prior to *The Merry Devil of Edmonton*, fueled English conflicts with Spain, backed by Rome. Papal bulls in 1570 and 1588 excommunicated Elizabeth I, relieving her subjects of their duty to be faithful to her and her government, and the latter bull even called on English Catholics to support a Spanish invasion. The English government responded with a similar blending of political and religious loyalty. The 1581 Act to Retain the Queen's Majesty's Subjects in Their Due Obedience deemed it treason to convert or to seek the conversion of others back to Roman Catholicism. Ultimately, this intermingling of religious and national affiliations affected those who thought of themselves as either English subjects or Anglicans, and James's institution of the Oath of Allegiance in 1605 ritualized this way of thinking. By extending the link between religious conformity and national loyalty, certain precepts about sexual life within Catholicism, such as the elevation of virginity, clerical celibacy, and monasticism, would entail not only religious error, but also foreign eccentricity and treason – threats from without and within, respectively. The post-Reformation elevation of marriage is, then, not only a tenet of Anglican orthodoxy, but also of English nationalism and loyalty to the sovereign. Indeed, the elevation of marriage and these national ideologies mutually reinforce each other. Because marriage increasingly rendered in bodily terms the nation's figuration of international political and economic relations, as we saw in *Friar Bacon and Friar Bungay*, anxieties surrounding non-marital intimacies, such as convent life, resonated on a national level. In the case of *The Merry Devil of Edmonton*, the threat is to the state's spatial and political integrity.

The play's generic association with New Comedy is supposed to ensure that there is no future for Milliscent in the convent – either her parents or Raymond will release her. Other traces in the play, however, suggest the presence of female-female intimate bonds formed by virtue of the fact that nuns make their lives together. Just as he did in his plan to send spirits into the forest to create confusion, Fabell imagines sending spirits into the convent:

> Ile send me fellowes of a handful hie
> Into the Cloysters where the Nuns frequent,
> Shall make them skip like Does about the Dale,
> And with the Lady prioresse of the house
> To play at leape-froge, naked in their smockes,
> Until the merry wenches at their masse
> Cry teehee weehee;
> And tickling these mad lasses in their flanckes,
> They'll sprawle, and squeke, and pinch their fellow Nunnes.
> Be lively boyes, before the wench we lose,
> Ile make the Abbas weare the Cannons hose.   (2.2.87–97)

Though the "they" to whom Fabell refers in line 95 may seem unclear, the male spirits are to provoke the women into physical and sexual contact with "their fellow Nunnes." Though the provocation is from outside the convent, Fabell appears to be taking advantage of some erotic charge barely latent within the structure of convent life. As Robert Burton's discussion of nuns' melancholy in *The Anatomy of Melancholy* (1628) claims, this charge is a function of enclosure itself: "this enforced temperance," he charges, turns nuns into "*tribadas* [tribades], *ambubaias* [promiscuous women], &c."[39] Refusal to enter into the mediated circulation of marriage produces excessive sexual circulation according to Burton. The communal intimacy suppressed by the Prioress's description returns in Fabell's imagination. When he imagines that the Abbess will put on the Canon's hose, he is not only invoking the charge in much anti-Catholic polemic that female and male monastics were often involved in sexual shenanigans. The Abbess is also taking on a male role, a commonplace in representations of female-female intimacy in the period that Valerie Traub argues "functions as a discourse of containment, a way of joining insignificance and immateriality on performances of . . . female masculinity."[40] Thus, even as he suggests their homoeroticism, he contains it as the perversion of something else.

Too threatening in making the convent a space of pleasure without relation to men, this imagined female homoeroticism is heterosexualized not
only when Fabell sends male spirits into the convent, but also when Raymond ultimately breaches the convent disguised as a friar coming to confess
her. The nuns need access to male priests for sacramental administration,
and here is where the charge of sexual activity between nuns and priests is
picked up by the play. Milliscent and Raymond even appropriate the confessional for courtship, for she tells Raymond, "If chaste pure love be sin, I
must confesse, / I have offended three yeares now with thee" (3.2.106–107).
Emerging successfully from the convent, Raymond recommends that all
his friends find brides this way: "there is / a company of girles would turn
you all Friers" (3.2.125–126). Raymond imagines the repeated, perpetual
penetration of the convent and the bodies of the women therein. Insofar
as the play offers no respite for the nuns from this fantasy, the narrative
forecloses on the convent as an alternative way for women to organize their
lives together. However, the potential desirability of the nuns' interrupted
intimacy is presupposed when it is targeted by the anti-Catholic satire that
punctuates the limited access to representation granted to convent life.

"SAY YOU WILL BE MINE": THE CONSOLIDATION OF SOVEREIGN POWER THROUGH MARRIAGE IN *MEASURE FOR MEASURE*

Measure for Measure also acknowledges the spatial and political concerns
that motivate the regulation of intimacy in *Friar Bacon and Friar Bungay*
and *The Merry Devil of Edmonton*. When, as part of Angelo's crackdown,
the brothels in the suburbs are closed, ungoverned sexuality is connected
to extraterritoriality. Like some authorities in Shakespeare's London, the
Duke sees as in Vienna's interests the imposition of Viennese laws adjacent
to its borders, bringing those whose affiliation to the city state is tenuous
under its juridical scope, even while an alderman saves the brothels within
the city limits from similar closure. The play's prostitutes are only one part
of this consolidation of state power.[41] Extending and sharpening the treason issues of *The Merry Devil of Edmonton*, Shakespeare engages the uneasy
relationship of Catholicism and loyalty to the state, for even Duke Vincentio's sovereignty potentially conflicts with the supranational network of
affiliations that structure the Catholic Church. The Duke himself points
to this network when, disguised as a friar, he claims a foreign friar's exemp-
tion from the law: "His subject am I not, / Nor here provincial."[42] Of
this extrajudiciality, Thomas Robinson complains in *The Anatomy of the
English Nunnery at Lisbon* (1622) that "Whereas all other Religious Houses

are under the Jurisdiction of *Provincials* of their owne Order *mediatè*, and under the Bishop of the Diocesse *immediatè*, yet this is not subjected to either" because the nuns in the English convent in Portugal are not Portuguese and the Bishop did not want to have to pay for the upkeep of foreigners.[43] Their legal status is ambiguous much in the way Duke Vincentio claims foreign friars in Vienna are. Yet what Vincentio seeks is to make such non-affiliation with the state impossible, whether for suburban prostitutes or urban nuns.

Though threats still loomed from abroad, the loyalty of English Catholics and the effect of their presence on the state's authority came under increased scrutiny in the first years of the seventeenth century. Near the end of Queen Elizabeth's reign, English Catholics made overtures to the Queen indicating that they desired to resolve the apparent contradiction between their relationship to the Catholic Church and to the state. On January 31, 1603, the Queen received "A Protestation of Allegiance made by thirteen Missioners," in which the petitioners, all ordained religious, pledged allegiance to and submitted to the authority of both the Queen and the Pope. Moreover, they claimed that their multiple affiliations did not conflict: "We will obey [the Pope] so far forth, as we are bound by the laws of God to do; which, we doubt not but, will stand well with the performance of our duty to our temporal prince, in such sort as we have before professed."[44] According to John Bossy, this declaration of loyalty was unacceptable to the Privy Council because it did not indicate that the petitioners would cease their priestly activities in England.[45] Available to remind those who might consider tolerance for Catholics of the history of foreign and domestic Catholic intrigue against Elizabeth, Samuel Harsnett's *Declaration of Egregious Popish Impostures* (1603), a text typically read for its role in Shakespeare's writing of *King Lear*, tells of "the bewitching of the poore people with an admiration of the power of theyr Romish Church and priesthood by these cogd miracles and wonders, and thereby robbing them of theyr fayth towards God and theyr loyaltie to theyr Prince, and reconciling them to the Pope, the Monster of Christianitie."[46] He also argues for the expediency of cracking down on Catholic clergy as a preventative measure: "if the sword of justice were drawne, and inflicted according to the waight and measure of [Catholic priests'] detestable designes, that fewer of them would come over."[47] In the first months of James's reign, a group of Catholic laypersons, largely from the English gentry, revived and revised the earlier priest-led cause by presenting a "Supplication unto the King's Majesty, for toleration of Catholic Religion in England." While affirming their allegiance to the new King, they noted the ill effects Catholic persecution has had on England's economy and the discontent it has brought to England generally: "Trade and traffic is decayed; wars and blood hath seldom ceased; subsidies and taxes never so many; discontented minds innumerable."[48] Moreover, official tolerance for English Catholics would resonate with the international community: "how grateful will it be to all catholic princes abroad, and honourable to your majesty, to understand how queen Elizabeth's severity is changed into your royal clemency."[49] The promise of national glory was clearly not sufficient for the King, who, even before the Gunpowder Plot, asserted that laws persecuting Catholics enacted under Elizabeth would continue to be enforced.[50]

Though *Measure for Measure*'s Pompey and Mistress Overdone seem to belong to English city comedy, the play's explicit setting is not Protestant London, but Catholic Vienna. Nevertheless, the play's setting cannot fully obliterate connections to the new discussions about English policy toward Catholics that James's succession prompted. Though ungoverned sexuality, not Catholicism, is targeted in *Measure for Measure*, these only appear to be two separate issues. Just as Catholicism provides subjects with models of non-national forms of affiliation, it also provides subjects with models of non-marital forms of intimacy in monasticism. The play lumps together these two relational models – one political, one sexual – as threats to the Duke's sovereignty. The Duke consolidates his power by combining two other relational models – the supreme authority of the Viennese city-state over its inhabitants and the primacy of marriage – to oppose the supranational Catholic Church's models of affiliation. The implantation and confession of interiorized desire helps to consolidate the intimate sphere and state power in the play. To achieve a docile citizenry that monitors and disciplines itself, the state casts interiorized desire as potentially transgressive of the relationship between the state and the subject who, obliged to maintain the relationship, perpetually focuses inwardly, looking for signs of transgression. The more interiorized the desires seem, the greater the need for their confession and the more justified the state becomes in extending its sovereignty over its subjects.

By suggesting the possible value of intimate content outside marriage, relational forms not governed by the norms of the heterosexual couple, such as communal life in convents, threaten the nation's strategies for asserting sovereignty over its subjects. As we know from the work of Lena Cowen Orlin, marriage – through its concomitant structures of the domestic sphere and the household – also provides a model for individual relations with the post-Reformation state.[51] In its articulation as dominant ideology, marriage helps the early modern subject to understand his or her subjection to the state and his or her relationship to others subjects of the state. Defining intimacy as coextensive with marriage, then, not only makes marriage more desirable, but also furthers the state's interests by regulating affiliation among its subjects in such a way that models on a microcosmic level the individual's macrocosmic subjection to the state. The exclusion of non-marital relations from both the intimate sphere and public life resembles what Michael Warner and Lauren Berlant, in a contemporary American context, call "the project of constructing national heterosexuality."[52] While I am not suggesting that heterosexuality and marriage are equivalent, the imagined community of the early modern state depends on marriage. In an uncanny anticipation of the modern rhetoric of "family values," Edmund Tilney, in *The Flower of Friendship* (1568), even calls marriage "the Preservation of Realmes."[53] His rhetoric piques nationalist sentiments in order to persuade his readers of the importance of marriage at a time when it was not self-evident.

The nation predicates political participation on marriage's reproductive function. Participation in a nation's politics is commonly construed as shaping the future of the nation. As I noted in the introduction, Lee Edelman has recently argued that politics is saturated with "the Child as the image of the future."[54] Political arguments advanced under the banner of taking action for "the sake of the children" suggest that full citizenship is located in the future and is coextensive with heterosexual reproduction. Like Berlant and Warner, Edelman discusses participation in the life of the nation in terms of democratized citizenship, which in US history, in its idealized form if not always in reality, has not been as explicitly linked to patriarchal subjection in the way early modern national membership would have been. While democratic citizenship and patriarchal subjection involve imagining the nation as two different types of families, both contexts construct the nation in familialist, reproductive terms. Since marriage is constructed and represented in the early modern period as the bond with access to futurity through legitimate sexual reproduction, marriage can provide access to national membership. For women in the early modern period, access to this politics of futurity was endlessly deferred because through marriage and reproduction, they perform labor for the nation but are not fully invested in the life of the nation; their husbands and male children are.

In literary narratives, participation in the future of a culture is frequently predicated on marriages or betrothals that occur at moments of narrative closure. Especially in comic narratives, these marriages suggest the production of offspring who, in turn, will guarantee the longevity of the social order whose constitution – or, often, reconstitution – coincides with the closural moments of that narrative. These closural moments encode the consolidation of national power through marriage and through the exclusion of alternate forms of affection from political life. We have seen, however, in the political, geographical, and economic concerns of *Friar Bacon and Friar Bungay* and *The Merry Devil of Edmonton* both the attempt to exclude convent life from the category of intimacy and the strains within the plays that resist the convent's exclusion. The indeterminacy of *Measure for Measure*'s ending affords an opportunity to recuperate the representation of the convent as a gesture toward modes of affection outside of married life and of modes of political affiliation ungoverned by the nation state.

Duke Vincentio's deputization of Angelo seeks to assert "the needful bits and curbs to headstrong weeds" (1.3.20). The Duke intends to bridle his subjects' erotic lives, but a bridle does not only stop a horse's movement; it also controls the horse so that its movement matches the rider's purpose. Thus, he will not eradicate eroticism, but make it match his purpose, the extension of his own sovereign authority. The form of his exercise of power also changes over the course of the play: the Duke, who leaves saying, "I love the people, / But do not like to stage me to their eyes" (1.1.67–68), returns to exercise his authority publicly when exposing Angelo's hypocrisy and Lucio's slander in the final scene. More than simply shifting from a private mode of asserting his sovereignty to a public one, however, the Duke combines the resources of both modes to consolidate his power. That is, he appropriates the private strategies of the confessional to create a space for interiority, which he then stages to the public so as to reveal his subjects' utter dependence on him for their lives and notions of selfhood. Therefore, the strategy employed by the Duke not only detects "what our seemers be" (1.3.54); it in fact creates the rift between private seeming and public being.

In his subjects, the Duke implants an urgency to translate their seeming into the public truth of their being, or their identity, through public and private acts of confession and submission. This process has psychological and temporal aspects, involving the very inwardness and futurity through which marriage was constituted as coextensive with intimacy in the period. While dressed as a friar, the Duke tries to foster in both Juliet and Claudio the correct attitude toward their sins and, through their confessions, ultimately positions them under his authority. He provides them comfort and the possibility of salvation, first spiritually (when dressed as a friar) and then corporeally and juridically (when he resumes his role as the Duke).

The Duke is also responsible for their need of comfort, for he originally wanted the law under which they suffer to be enforced. The Duke is like a firefighter who, hoping to demonstrate his firefighting prowess, sets fires that he will put out himself. In this way, he manipulates characters' feelings of hope and despair to instill in them a sense that their futures depend on him. That is, to borrow Jonathan Goldberg's phrase, the Duke "authorizes and authors" these characters' attitudes toward their futures.[55] Moreover, their desires for a certain kind of future are functions of an interior space that the Duke has invested with importance through his appropriation of the power of the confessional. As Michel Foucault writes about the relation of sexuality and confession, "it is in the confession that truth and sex are joined, through the obligatory and exhaustive expression of an individual secret."[56] Combining the roles of confessor and lawgiver, the Duke seeks to convince his subjects that they feel a hidden, inward sexual desire that must be externalized through confession because this desire is out of control. If desire is unrestrained when hidden inside the subject and only restrainable when publicized, then, the state is justified in prying even further into their sexual lives to effect such publicization. This spiral of confessions and investigations has the ostensible but unobtainable goal of the mastery of sexual desire as well as the more subtle one of submission to state authority.

Though the Duke does not invent confession or the inwardness that is privileged within confessional subjectivity, his subjects' inwardness does not precede his appropriation of the power of the confessional through his friar's disguise. Inwardness is constituted as a zone of state surveillance when the Duke insists that other characters confess to him, and that is precisely the moment when his subjects' dependency upon him is inaugurated. For example, he tells Juliet that she should feel anxious about whether or not her penitence is valid: "I'll teach you how you shall arraign your conscience, / And try your penitence if it be sound / Or hollowly put on" (2.3.22–24). First he scripts her anxiety about the state of her repentance and then instructs her to respond to that anxiety with further introspection and doubt of her own motives, which she can then confess to him in return for relief from the anxiety that he first authored. The implantation of the anxiety precedes its arousal and manipulation for the purposes of furthering the dependence of the Duke's subjects on him and extending his power.

Inwardness, therefore, is both the creation of and instrumental to a power relation in this play. This dual function is probably most evident in the Duke's treatment of Isabella. When the Duke proposes the bedtrick, he is careful to suggest that the ends justify the deceptive means. Because "by this is your brother saved, your honour untainted, the poor

Mariana advantaged, and the corrupt deputy scaled," the Duke tells her, "the doubleness of the benefit defends the deceit from reproof" (3.1. 255–257, 259–260). Isabella is thus bound to him for finding the means, however dubious, to achieve what to her seem mutually exclusive goals. Later, he keeps the knowledge of her brother's safety from her "To make her heavenly comforts of despair / When it is least expected" (4.3.107–108). He produces despair in her so that he can pose as an instrument of mercy and comfort. Not only will he foster her gratitude; he will also make a spectacle out of her subjection to him. At first, Isabella's gratitude is not the result of confession and pardon, for Isabella has nothing to confess when the play opens. However, as the Duke augments her sense of obligation to him, he fabricates a sin for her to confess, telling her "to the head of Angelo / Accuse him" (4.3.139–140) of violating her chastity. This accusation takes the form of a publicly staged false confession of her own sinfulness, however: "after much debatement, / My sisterly remorse confutes mine honour, / And I did yield to him" (5.1.99–101). She has not even broken any laws, but the Duke gives her the identity of violated virgin and asks her to publicize it to further his own political ends. Later appearing as himself, the Duke responds with feigned incredulity at her accusation and asks her to "confess the truth, and say by whose advice / Thou com'st here to complain" (5.1.113–114). Her confession has prompted the state to inquire further for the truth, even though the representative of the state doing the inquiring both already knows the truth about who sent her and, in a way, is the truth because he is the one who sent her.

When Isabella discovers that the friar who sent her was the Duke in disguise, her sense of obligation to him produces yet another, somewhat more formal confession: "O give me pardon, / That I, your vassal, have employed and pained / Your unknown sovereignty" (5.1.382–384). The Duke's pardon and absolution only furthers her debt to and dependency on him and allows her the opportunity to name herself as his subject. This cycle of confessions, revelations, pardons, and increased obligations culminates when the Duke presents Isabella with her brother, pardons him, and asks for her hand in marriage. These three acts are so much part of the same project for the Duke that the play contains them within the very same sentence: "If he be like your brother, for his sake / Is he pardoned; and for your lovely sake / Give me your hand, and say you will be mine" (5.1.489–491). His assumption that she would wish to marry at this point is the logical consequence of his positioning her as a confessional subject, for the same strategy led to marriage for Angelo and Mariana and Claudio and Juliet.

Confession informs characters' relationship to the state in Vienna and eases the channeling of sexual desire into marriage. Yet what interests me is how and why the state arrives at the determination that marriage is the only form of intimate affiliation that is licit for citizens of Vienna. As the advice literature of William Whately and others indicate, marriage insists on the expression of desire, but places strict limits on its expression. Thus, it is the perfect relational form through which a docile citizenry can be produced, for without interiorized desire to confess, the subject would cease his or her confessional relation to the state. Mario DiGangi notes that, in *Measure for Measure* and early modern culture in general, this need to activate and channel desires produces the categorization of female sexuality based on "the number and kind of a woman's sexual partners."[57] More generally, the married couple has the right number and kind of partners for navigating the state's paradoxical activation and bridling of desires. In marriage, the subject senses his or her desires are uncontrollable and disciplines him or herself into managing their expression.

Positioning its characters in right relation with the state, *Measure for Measure* dramatizes the state's foreclosure on other forms of affiliation that do not operate in the same way as marriage. Gail Kern Paster characterizes the Vienna of *Measure for Measure* as a "city inhabited not by a community, but by an aggregate of selves."[58] Indeed, at the outset of the play, there is a lack of traditional forms of affiliation, such as kinship, and the spaces, such as the household, in which such affiliations can take place, but these do not represent all possible forms of community. Isabella does attempt to join one available community, the convent. It is a space of restraint, as Isabella acknowledges, and thus it may be thematically aligned with the prison, but Isabella enters the convent voluntarily; thus the convent space and the restraint therein is distanced from the state-sponsored carceral space and the state itself. Though the play only offers the briefest of glimpses into the convent community, the narrative strand wherein the Duke positions Isabella as a confessional subject is nonetheless preoccupied with the state's attempted destruction of this communal option for her. What is striking about Isabella's silence at the end of the text, then, is that it signals the limits of state power to define intimacy. Kathleen McLuskie argues that this silence reflects the way that feminist concerns are silenced by the play's narrative. "Feminist criticism of this play is restricted to exposing its own exclusion from the text," she writes, because "the dilemmas of the narrative and the sexuality under discussion are constructed in completely male terms."[59] Isabella's silence seems to indicate one female character's exclusion from the trajectory of the narrative. In the final moments of the play, the complicity of the comic narrative with the extension of the Duke's power, effected largely through enforced marriages, is exposed, but we need not be limited to bewailing our dissatisfaction at either the narrative's complicity or its rather uncomic failure to conceal its ideology. To read it otherwise, McLuskie claims, "would require a radical rewriting both of the narrative and of the way the scenes are constructed."[60] It is precisely this radical critique of the traditional approaches to narrative structure that I have been advocating and that I will elucidate for this play. Specifically, I show that *Measure for Measure* imagines modes of resistance to the ideology of its own narrative structure and opens up possibilities for Isabella and other women who wish to organize their intimate lives around a community of women.

The play appears to prompt us to think of Isabella's postulancy in terms of sexual renunciation or sexual insufficiency. Even as Julia Reinhard Lupton acknowledges that marriage in the play is tied to participation in the life of the nation and for Isabella it "is the legal and ritual means of her registration in the civic body," her understanding of Isabella's postulancy as "nonrelation" and a "willed exit from sexual circulation and its fluid exchanges" effaces that which the play itself cannot: the forms of affiliation in the convent.[61] Isabella's opening exchange with Francesca, her first-day-in-the-convent tour guide, suggests that they have been discussing the house rules, and Isabella corrects Francesca's interpretation of her question about the privileges of the nuns: "I speak not as desiring more, / But rather wishing a more strict restraint / Upon the sisterhood, the votarists of Saint Clare" (1.4.3–5). Granted, part of the "strict restraint" on life in the convent is the renunciation of free interaction with men. The Rule of the Holy Virgin Saint Clare, which would govern the order that Isabella is joining and which mentions a rule governing speech with the outside world similar to one mentioned in the play, indicates that when a nun joins a convent, "there shall be declared unto her the contents of [her] manner of life" and that "the Abbesse shall carefully provide a mistresse" – that is a mentor nun – to teach the novice the ropes.[62] The rule offers a guide for relations within the convent when a postulant arrives needing the mentorship that Francesca is shown providing Isabella.

What is not mentioned in the play is that a postulant has to be accepted by all the nuns; according to the rule, "the Abbesse shall be bound to ask the consent of all the Sisters: and if the greatest part give their consent . . . the Abbesse may receive her."[63] Thus, a nun's reception in an order of Clares involves the other nuns choosing whether to have a relationship with the new member. Though Shakespeare demonstrates a familiarity with

convent regulations, he represents only those regulations concerning relations with the outside world, as opposed to the full cluster of regulations,
including intraconvent relations, the Rule of Saint Clare addresses. I am
not faulting Shakespeare for not representing the entire Clarists' rule, but
the differences tellingly account for why so many critics mistakenly assume
Isabella desires non-affiliation by joining the convent. Though the Duke's
proposal presents Isabella with a choice between two ways of organizing
her sexual experience, this choice is presented asymmetrically. Non-marital
relations are at the margins of representation because they do not support
the Duke's political aims.

    From a counternarrational perspective, however, Shakespeare shows
Isabella seeking these affiliations within the convent, even if the Duke
ignores this by proposing marriage. Janet Adelman argues that Isabella's
"initial flight to the nunnery and her desire for more restrictions
there... suggest that she... wishes to be exempt from ordinary human
sexuality and the ordinary bonds so engendered."[64] While Isabella can
expect from the convent a different erotic life from the kind experienced
throughout Vienna, Adelman assumes a woman could not wish to organize her intimate life around a community of women without first rejecting
another model of affective relations deemed "ordinary human sexuality."
Her postulancy emerges independently in the play, unlike Milliscent's,
which is part of an elaborate arranged marriage plot in *The Merry Devil of
Edmonton*, and unlike Margaret's, which is a reaction to a negative experience with a man in *Friar Bacon and Friar Bungay*. Isabella offers us a
brief glimpse into her past that supports the idea that she might seek the
company of women independent of any distaste for marriage. Isabella calls
Juliet "my cousin" (1.4.44), and Lucio insinuates that there may be an
incestuous angle to the unfolding family drama, which precipitates this
second moment in the scene where something said by Isabella, she of
the alleged "prosperous art / ... with reason and discourse" (1.1.172–173),
requires clarification. Isabella replies that she is only her cousin "adoptedly,
as schoolmaids change their names / By vain though apt affection" (1.4.46–
47). Though Isabella downplays this relationship as youthful folly, she
points to a history of female bonds that take affection rather than blood
as their primary generator, and convent life would be an extension and
enlargement of these fondly recalled female bonds. As a part of her earlier
clarification to Francesca, she even invokes the "sisterhood" to convey that
the multiple relations she will form with the other nuns are valuable and
important to her as she is about to join this intimate community.

    A different Isabella also emerges from the text if we entertain the idea
that one could wish for restraint for its own pleasures, rather than out of

revulsion at other kinds of erotic experience, much in the way we need not see the convent as a space of lack or absence of affiliation. The pleasures of life in an ascetic community of women are not fully effaced in the play, although the traces of such pleasures that remain are largely obscured. While it is the only regulation specifically mentioned, the protocol for speaking to male visitors may not be the only aspect of convent life Isabella seeks by joining. Since Francesca does not appear to be repeating herself when she mentions this rule, we can assume that she and Isabella were speaking of other matters before the scene opens. Presumably, the part of their conversation that takes place before the scene opens involves more generally the rules governing bodily comportment within the convent, such as those listed in the Rule of Saint Clare, and the relations between the nuns themselves, since those rules would be exercised on a much more regular basis than the rules governing interaction with outsiders. We do not hear a reaction from Isabella to the restraint governing interactions between nuns and male visitors to the convent, and even though they cannot quite be named in the text, the more general ascetic aspects of the convent arouse Isabella, producing her clarification to Francesca about desiring more restraint. Partly involving but irreducible to highly-regulated interactions with men and outsiders in general, this conjunction of intimate life and restraint experienced in a community of women is what attracts Isabella to the Votarists of Saint Clare, an order reputed for its strict asceticism.[65]

Restraint is not the same as renunciation, and it is important to maintain the difference: they point to very different experiences of sexual pleasure, and their conflation blinds us to the pleasures available to Isabella through restraint. If we assume that Isabella's understanding of pleasure is the product of sexual renunciation, we cast the masochistic erotics of restraint as a passive and aberrant position rather than an actively inhabited one. When Angelo asks her, only quasi-hypothetically at this point, if she would have sex to save her brother's life, Isabella's response seems to support the sense that her masochistic eroticism is the product of renunciation. She claims that she would not have sex even to save her own life:

> That is, were I under the terms of death,
> Th'impression of keen whips I'd wear as rubies,
> And strip myself to death as to a bed
> That longing have been sick for, ere I'd yield
> My body up to shame.   (2.4.100–104)

Angelo forces her to choose between forced sexual acts and torture, so her rejection of an abhorrent heterosexual encounter seems to produce her masochistic desires. However, her lines to Francesca about wished-for restraint occur before she has even met Angelo; she speaks them when attempting to organize her intimate life by joining the convent. Since she is rejecting sexual blackmail, not pleasure, we should not read Isabella's preference for torture to sex with Angelo retroactively on to her previous utterance in order to denigrate masochism or to suggest her sexuality is pathological. Just as seeking female-female bonding need not be the result of rejecting cross-gender bonding, neither does the pleasure of restraint necessarily derive from the renunciation of pleasure. To assume so exiles masochistic practices from the category of the intimate. For Isabella, restraint can be the means of attaining such sexual pleasure. The female community Isabella seeks in the convent and the kind of pleasure from restraint she envisions are part of a singular understanding of intimate life, as Isabella's clarification to Francesca about her attitude toward "farther privileges" so concisely conveys (1.4.1).

Isabella does not invoke torture simply for rhetorical effect with Angelo, then. The play offers a previous reference, Isabella's wish for restraint in the convent, as a context for her statements about torture. Thus, instead of projecting her description of torture back onto her desire for restraint, I would suggest that the masochistic desire for restraint she expresses upon entering the nunnery lends her the conceptual resources to reimagine torture as pleasure and, by implication, to resist the state's assertion of its authority over her relationship to her body. With this relationship between Isabella's two references to masochistic pleasure in mind, we can see more clearly how the text presents her relation to the pleasures of her body. She imagines that the whips make impressions as they attempt to penetrate the surfaces and break the boundaries of her body, but, imagining her body as encrusted with jewels rather than punctured, she indicates that she would respond to that attempted penetration with a spectacularized display of bloodied surfaces. In her comparison of flaying to undressing for bed, the removal of skin satisfies longing. Undressing reveals only another surface, and the comparison holds on this level too. As she imagines it in her speech, flaying does not create an interiorized space for the state's manipulation of identity through perpetual cycles of confession and obligation, but instead she reimagines the body's surfaces as a space for resistance through unabashed pleasure in the face of a state seeking to make political use of its subjects' erotic lives.

The Duke attempts to eradicate Isabella's resistance to state-mandated intimacy. Affiliations between women characterize Isabella's intimate life until familial obligations take her out of the convent and expose her to the

Duke's machinations. At first, the Duke promotes Isabella's relations with another woman, Mariana, but this ruse allows him to wrest control of the unfolding events away from them. When introducing Mariana to Isabella, he says, "I pray you be acquainted with this maid. / She comes to do you good" (4.1.50–51) and Isabella adds, "I do desire the like" (4.1.51). While her response potentially encodes her desire for the acquaintance of one who is "like" her in terms of gender, Isabella desires female community now as an echo of what the Duke wants for her. When Mariana and Isabella come together in Act 5 to accuse Angelo, he correctly suggests that they are "instruments of some more mightier member" (5.1.235); the Duke has staged this scene and has appropriated Isabella's commitment to female solidarity for his own purposes, just as in *The Merry Devil of Edmonton*, where Fabell piques female-female intimacy in the convent in order to promote marriage. When Isabella kneels at Mariana's behest to ask the Duke to pardon Angelo, the women engage in a form of female solidarity that seeks to undo itself. Mariana pleads, "Lend me your knees, and all my life to come / I'll lend you all my life to do you service" (5.1.428–429). She recasts their female solidarity as servitude, but what will undo their bond is the success of their suit, for Mariana's marriage will organize her intimate life around Angelo.

Seeing female bonds work to end themselves, the Duke brings in Claudio, redirects Isabella's attention to her obligation to him, and stages more confessions from her. He has already prompted Isabella to confess an act that she has not committed so as to open up a space for interiority. In addition, he has filled that space with a sense of obligation for the maintenance of her chastity, for when Lucio unmasks the friar as the Duke, she asks his forgiveness as a vassal having troubled him with a personal matter. This confession, in a way, also involves a crime that she has not committed, since the disguised Duke becomes involved in her affairs of his own accord. Revealing that her brother is still alive, the Duke finally asks her for one more confession: "Give me your hand, and say you will be mine" (5.1.491). Having manipulated female-female affiliations and interiority for the purposes of extending his own sovereignty and having created in Isabella a sense of obligation to him, the Duke has arranged all of Isabella's affiliations so they put her in right relation with the state. To complete this process, he offers her marriage, the same condition on which the re-establishment of the other characters' right relationship with the state is predicated.

In one of the moments in the play where the audience views the inefficacy of the Duke's stage-management of the play's resolution, Isabella remains silent, with no love to confess to the Duke. The process of her subjection to the state is interrupted. Isabella's silence can be placed in a network of local resistances to the exercise of the state power that the narrative seems to underwrite. By not confessing love for the Duke, Isabella resists understanding her subjectivity as interiorized, requiring verbal exteriorization through confession, which, in turn, produces submission to his authority. This act of resistance aligns Isabella with Barnardine, who also does not allow the Duke to arraign his conscience so that the state can execute him. Katharine Eisaman Maus maintains that the Duke encounters limits to his power because of "the way that the characters' inwardness . . . recedes almost instantly into unknowability in the midst of what is structured as a scene of revelation and pardon."[66] Barnardine's resistance to confessing to the disguised Duke and Isabella's silence at the Duke's proposal could, following Maus, be part of a strategy to assert the unknowability of interiority to ward off the Duke's farther incursions. I would, however, suggest an alternate relationship between Barnardine and Isabella's silences that nevertheless maintains the possibility of Isabella's resistance to the Duke's power over her subjectivity. In the final scene, Barnardine's inwardness does not so much become unknowable as much as his silence reveals that inner life and futurity in general is a fantastical construction of the state. Despite Barnadine's continued silence, the Duke pardons him, citing his "stubborn soul / That apprehends no further than this world" (5.1.478–479). He is constructed, like the queer in Edelman's *No Future*, as the enemy of futurity, and in this case embraces it. On one level, the Duke indicates that Barnardine is insensitive to his own mortality and the damnation he faces in his unconfessed condition. Though the Duke commands him to "provide / For better times to come" (5.1.483–484), that lesson remains unlearned in the play and futurity is separated from the space of representation. Barnardine apprehends only this world of sensory perception and surfaces. Even as the Duke voices it, Barnardine's sense that the truth exists at the surface of things, in exteriority, and not in their depths cuts at the very heart of the Duke's strategy for positioning his subjects under his sovereign power. Thus, the inwardness the Duke privileges as the reality about his subjects' identities fades not into unknowability so much as it fades into nothingness or unreality; at the same time, the future of the nation secured by marriage encounters the limits of representability.

The Duke's marriage proposal seems to be the logical outcome of reseducing back into the national fold a "seduced . . . Catholic," but in so doing, his means become contaminated by their similarity to those of the Catholic exorcists against whom Harsnett inveighs. Borrowing the costume of a Catholic friar, he has attempted to produce inwardness and foster dependence on the state for the future, and, in a rewriting of Harsnett's polemic against Catholic exorcism, used the "cogd miracle" of producing the living Claudio to renew, rather than rob Isabella of, her "loyaltie to [her] prince."[67] Even Lucio is given a future in exchange for marriage when the Duke threatens him with execution and then forgives his slanders and remits all punishment of him other than marriage. The play figures marriage as a kind of movement through time when Mariana says that if her claim that Angelo "knew me as a wife" is not true, then she should "forever be confixèd here, / A marble monument" on her knees begging (5.1.230–231). Whereas this image is one of permanent subordination and supplication, it is also an acknowledgment that without marriage, she might as well be stuck there. Isabella's silence may indicate that she would rather be stuck there than be part of the marriage movement that Juliet, Mariana, and even Kate Keepdown will be happily claimed by. The Duke encounters the resistance of one who refuses to acknowledge the existence of the state's privileged realm of truth – he has failed to make "thoughts" the basis for her being a "subject," the terms Isabella opposes in her final lines in the play (5.1.450). There is a breach between these two conceptions of embodiment, interiority and exteriority, across which language cannot travel. The Duke is left only with the ability to tell "what's yet behind," that is, the past, not the future (5.1.538). Isabella, the character who had graphically situated the pleasures of the body on her body's surfaces, takes a cue from Barnardine's exteriorized subjectivity and resistance to futurity. By remaining silent, she denies the existence of an inner world from which her confession of love should come, and she exposes that world as a discursive construction that leads, in this play, to marriage and participation in the reproduction of the life of the nation.

This chapter began by suggesting that it would be useful to situate Isabella's postulancy in its dramatic context. My readings of *Friar Bacon and Friar Bungay* and *The Merry Devil of Edmonton* bring to the fore the geographic, psychological, political, and narrational stakes involved when a dramatist presents a heroine with the choice between the convent and marriage. The consolidation of intimacy is tied up in these texts with other historical processes and institutions, such as the Reformation, absolutist rule, and nation formation, and insofar as they make use of women's bodies, desires, and affections as conceptual resources, the intimacy of convent life stands in for the ways that women might refuse to collaborate with dominant culture. Though these texts appear to suppress the convent alternative, there remains in each a limited investment in the female-female intimacy of convent life that challenges marriage's dominance over the intimate sphere and comic narrative. By reading against the grain, I have put together an intimate counternarrative out of representations of what we might be tempted to assume an early modern, post-Reformation reader or audience member would have seen as an outmoded, foreign way of life for women. Instead, these texts' ambivalence about convent life allows a reader to be piqued by the possibility of building a way of life that resists integration in the projects of amassing authority to marriage, the nation, and the monarchy.

CHAPTER 5

Female homoeroticism, race, and public forms of intimacy in the works of Lady Mary Wroth

INTRODUCTION: INTERSECTIONS OF RACE AND SEXUALITY

To extend the previous chapter's discussion of representations of female same-sex intimacy in early modern texts, this chapter focuses on the public status of bonds between women in the work of Lady Mary Wroth. While I have discussed drama in the last three chapters, by shifting genres I hope to show that the definitional struggle over intimacy was carried out in multiple literary venues in the period. Wroth's prose romance and verse are not literary in the same way as the period's commercial drama, though the dramatists themselves hardly agreed on the literariness of plays. Nevertheless, Wroth's texts and the dramatic texts I discussed in previous chapters share many of the same concerns about relationality. I hope that the scope of my analysis will encourage Renaissance scholars to develop their own rubrics through which they might assemble unexpected canons, break down traditional generic boundaries, and bring women writers into further dialogue with male-dominated milieux of literary production, such as the commercial theatre.

Several affective economies structure Wroth's work, but the relationship between Pamphilia and Amphilanthus seems to be the organizing principle of both the prose romance *The Countess of Montgomery's Urania* and the sonnet sequence that bears their names. Yet the centrality of this relationship is complicated by the significance Wroth invests in her texts' female-female relations, which interact with the cross-gendered bond of Pamphilia and Amphilanthus and other heteroerotic bonds. Wroth repeatedly returns to the problem of publicizing intimate bonds that are based on private, interiorized desire. This psychic depth model's near-exclusive control over intimacy in Wroth's work is also exclusionary. As I will show in this chapter, homoerotic and heteroerotic bonds do not achieve representational parity despite both being underwritten by interiorized desire in her work. In fact, the psychic depth model inhibits the achievement of

parity. Though her sonnet sequence and prose romance are different as narratives, the teleology structuring both erases, appropriates, and transforms
female-female bonds in order to advance the public status of marriage and
heterosexual coupling.

In part, this transformation of female-female bonds occurs in conjunction with the narratives' strategic deployment of representations of blackness. Like many of her contemporaries, Wroth introduces male and female
black bodies in her texts in order to construct white subjectivity and more
particularly white femininity. Wroth's texts demonstrate how important it
is to approach early modern intimacy intersectionally – that is, to examine
multiple features of identity and their interactions.[1] Building on the critical
discussion of race and gender in her work, I seek to attend to the nexus
of race and sexuality in her articulation of an intimate sphere organized
around the heterosexual couple. In the manuscript continuation of the
romance, this intimate economy can partially accommodate blackness in
the context of the public relationship between Pamphilia and Rodomandro, but Wroth's texts articulate female-female cross-racial bonds, such as
Pamphilia's affection toward Night in the sonnets, in order to disavow
them. The blackness of these female figures is divisive, ultimately reaffirm-
ing otherwise problematic forms of heterosexual coupling. In this chapter,
I examine this deployment of blackness and the opportunities for a reader
to reopen the texts' conditional space of cross-racial female-female affection. The intimacy of heterosexual coupling in Wroth – at least insofar as
Pamphilia and Amphilanthus are to be understood as icons of heterosexual love – is a representational illusion created by denying signification to
other affective relations. Within the world of the romance and the sonnet
sequence, Wroth's characters frequently fail to publicize their interiorized
heteroerotic desires, and as a result her representations of heterosexual coupling fail to signify publicly the full scope of intimate life. In the process
of discussing the interpretive possibilities that emerge from Wroth's counternarrative to the failed project of publicizing interiorized heterosexual
desire, I also argue that we need to rethink what constitutes evidence of
desires, especially non-normative ones, in Renaissance texts.

"TRULY POORE NIGHT, THOU WELLCOME ART TO MEE": MANAGING THE INVITATION TO FEMALE HOMOEROTICISM IN *PAMPHILIA TO AMPHILANTHUS*

Primarily a reflection on the speaker's emotional state rather than an assem-
bly of events that can be plotted, *Pamphilia to Amphilanthus* is a narrative

in only the broadest sense. While they certainly do not have the narrativity of nineteenth-century novels, Renaissance English sonnet sequences did not avoid narrative temporality altogether. Wroth's uncle, Philip Sidney, begins *Astrophil and Stella* in typical Petrarchan mode with a lover pleading for his beloved lady's favor, and while the sonnets reflect mostly on the speaker's hopes and despairs, eventually a kind of plot development gives the sequence a semblance of narrativity. In sonnet 69, we reach a turning point where Astrophil's wooing seems to have succeeded: "Stella hath, with words where faith doth shine, / Of her high heart given me the monarchy."[2] However, we find out that "she give but thus condition'ly" (69.12). The promise of sexual union is qualified, deferred, and ultimately denied when the speaker must "By iron laws of duty . . . depart" (87.4). As a sort of narrative closure, the speaker reflects in the remaining poems on absence and sorrow. While the English sonnet sequence is not a monolithic genre, narrativity, loosely defined, may have been generically important in the period's sonnet sequences.

To a degree, Wroth's printed sonnet sequence follows in the footsteps of her uncle by adhering to generic expectations of a semi-teleological temporality.[3] Pamphilia's equivocation about love makes the sequence somewhat recursive, but overall the sequence appears to have a narrative-like structure that moves it toward the resolution of Pamphilia's qualms. The first sonnet hearkens back to a dream vision of Cupid and Venus implanting a flaming heart into her chest, and she concludes, "Yett since: O mee: a lover I have binn."[4] Thus, this sonnet sequence begins *in medias res*, with Pamphilia already in love, and the reader follows her as she deals with the implications of her feelings. In P55, the experience of love has become more and more intense, as Pamphilia observes, "How like a fire doth love increase in mee" (P55.1). Despite this intensity, Pamphilia asserts "Yett love I will till I butt ashes prove" (P55.14), and she signs her name at the end of the poem. Even if she is not "signing off" with her signature, Pamphilia here represents herself as fortified with enough resolve to conclude this part of the sequence and predict for herself a future of constant love. As it is printed, the sequence does not end here, and she offers additional reflections on the experience of loving Amphilanthus, which prompts one to question whether she has secured the future for herself that the final line of P55 indicates. At the end of P103, the last sonnet, she again signs her name and explains why she can now "leave off" writing poetry (P103.13). Now that she has secured futurity for her relationship with Amphilanthus, she can offer the reader narrative closure: "my muse now hapy, lay thy self to rest / Sleepe in the quiett of a faithfull love"

(P103.1–2). Her muse seems to be the embodiment of the formal demands of the sequence, and pleasing her muse means fulfilling those demands in order to achieve narrative closure. As in P55, she has achieved some resolution about her constancy, but in P103 she has also pleased her muse and thus can finally command, "write you noe more" and "wake nott to new unrest" (P103.3, 4). Unrest has structured the narrative of the sequence, and, if she is able to avoid it, there will be nothing to report and no more need to write. Somewhat tentatively, she cannot entirely rule out future unrest, so instead she commands her muse to sleep through it. An act of will to avoid unrest in love precipitates narrative closure.

Exactly how has Pamphilia made her muse happy, though? What does her muse want from her in the first place? To begin to answer these questions, we encounter the fact that, as Josephine A. Roberts notes, the printed sequence "devotes relatively little attention to Amphilanthus, whose inconstancy serves as merely the condition which prompts the persona's reflections."[5] Roberts may even be overstating his presence, for many individual sonnets meditate on other, more palpably present figures, such as Venus and Cupid in the first sonnet, where no explicit mention of Amphilanthus is made. When Pamphilia does address sonnets to him, they are often occasioned by his departure, as in P28, where she begs him to "make nott too long stay" (P28.2); or by his absence, as in P91 where she begs him, "lett me injoye thy sight" (P91.1). His presence can even be illusory, as in P98, where Pamphilia reflects on "the Image of my deere" (P98.1). Despite Amphilanthus's absence from many of the poems, this sequence's narrative demands that Pamphilia integrate her private experience of desire into her publicly visible and circulating social identity, thereby achieving the status of a constant lover. She, however, believes that to publicize her love would be to falsify it. Though they seem to disagree, Jeffrey Masten, who argues that the sonnets "seem to speak an almost inscrutable private language," and Daniel Juan Gil, who argues that Wroth "never imagines a private sphere that is separate from public, explicitly conventionalized spaces," are both right about the public and private spheres in the sequence, as long as we do not confound the speaker and the form of the sequence.[6] Publicness saturates the sequence's form while its star Pamphilia privatizes her experience of affective relations.

The existence of this formal demand for publicness can be inferred from Pamphilia's tone and her use of the language of testimony. In P46, she responds to imagined interlocutors demanding testimony of her love that "Itt is nott love which you poore fooles do deeme / That doth apeare by fond, and outward showes" (1–2), after which she lists and distances herself from several actions that might count as outward shows. As Hamlet might say, these are "actions that a man might play" (or here a woman), and she has "that within which passeth show."[7] To answer this fantasmatic public that defines love in terms of "outward shows," Pamphilia can only describe what her love is not, asking her audience to take at face value that "in the soule true love in safety lies" (P46.12). She cannot demonstrate her love without endangering the safety and, ultimately, the truth of it. Like her muse, these "poore fooles," as she deems the interlocutors, are the manifestation of the sonnet sequence's requirement that she publicize her desire in exchange for recognition of her identity as a constant lover.

In the course of the sequence, the conflict between the form and the speaker of the sequence separates the spaces of public representation and private affection. This separation emerges even in the first sonnet. In Pamphilia's private dream vision, Venus holds burning hearts aloft, displaying them as her plunder in a highly theatrical manner, and Cupid implants one such heart into Pamphilia's breast. Instead of allowing Pamphilia the solitary experience of loving the absent Amphilanthus, the vision compels her to testify that she is a lover. However, the evidence is hidden in the space occupied by the burning heart that was implanted in her during this metaphorical cardiothoracic surgery. Through its demand that Pamphilia's desire be made public, the sequence seeks to return this burning inward heart to the originary moment of its own triumphant display. To satisfy the requirements of the sequence, Pamphilia must go further than admitting that she is a lover in P1's private context of a dream vision. She must confess that her desire for Amphilanthus constitutes her public identity.

In P41, Pamphilia examines her vexed attempts to bridge the gap between interiorized desire and her public status as a lover. Exposing the interior, she externalizes her own heart through an apostrophe: "How well poore hart thou wittnes canst I love" (P41.1). When she says that the heart's "chiefe paine is that [she] must itt [her love] hide" (P41.11), she changes what her heart witnesses from her love itself to the existence of a secret. Thus, what the heart is supposed to signify changes from affection to privacy. In the final couplet, she refutes the idea that love is always accompanied by great shows of passion: "For know more passion in my hart doth move / Then in a million that make show of love" (P41.13–14). Here Wroth echoes Sonnet 54 from *Astrophil and Stella*, which similarly concludes, "Dumb swans, not chatt'ring pies, do lovers prove; / They love indeed who quake to say they love" (54.13–14). Pamphilia defends herself against a skeptical public made up of those who would say that "sure love can nott bee / Wher soe small showe of passion is descrid" (P41.9–10). If the final lines are addressed to the heart, as the rest of the poem is, Pamphilia tries to convince it of what it was originally supposed to witness. If they are addressed to her interlocutors, the passion moves *in* her heart, available to the addressees only through Pamphilia's bald assurance. Either way, her intimacy never achieves publicness as her address to an unspecified audience collapses back into the unrepresentable space of interiority.

The tentativeness of the end of the sequence still holds out the possibility of "new unrest" while hoping to avoid it. Thus, Pamphilia at most comes to terms with the narrative's demands. At the end, she concludes to herself that "what's past showes you can love" (P103.13), but what is past is not her desire's achievement of publicness exactly, but the struggle to reconcile the sequence's need for public recognition with her notion that the more private the experience of desire, the truer it is. She claims that her ability to say she is truly a lover after such a struggle will have to satisfy these posited interlocutors of her desire, and she identifies this constancy as the principle through which to negotiate the division between the public space of representation and the private space of an intimacy grounded in interiority. Instead of positing a future of loving Amphilanthus, she commands herself, "lett your constancy your honor prove" (P103.14). As many critics have noted, Pamphilia publicly declares her constancy to constancy, an abstraction she substitutes for Amphilanthus – or, more precisely, an abstraction that fills Amphilanthus's absence in order to satisfy this sequence's demand for a public statement. Because Amphilanthus does not figure into this public statement more than obliquely, Pamphilia only appears to resolve the separation of the spaces of intimacy and representation. Her declaration of constancy allows her to be public in order to cover the absence of the object of her desire and, quite possibly, the absence of desire for him altogether.

This representational conflict between Wroth's sonnet sequence and its speaker is implicated in the division between public and private spheres that was emerging in the early modern period. According to Philippe Ariès, the period saw interarticulated public and private spheres disentangle themselves to become distinct, though interactive, conceptualizations of space.[8] Examining one aspect of this process, Jürgen Habermas contends that constitution of the private sphere originally involved "exclusion from the sphere of the state apparatus" or the public authority.[9] The private sphere, thus, was actually privative, characterized by deprivation and disempowerment, and this connection operates even at a linguistic level, since both "private" and "privation" derive from *privare*, the Latin verb meaning "to deprive." According to Habermas, the bourgeoisie rearticulated the distinction between public and private. No longer was it the space to which they were relegated because of their exclusion from sites of power, such as the court; it instead was the staging area from which they emerged into public life and power. For Habermas, the relationship between public and private spheres was revised somewhat later than the Renaissance, but Francis Barker has demonstrated that this process was already inchoate in the seventeenth century's increasing investment in interiority. The subject replicates the division between the public and private sphere in his or her (though usually first "his" in patriarchal culture) mode of embodiment, thereby producing a space for inwardness. Though interiority appears to be a space from which one emerges into agency, much like the private sphere of the bourgeoisie, it "constitutes . . . the potential instead for a very profound subjection."[10] Barker here exploits the linguistic connection between "subjectivity" and "subjection," similar to that which exists between "private" and "privation," for whereas interiorized forms of subjectivity promise freedom from subjection, they entail their own restrictions on agency. Moreover, because of the emerging parallelism between privacy and inwardness in the early modern period, there is always the specter that the inward space is just as privative as the private sphere was in its earlier constitution.

This emerging link between the public and private spheres provides a context for Wroth's perhaps ambivalent articulation of conceptions of female subjectivity or authorship. By bringing queer scholarship on the public and private spheres into dialogue with Renaissance literature, we can also see that this division between public and private is also implicated in the forms of intimacy that Wroth can imagine. The sequence privileges Pamphilia's relationship with Amphilanthus, despite its apparently unsatisfying aspects, by positioning it as Pamphilia's exclusive route to narrative closure and to the agency of publicness. The sequence's advancement of the relationship of Pamphilia and Amphilanthus might be understood as an early example of the process through which heterosexuality became diffused through modern Western culture by exploiting the division between public and private spheres. Lauren Berlant and Michael Warner make two compelling arguments in this regard: first, "the normativity of heterosexual culture links intimacy only to the institutions of personal life, making them the privileged institutions of social reproduction, the accumulation and transfer of capital, and self-development"; second, "by making sex seem irrelevant or merely personal, heteronormative conventions of intimacy block the building of non-normative or explicit public sexual cultures."[11] For Berlant and Warner, public means "accessible, available to memory, and sustained through collective activity."[12] Sexuality is relegated to the private sphere, then, in part to cover over the public sphere's saturation with conventions associated with heterosexual coupling. Intimacies not governed by the norms of heterosexual coupling seem intrusive or out of place in the public sphere, thereby making it difficult, if not impossible, to imagine or represent such alternatives, which is a prerequisite to making them accessible, memorable, and sustainable to those who might find them more satisfying than long-term heterosexual monogamy.

Engaging this emergent division between public and private spheres, Wroth anticipates some of the problems in imagining and representing intimacy that Berlant and Warner discuss as characteristic of more recent historical contexts. Because of this sequence's aim that Pamphilia publicize her desire, there seems to be little room in the intimate economy of the sonnets for the representation of other potentially more satisfying bonds. Yet this importance of narrativity and teleology in literary texts has its detractors, as we saw in Chapter 1 in Marlowe's *Hero and Leander*. Indeed, the many texts I have discussed throughout this book register a teleological narrative impulse with strong counter-impulses, and it has been my contention that the latter have been ignored or discounted, especially in discussions of the forms of affection that a text makes available to its audiences. Wroth represents just such a bond between Pamphilia and the female figure of Night who, in providing comfort and care to Pamphilia, threatens to supplant Amphilanthus as an object of Pamphilia's desire. Through her representation of Night, Wroth creates a temporary space for a non-heteroerotic intimate economy and opens up room for a reader to question the heterosexualizing impulses of narrative closure.

Nighttime is mentioned frequently in the sequence as an abstraction but Night is also a female personification with whom Pamphilia interacts. Barbara Lewalski and Wendy Wall view Night as a projection of the speaker's psyche, but the resemblance between Pamphilia and Night does not preclude Night's being treated as an independent figure for whom Pamphilia feels an affection, howsoever rooted such affection is in identification.[13] The sequence's few references to Amphilanthus mostly involve simulacra that only further emphasize his absence, as in P24, where Pamphilia recalls, "When last I saw thee, I did nott thee see, / Itt was thine Image, which in my thoughts lay" (P24.1–2). Thus, he has the disembodied qualities of a psychic projection, but it would be unlikely for a critic to suggest that he was somehow fantasmatic. Although she is technically a personification and not a character in the traditional sense, there is even less evidence from the sequence to treat Night in this way. In the sonnets where Night is a sustained presence, she offers Pamphilia an embodied and pleasurable same-sex affective relation. When we are introduced to her, Night competes with day for Pamphilia's attention, and because of the similarity between the two women – Night's appearance reflects Pamphilia's inner torment – Pamphilia issues an invitation to intimacy:

> My thoughts are sad; her face as sad doth seeme:
> My paines are long; Her houers taedious are:
> My griefe is great, and endles is my care:
> Her face, her force, and all of woes esteeme:
> Then wellcome Night, and farwell flattring day
> Which all hopes breed, and yett our joyes delay.
> (P13.9–14)

This sonnet resembles *Astrophil and Stella* 89, where Sidney treats the inter-action of day and night as a kind of battle and even calls night "tedious" (89.6). In Sidney's poem the competition results in what Astrophil calls the "bad-mixture of my night and day" (89.12). Alternately, Night is victorious in Wroth's poem. Moreover, while Astrophil seems to be in a position of powerlessness in a conflict whose stakes are not spelled out, Wroth places Pamphilia as both judge of the outcome of the competition and that com-petition's prize. Day offers Pamphilia "flattring" hope that turns out to be false because it never really precipitates the joy of union with Amphi-lanthus. In fact, she accuses day of delaying her joy, whereas Night offers Pamphilia immediate comfort through identification. Night's resemblance to Pamphilia associates Night with presence and embodiment. Pamphilia sees Night's face, not just her image.

Moreover, Night's resemblance to Pamphilia potentially allows their affection to heal the breach between inner and outer that vexes her rela-tionship to Amphilanthus. In P17, Pamphilia welcomes Night, again on the basis of their similarity:

> Truly poore Night thou wellcome art to mee:
> I love thee better in this sad attire
> Then that which raiseth some mens phant'sies higher
> Like painted outsids which foule inward bee;
> I love thy grave, and saddest lookes to see,
> Which seems my soule, and dying hart intire,
> Like to the ashes of some happy fire
> That flam'd in joy, butt quench'd in miserie:
> I love thy count'nance, and thy sober pace
> Which evenly goes, and as of loving grace

To uss, and mee among the rest oprest
Gives quiet, peace to my poore self alone,
And freely grants day leave when thou art gone
To give cleere light to see all ill redrest.

(P17.1–14)

Following Petrarchan convention, Pamphilia blazons Night as an available female erotic object. Though the catalogue is not extensive, her appreciation of Night's clothes, face, and gait are telling in the absence of such a blazon for Amphilanthus. Although Pamphilia invokes phallocentric tropes of arousal that are appropriate to the masculinist form of the blazon, she does so only to disavow and replace them with an account of her arousal by another woman based on sameness rather than difference. Instead of slicing Night into pieces in the way that blazons often do to women, her catalogue of the various aspects of Night form a unitary display all the more attractive to Pamphilia because the characteristics she observes are so familiar to her. Night's clothes do not produce in Pamphilia the false hope that otherwise causes her much suffering. Instead, they complement the grave look of her face and entice Pamphilia to the person and body beneath. Her relation to Night is cast in positive terms: it can sidestep, because of Night's choice of attire, the aesthetics of division between inner and outer selves that seems to underwrite male heteroerotic desire. Pamphilia claims that Night's clothes arouse her more than those that, by covering up defects, conventionally "raiseth some mens phant'sies higher" (P17.3). She equates her arousal and male arousal because it can be heightened prosthetically, for it is not so much that men's "phant'sies" are higher than hers but that both she and the men that she posits require additional stimulation. The difference is, however, that she sees complementarity in clothes whereas men look to clothing as supplements to provide a pleasant façade for thoroughgoing corruption. Other men and women are objects of her scorn in this poem: women for covering their foulness and men for being, or perhaps for needing to be, deceived. Night, saved from such derision by not being deceptive, stands out by contrast. Thus, Pamphilia sees and values in Night resemblance to herself and difference from everyone else.

In P17, then, Pamphilia somewhat paradoxically associates sadness and arousal by finding pleasure in what traditionally might be regarded as aesthetically unpleasant or even foul, but behind the split such a paradox enacts, Pamphilia insists there is a unity of inner and outer personhood that is attractive about Night. One might compare this poem to *Astrophil and Stella* 96, where Sidney writes that Thought and Night, both personified, have "one livery" (96.2). Sidney detaches Thought from his speaker and makes Thought the addressee; thus, the relationship he creates is mediated by Thought, for it is Thought, and not Astrophil himself, who "with good cause . . . likest so well the night" (96.1). In contrast, though she notes the resemblance between Night and her "soule, and dying hart intire" (P17.6), Pamphilia is shown directly interacting with Night, her clothes, and her countenance when she addresses her with phrases that begin with "I love thee" (P17.2) or "I love thy" (P17.5, 9). Though the tone of Wroth's poem is more somber than excited, Pamphilia's relation with Night is undeniably amorous, unmediated, and welcomed by Pamphilia.

This bond represents an alternative to publicizing her desire for Amphilanthus. However, Pamphilia's vision of a homoerotic relation, suffused with affection, care, and identification, does not offer her a route toward a public declaration of desire, the aim of the sequence. If it did, the sequence could end at P43. Even if her relation with Night is everything that, according to the logic of the sequence, her relationship with Amphilanthus ought to be – that is, pleasurable, articulable – access to public signification turns out to be asymmetrical for different intimacies. Particularly affected by this asymmetry in the early modern period, female same-sex erotics, according to Valerie Traub, "were culturally practiced and represented in a variety of ways, although often according to a governing logic that attempted to reinscribe their impossibility."[14] Such representations often remained incompletely subordinated, as Traub's "attempted" implies. The potential for recuperating an affirming representational economy of female homoeroticism lies in these moments where representation exceeds its originary purposes, such as when Night offers Pamphilia the satisfaction that Amphilanthus can never seem to offer her.

Love, then, is politicized, at least insofar as homoerotic and heteroerotic affects have asymmetric access to the forms of signification that will precipitate narrative closure in this sequence. This politicization of love is too often forgotten in the wake of approaches to sonnet sequences that understand love discourse as merely the vehicle by which other political matters are expressed within a setting, such as the court in Renaissance England, where direct expression of political ambition was tacitly prohibited.[15] As a proud Sidney and courtier, Wroth was certainly engaged with Jacobean politics, but when we insist that expressions of love are only metaphors for political matters, we risk suggesting that amatory discourse in itself is not already political prior to its particular figurative uses by ambitious courtiers. Love becomes, to borrow a phrase from Berlant and Warner, "the *endlessly* cited elsewhere of political public discourse."[16] That is, in the critical insistence on amatory discourse's utility for political ends, love is itself depoliticized, which obscures the fact that certain forms of affection were unthinkable and those that were imaginable were arranged in a hierarchy of value within early modern English culture, as within modern Western culture. Amatory discourse has an ideological valence predetermining what can and cannot be represented as "love" even before sonneteers couch their political ambitions in it. *Pamphilia to Amphilanthus* contains this already politicized amatory discourse, for what can count as the private experience of love is circumscribed by what can be publicized.

Critics have not examined the way that the availability of different forms of affection is always already politicized in the sequence because they have followed the lead of Pamphilia, who relentlessly evaluates her experience of affection through a rubric of privacy. Attempting to foreclose on these homoerotic possibilities for Pamphilia, Wroth introduces a way for her to differentiate between forms of privacy in order to keep her on the trajectory toward publicizing her heteroerotic bond with Amphilanthus. Naomi J. Miller argues that "same-sex bonds consistently allow [Wroth's] female characters to re-view and sometimes revise the conventionally hierarchical dynamics of heterosexual desire."[17] My view, however, is that the service to which female-female bonds are put in the sequence is far less benign, because such service effaces their homoerotic content in order to emphasize the desirability of heterosexual relations with Amphilanthus, which would otherwise appear unsatisfying or impossible because of his absence. Wroth sets up the following distinction in response to Pamphilia's affection with Night: her bond with Amphilanthus represents one kind of privacy – characterized by the presence of love and her beloved and linked to the truth of her personhood – and her bond with Night represents another kind of privacy – characterized by absence and not associated with her personhood at all. In this way, the sequence turns the privacy of her bond with Night into privation. However, this difference is difficult to sustain, and the distinction the sequence sets up threatens to collapse because the absence that is projected onto Night in order to differentiate the bonds actually characterizes her relation to Amphilanthus. That is, her experience of this heteroerotic bond may in fact be privative as well as private.

Wroth repeatedly associates Amphilanthus with daylight and sunlight, and she draws on this association when she suggests that Pamphilia's bond with Night involves privation, whereas her bond with Amphilanthus occurs within a private space of inwardness that is the potential source of her subjectivity. The daylight figures the outward expression or public face of that inwardness in order to testify that her bond with Amphilanthus is characterized not by absence but presence. This apparent agency is offered in exchange for conceding to the sequence's understanding of relationality and publicness. Yet Pamphilia only makes this concession after she has articulated in P7 that her fear that her bond with him is actually privative:

> The Sunn which to the Earth
> Gives heate, light, and pleasure,
> Joyes in spring, hateth dearth,
> Plenty makes his treasure.
> His heat to mee is colde,
> His light all darknes is
> Since I am bar'd of bliss
> I heate nor light beeholde.
>
> (P7.9–16)

Being with Amphilanthus is like being under the sun but, paradoxically, feeling cold and being cloaked in darkness. Though she says that she cannot feel heat or light in line 16, the preceding lines indicate that the sun actually takes away heat by making her cold, takes away light by making it dark, and takes away plenty by bringing in dearth. Thus, she experiences lower than normal levels of the light, heat, and plenty that she expects her bond with him to augment.

In the sonnets to Night, Pamphilia receives added comfort and pleasure from Night even in the context of darkness. She does not deplete Pamphilia as Amphilanthus does; she gives "quiet [and] peace" (P17.12). Eventually, the tables are turned such that Night supplants Amphilanthus as the agent of her deprivation. In P42, Pamphilia addresses his eyes:

> See butt, when Night appears,
> And Sunn hath lost his force
> How his loss doth all joye from us divorce;
> And when hee shines, and cleares
> The heav'ns from clowds of night
> How happy then is made our gazing sight,
> Butt more then Sunns faire light
> Your beames doe seeme to mee,
> Whose sweetest lookes doe tye and yett make free;
> Why should you then soe spite
> Poore mee as to destroy
> The only pleasure that I taste of joye?   (P42.13–24)

Invoking the idea from Renaissance optics that the eyes see by emitting beams through which objects are made visible, Pamphilia laments that Amphilanthus deprives her of joy by not looking upon her enough. This current, wherein he is the source of her deprivation, is in tension with the way that she organizes and hierarchizes his eye beams, sunlight, and Night; this tension, in turn, allows Pamphilia to project onto Night the fault he should bear for his neglect. Pamphilia claims that Amphilanthus's gaze warms her and that the sun imperfectly recreates and approximates this pleasure in his absence. Night no longer fills the absence of Amphilanthus; instead, Night is the absence of both Amphilanthus and anything that might give Pamphilia substitute pleasure. Thus, instead of being an object of erotic attachment, Night gives substance by contrast to heterosexual coupling, just as she provides a "shade for lovers" (P65.2).

The restructuring of Pamphilia's relationship with Night proceeds unevenly through the sequence. One poem will note how tedious Night is because of Amphilanthus's absence, and another will welcome Night as the embodiment of an economy of pleasure not routed through an absent male figure. Wroth allows Night to return to re-establish a claim on signification within the intimate economy of the sequence. In P63, for example, Pamphilia assigns to Night the light imagery that had formerly differentiated her from Amphilanthus:

> In night yett may wee see some kind of light
> When as the Moone doth please to show her face,
> And in the sunns roome yeelds her light, and grace
> Which otherwise must suffer dullest night.
>
> (P63.1–4)

Wroth reasserts Night as presence in the light of the moon, but, in line 3, she qualifies this reassertion by noting that the light of the moon has its source in the sun. The moonlight becomes an approximation of the sun-like Amphilanthus, and Pamphilia compares the moon's phases to her own changing fortunes in the quest to enjoy "true delight" (P63.5), which can only be experienced with him, or so we are to assume, since Wroth gives her no experiential basis on which to make that claim in the poems.

As the basis for a public identity, Pamphilia's constancy assures that her relation to Amphilanthus remains "true delight" instead of privation. Thus, the kind of subjectivity Wroth, through Pamphilia, is able to articulate publicly is derived from the representational strategies that the sonnet sequence uses to valorize certain kinds of intimacy. As Michael Warner notes, "being in public is a privilege that requires filtering or repressing something that is seen as private."[18] Pamphilia's emergence as a public, constant female subject requires her to filter out her erotic attachment to Night because it threatens to expose the fiction on which that subjectivity is based. Yet Pamphilia's attachment to Amphilanthus is also filtered out as soon as she publicly declares her constancy. In the final sonnet, she is ready to "leave the discource of Venus, and her sunn" (P103.9). Throughout the sequence, Venus and Cupid figure prominently in the production of Pamphilia's attachment to Amphilanthus, which propelled Pamphilia into the crisis of navigating the public and private spheres. Leaving behind this discourse implies leaving behind the attachment to Amphilanthus that exists solely within that discourse. Moreover, while the reference to Venus's "sunn" points to Cupid, Wroth's spelling suggests another layer of meaning. Pamphilia is also leaving behind the "sun" that she associated with Amphilanthus in order to continue as a publicly constant subject, though, perhaps ironically, his presence, which would be required for her to take leave of him, has not been made manifest by the time she makes this declaration. Ultimately, then, homoerotic and heteroerotic bonds are subject to similar treatment from Pamphilia, even as there is an apparent relationship between her public constancy and her private heteroerotic desire for Amphilanthus, in order to privilege the eponymous heterosexual couple.

This effacement of heteroerotic desire is the inadvertent outcome of Wroth's reinscription of female homoeroticism as absence. Furthermore, I would argue, it is a necessary consequence of the interiorization of desire and privatization of affective relations, both of which in turn require the separation of the intimate sphere from the space of representation. While this separation appears to preclude non-normative desires from entering the scene of representation and publicness on their own terms, it also creates a public sphere without any intimate content at all. Instead, the public sphere is filled with abstractions, such as constancy, that only tenuously point to bodies, sexual contact, or pleasure. Wroth's sequence ends on a melancholy note, then, for the reader can see what Pamphilia cannot: whereas dispensing with Amphilanthus to embrace the abstraction of constancy promises to mitigate her suffering, she must also ignore the pleasurable intimate possibilities of her relationship with Night as the price of her publicness.

"BETTER ARE THEY WHO THUS TO BLACKNES RUNN": RACE AND FEMALE HOMOEROTICISM IN *PAMPHILIA TO AMPHILANTHUS*

To associate Pamphilia's attachment to Night with a privative privacy to which public signification is unavailable, Wroth deploys images of blackness derived from early modern constructions of racial difference. As the word was used in the Renaissance, "race" does not translate precisely into the modern uses of the term that are derived in large part from social and biological sciences, as many critics and historians have shown. Yet such differences do not negate the existence in the Renaissance of systems for parsing differences in religion, skin color, ethnicity, or geographic origin. From her blackface participation as Baryte in Ben Jonson's *Masque of Blackness* (1605), Wroth was no stranger to the complex and contradictory ways in which race, and specifically blackness, could be represented in the period. In *Pamphilia to Amphilanthus*, Night is paradoxically racially marked and put under erasure. Her markedness differentiates her from Amphilanthus as an object of desire, and thus her presence helps construct his whiteness in the absence of his body. Kim Hall notes that, in Renaissance texts, "the polarity of dark and light is most often worked out in representations of black men and white women," but the treatment of blackness in Wroth's sonnet sequence is not confined to this heterosexual formulation.[19] Critical work on the nexus of race and gender in the period often proceeds within the context of gender difference and, when discussing fears of miscegenation, reproduction; consequently, modern readers of Renaissance texts have ignored the role of racial difference in structuring understandings of same-sex affection.[20]

In her treatment of the origins of blackness and its erotic and aesthetic possibilities, Wroth rearticulates and reformulates the intersection of race and eroticism that Ben Jonson engages in *The Masque of Blackness* (1605) and *The Masque of Beauty* (1608). Wroth's participation in the masque signals her material participation in shaping early modern racial discourse, so it might be more accurate to say that she reworks issues of race that she, Jonson, Inigo Jones, Anne of Denmark, and other courtiers first collaboratively articulated in the masques. As the masques cover important territory in the early modern racial imaginary, it will assist our analysis of Wroth if we look at the way these court performances bring together race and eroticism. *The Masque of Blackness* begins with two competing narratives about the origins of blackness: in the first, Niger's daughters' blackness is the sign of the sun's "fervent'st love"" and their "perfectst beauty," and in the second, their blackness is the calamitous result of Phaeton's fateful chariot ride which brought the sun too close to the earth, before which "the *Aethiopes* were as faire, / As other *Dames*."[21] Though Niger fights to authorize the first, the second narrative, wherein blackness is a deviation from white beauty rather than a different kind of beauty, takes on the authority of the truth, for the rest of the masque is absorbed with the possibility of undoing their blackness. Aethiopia indicates that the nymphs desire to see "those beauties, that which so much fame / the sacred MUSES sones have honored" (243–244) – that is, their desire is directed toward women reputedly more beautiful than themselves. The nymphs are desiring gazers like the muses' sons, but they are women gazing at other women. This same-sex desire to behold white women mutates into a desire to become like them. When they arrive in Britannia, "Their beauties shall be scorch'd no more" (263), and this transformation, in turn, would reposition them as the potential object of the heteroerotic desire of the "Muses' sons," or poets. Ultimately, the masque reroutes their desire toward a male monarchical figure, for Britannia is "Rul'd by a SUNNE, that to this height doth grace it: / Whose beames shine day, and night, and are of force / To blanche an AETHIOPE, and reviue a *Cor's*" (253–255). Aethiopia goes on to note the benefits of being in the presence of this sun king, one of the figures for James in the masque: "His light scientiall is, and (past mere nature) / Can salve the rude defects of every creature" (256–257). This intervening male figure effaces female homoerotic desire and blackness, both of which consequently have the status of "rude defects." Whereas James, the sun, is both part of and past nature in his corrective powers, these "defects" are part of and yet less than nature according to the conflicting origin myths.

Managing the racial and sexual valences of the masques proves difficult, perhaps because race is culturally no more stable as a form of difference than is the binary between same- and opposite-sex desire. Racial discourse brings its inconsistencies, instabilities, and contradictions along when invoked to stabilize the uneasy difference between homo- and heteroeroticism; as Kathryn Schwarz notes of *Blackness*, "the masque cannot repress racial and sexual dissidence at the same time."[22] When the daughters of Niger come on shore in Britannia, Aethiopia bids them to "Indent the *Land*, with those pure traces / They flow with, in their native graces" (260–261). Their blackness threatens to mark the whiteness of Britannia as they become female penetrators of the land. The masque departs from the traditional feminization of the landscape, identifying it as male, for "*Albion* the faire" (206) is James, named for and embodying his kingdom. Avoiding the homoerotic image of the female penetration of a feminized landscape by masculinizing the land, Jonson exposes the King himself to penetration by these tribadic black women. Dudley Carleton, in the audience at the court performance, even reported that James feared he would be marked by the female masquers' blackface.[23] The masque flees from this imagery of the penetrating woman, peculiarly displacing the King's authority to wash the women white by instead ordering the daughters of Niger to stay in the ocean to wash their blackness off before they can return to Britannia. Then, their entrance into the land will be more incorporation than penetration, but this masque stages only their return to the sea. When the masque tries to repress racial and sexual dissidence, it can repress neither and thus forgoes representation altogether.

In *The Masque of Beauty*, this failure of representation is displaced onto the conveniently named Night, who is blamed for the disappearance of the daughters of Niger from Britannia. Night feels threatened by the daughters of Niger and the four new nymphs who want to follow their example because "men should deeme / Her colour . . . of small esteeme" if so many nymphs take it upon themselves to go from black to white (82–83). The four nymphs are driven by an attachment to what they believe is the twelve daughters' new beauty; here, homoeroticism privileges whiteness. In *The Masque of Blackness* the original nymphs had first desired to gaze upon white female beauty in Britannia; this homoerotic desire is rewritten such that they desire to become white female beauties, the potential objects of the heteroerotic desire of the muses' sons. In *The Masque of Beauty*, the originary homoeroticism is less explicit, but the result is similar: the nymphs seek their sisters, and Boreas explains that they must be looking for "like favor, as like worth" (79). In Boreas's imagination, they cannot be motivated by a homoerotic desire for female beauty; they must be seeking the transformative "favor" of Albion to be worthy objects of male heteroerotic affection, as their sisters have become. Yet homoeroticism returns when their potential attractiveness to men threatens a female figure. Night's sense that these women should not be changed because they are already desirable as black also involves a female figure imagining the erotic desirability of other women, but this desire is quickly incorporated into a heteroerotic economy when she posits the men whom she fears may no longer desire her if whiteness becomes the standard of beauty. Blackness is centralized in the figure of Night, for not one of the nymphs appears prior to their actual transformation. Along with its role as a narrative obstacle, blackness's absence reinforces the disavowal of its status as an object of desire, after such status had been made imaginable in *The Masque of Blackness*.

Through her use of darkness and blackness in *Pamphilia to Amphilanthus*, Wroth portrays Night as a racially marked figure to displace Amphilanthus's absence onto Night, a displacement much like the one in *The Masque of Beauty*. Once Night is associated with absence, Pamphilia's bond with her becomes both unpublicizable and seemingly unrecognizable as intimacy within the sequence's affective economy. Before Wroth puts the bond between Pamphilia and Night under erasure, her representation of cross-racial female-female bonding creates a space in which a reader can resist the foreclosure on female homoeroticism and piece together instead an alternate economy of same-sex relations. Not just dark, Night is "black as spite" (P13.8), but this blackness does not initially preclude her desirability. Pamphilia focuses her attention on Night's black countenance in P17 because it matches her own psychic state. The racialization of Night leads potentially to a model of subjectivity, for in P17, Night's matching counte-nance and attire produce a more unified subject than would be attainable by those women who, through cosmetics, created "painted outsids" but who "foule inward bee" (P17.4). Night's black face not only reflects Pam-philia's interiority, but it also allows Pamphilia access to Night's interiorized subjectivity. Although she suggests that Night's black outside potentially reflects a foul inwardness, Pamphilia seems to be working against such an association, for when she blazons her, she indicates that Night's blackness provokes desire. Wroth has prepared the reader to expect this aesthetic and erotic appreciation of blackness in an earlier poem where Pamphilia says that Amphilanthus's unkindness

> makes mee now to shunn all shining light,
> And seeke for blackest clouds mee light to give,
> Which to all others, only darknes drive,
> They on mee shine, for sunn disdaines my sight.
>   (P9.9–12)

The disdain with which Amphilanthus, who is figured as the sun, has treated Pamphilia has prompted her to re-evaluate the terms of her desire. She still thinks of desire in terms of "shining" but she no longer sees "shining" as the exclusive property of whiteness. Instead, in the seemingly paradoxical image of the shining black cloud, she opens up a space for an alternative erotic investment in the blackness associated with Night.

In some ways, this sonnet reframes in affirmative terms what John Leo Africanus wrote of the *fricatrice* witches of Fez in *A Geographical Historie of Africa* (1600). Condemning female homoeroticism, he anticipates Jonson's masques by assuming that whiteness provokes desire in black females: "faire women" provoke the witches of Fez to "burne in lust towardes them."[24] But Africanus goes further than Jonson to suggest that some of the "faire" women, who for Africanus may be European or simply lighter-skinned than the witches, "which being allured with the delight of this abominable vice, will desire the companie of these witches."[25] Though cast in terms of corruption and degeneracy, Africanus imagines a female homoeroticism that would run contrary to the assumptions of many of his European readers that whiteness is the pinnacle of desire and that like desires like, for while Africanus is not clear about this desire being cross-racial, it at the very least crosses the gradations of complexion that Africanus is always ready to establish when writing of Africans. Finally, and this is what connects Africanus with Wroth's scenario in *Pamphilia to Amphilanthus*, the husband is so credulous that, when his wife fakes illness or possession, he "commits his false wife to their filthie disposition" by bringing a witch to her for the comfort that he cannot provide.[26] While Amphilanthus does not act as an unwitting procurer for Pamphilia and Night's relationship, Wroth charges him with the insufficient ability to please a woman that is implicit in Africanus's discussion of the "silly husband" whose fair wife cheats on him with a black *fricatrice* witch. Whereas Africanus provides witchcraft as a context for female same-sex desire in order to derogate it, Wroth temporarily allows the cross-racial female-female intimacy of Night and Pamphilia to have a positive valence, even if it does not quite emerge independently from heteroerotic desire.

Pamphilia's most explicit racialization of the blackness traditionally associated with Night, however, contributes more to her own self-definition than to her relationship with Night. In P25, she alternates between identification with and differentiation from blackness, only to settle on a difference that undermines desirability:

> Like to the Indians, scorched with the sunne,
> The sunn which they doe as theyr God adore
> Soe ame I us'd by love, for ever more
> I worship him, less favors have I wunn,
> Better are they who thus to blacknes runn,
> And soe can only whitenes want deplore
> Then I who pale, and white ame with griefs store,
> Nor can have hope, butt to see hopes undunn;
> Beesides theyr sacrifies receavd's in sight
> Of theyr chose sainte: Mine hid as worthles rite;
> Grant mee to see wher I my offrings give,
> Then lett mee weare the marke of Cupids might
> In hart as they in skin of Phoebus light
> Nott ceasing offrings to love while I Live.
>
> (P25.1–14)

Though she offers an account of the origins of pigmentation analogous to the Phaeton myth in *Blackness*, Wroth here is less interested than Jonson in the mythic origins of blackness, as she turns her attention more to the representational dynamics of race. The poem emphasizes, in Hall's view, a "disjunction between male public speaking/worship and her private art," but what might this disjunction between public and private, articulated as it is through racialized tropes of blackness and paleness, mean for the sequence's sexual economy?[27] Pamphilia's theorization of blackness associates it with the visibility of the public Indian sacrifice, which takes place in the full view of their god, the sun. This association could satisfy the sonnet sequence's requirement that she publicize her desire, but with Night as the object of a cross-racial homoerotic desire. Though Night is conspicuously absent from P25, the poem's discussion of blackness implicates her because the conclusion Pamphilia draws here affects the sequence's subsequent representations of Night and her blackness. Thus, the poem illustrates Joyce Green MacDonald's assertion that "allusion and displacement . . . mark a fundamental descriptive axis of the representational practices surrounding race in the early modern period."[28] As Night's displacement in a poem about blackness shifts attention away from Amphilanthus's physical absence from the sequence, the figures of the sun and Cupid allow Wroth to create the illusion of Amphilanthus's presence so that he may be reasserted as the proper object of her desire. Nonetheless, the illusion is fragmented, for Pamphilia wears Cupid's mark on her heart, where it remains inaccessible to the public signification it is supposed to effect.

The desirability of running to blackness is not the argument of this poem, however. Just as the black daughters of Niger search for white women only to be directed to a white man, Pamphilia's attachment to a black female figure leads her back to a white man. The poem suggests the possibility only to focus instead on how the marked black body may be appropriated to foster the public signification of Pamphilia's direct devotion to Cupid, whose "marke" confers on her the status of a lover and signifies indirectly devotion to Amphilanthus, whose role seems limited to providing an object in order for her to be a constant lover. Moreover, the pale Pamphilia differentiates herself from the black "Indians" in order to give ontological support to her own whiteness, which will, in turn, help to signify her status as a grieving lover. As a result, Pamphilia expresses a changed understanding of the relationship between blackness and black bodies. Unlike in previous sonnets, Pamphilia casts corporeal blackness as a surface feature in P25 and thereby insists that blackness is a derivation and a deviation in order to maintain the privileged status of her own whiteness. Wroth has Pamphilia renarrate the origins of her desire for blackness so that it derives from her true desire for Amphilanthus and causes her to deviate – in a way that stresses the connection of deviation and deviance – from her devotion to him. The extent of this reinscription can be seen in the juxtaposition of P25 with previous sonnets, such as P9 and P17, where she invokes blackness. Instead of being suffused through a unified body and psyche, as in the description of Night in P17, blackness in P25 is superficially "scorched" on the body to cover over an originary whiteness. Moreover, in P9 Amphilanthus's absence had precipitated Pamphilia's turn to Night and her desire for blackness, but in P25 blackness is caused by too much presence of the sun, the figure that stands in relation to Amphilanthus through the sequence. The unkindness of the sun in P9 prompted her to articulate an economy of desire for black bodies; however, blackness in P25 is caused by the white light of the sun darkening otherwise white bodies, and the focus on inwardness in these poems leaves little room for recuperating the surface as a site of intimacy. While in both poems the Amphilanthus-like sun has a causal role, in P9 the sun produces the search that leads Pamphilia to blackness, whereas in P25 it produces blackness itself. In P25, then, blackness becomes derivative of whiteness, thereby allowing Pamphilia's earlier search for an alternative in blackness to lead her right back to Amphilanthus and whiteness.

In Jonson's *Masque of Blackness*, both the origins and desirability of blackness were rewritten, but Wroth somewhat differently rewrites the origin of Pamphilia's love and the desirability of blackness when she displaces Amphilanthus's absence onto Night. In the sonnets, Night's obstruction of the narrative, similar to her role in *The Masque of Beauty*, undermines her availability as an erotic object. In P33, Pamphilia no longer turns to Night in Amphilanthus's absence; instead, Night signals and partly seems to precipitate that absence:

> While I injoy'd that sunn whose sight did lend
> Mee joy, I thought, that day, could have noe end
> Butt soone a night came cloth'd in absence darke,
> Absence more sad, more bitter then is gall
> Or death, when on true lovers itt doth fall
> Whose fires of love, disdaine rests poorer sparke.
>   (P33.9–14)

Night befalls Pamphilia like a tragedy; she does not seek her out here. She no longer finds Night's clothing appealing for its darkness, with which she can identify. Rather than inviting Pamphilia as a potential lover, Night's clothing signifies separation between lovers. What once was an object of comforting identification is now privative, and, because Night's privation also threatens to extend to Pamphilia's relationship with Amphilanthus – as though her desire for Amphilanthus were not thoroughly ensconced in his deficiency already – she laments Night's presence instead of welcoming her. To the extent that one can say the sequence has a plot, Pamphilia retrospectively reinterprets its events in relation to their effect on her heteroerotic bond with Amphilanthus. This bond gains a stranglehold on representation by exiling desire for blackness and homoerotic desire, the very desires necessary for her to define her heteroerotic desire. Yet Wroth still represents these other desires, as in Pamphilia's blazon, before she deploys them to produce the difference that structures the act of making heteroerotic desire public. If one reads against the grain of the sequence's trajectory – which, in the quest for Pamphilia's subjecthood, ultimately effaces heteroerotic desire too – those representations of other forms of affection can be shown to exceed their originary differential purposes to become the foundations of alternate economies of pleasure and affection.

"AFFLICTIONS SOUNDED BEST IN YOU, DARKE, BLACKE AND TERRIBLE": BLACKNESS AND DESIRE IN *THE COUNTESS OF MONTGOMERY'S URANIA*

Such reading against the grain becomes more complex when the sonnet sequence is brought into dialogue with the romance to which it was appended. Pamphilia and Amphilanthus are featured prominently among the scores of characters who populate *The Countess of Montgomery's Urania*, which provides an important context for the sequence's engagement with publicness, sexuality, and race. In the *Urania*, Wroth also explores both the split between public representation and private affection and the rerouting of same-sex desire by deploying a discourse of blackness. While she examines a broad array of heterosexual couplings without necessarily organizing affection around marriage, her open-ended romance encounters the limits of what might be representable as intimacy when affection is privatized and desire is interiorized. In the romance, even the signification of affection between women, because it too is grounded in privacy and interiority, is predicated on the impossibility of cross-racial same-sex affection.

The *Urania* is an expansive text: with two parts, one printed in 1621 and one existing only in manuscript until 1999, it has nearly 590,000 words, features an almost innumerable cast of characters both major and minor, and ranges in its setting from Europe to the Middle and Far East. Likely in imitation of Sidney's *The Countess of Pembroke's Arcadia*, the romance's two parts end mid-sentence, microcosmically reproducing the virtually boundless, digressive features typical of Renaissance romance. At the end of part one, Pamphilia and Amphilanthus prepare to go to Italy, but the reader is denied any sense of whether their reunion will last. In the manuscript continuation, after less than one folio page describing the couple's arrival in Italy – or, more precisely, refusing to describe the details of their arrival and defying anyone else to express them – the narrator indicates, "necessity of other princes calleth mee a little aside from this much more loved story."[29] This punctuated narrative structure continues throughout the second part of the romance when a second generation of characters crowds the narrative with their stories, which are situated alongside the continuing saga of the first generation. The manuscript ends with several mysteries unresolved, including how Rodomandro can have died only to reappear alive later in the narrative (II.406–407), who Faire Designe's parents are, how the enchantment of the true Sophy of Persia will be broken, and whether Pamphilia and Amphilanthus will ever be together after they marry other people.

Because its narrative structure makes closure elusive and detaches marriage from closure, the romance does not automatically presume marriage is the exclusive locus of affection, thereby opening up to representation a broader range of heterosexual experiences, summarized by Roberts: "Wroth offers more than merely a panoramic view of aristocratic marital practices, for she explores the genesis and nature of interpersonal commitment: she questions how, when, and even whether women should enter into exclusively monogamous relationships and how widely such unions need to be acknowledged."[30] At least where Pamphilia and Amphilanthus are concerned, marriage is the occasion for intensified but unresolved conflicts over public and private forms of affection. The romance situates Pamphilia and Amphilanthus's relationship in a broader milieu than in the sonnet sequence by contrasting the private affection Pamphilia has for Amphilanthus with her publicly visible marriage to Rodomandro. Pamphilia and Amphilanthus's private *de praesenti* spousal only seems to offer potential confirmation of Pamphilia's understanding that privacy grants authority to affection. The narrator remarks, "After the Contract ther was les outward cerimony butt more truly felt hapines then beefor: now appeering like one an others, without feare, their Countenances shooing a blessed content in assured injoying" (II.45). Though there were five witnesses, it exhibits a lack of "outward cerimony." Such lack, the narrator emphasizes, does not preclude "truly felt hapines"; instead, the couple feels more of it and expresses their affection "without feare." Yet the lack of public recognition of the marriage leaves Pamphilia without recourse when Amphilanthus is tricked into marrying the Princess of Slavonia. The events of the plot falsify any future "blessed content in assured injoying" that Pamphilia and Amphilanthus feel and that their countenances confirm, thereby undermining the narrator's privileging of the emotional state of the couple over and against wider public recognition.

At least from Pamphilia's perspective, her private relationship with Amphilanthus is understood to be the true site of affection in contrast to her agreeable but rather less passionate public marriage to Rodomandro. Rodomandro's suit for Pamphilia's hand begins humbly with his protest, "'Nor seeke I soverainitie over love, as that way to master, butt to bee a meanes for mee, poore mee, to bee accepted and receaved by you'" (II.271). Yet the more he woos her by expressing his respect for her private personhood, the more he suggests she will be the object of his publicizing gaze: "'Love your booke, but love mee soe farr as that I may hold itt to you that, while you peruse that, I may Joye in beeholding you; and som times gaine a looke from you, if butt to chide mee for soe carelessly parforming my office, when love will by chance make my hand shake, purposely to obtaine a sweet looke'" (II.272). Here, Rodomandro concedes that Pamphilia's affection will not be as strong as his desire for her, but that she will grow to love him and it will "'with all sweetnes shine in thos cleerest lights [her eyes]'" (II.272). Though it is not entirely clear if this light show will be just for Rodomandro, his gaze is supposed to produce publicly legible affection. The extent to which he wants to look at her suggests that she will not have any privacy when he is around, even though he says he will respect her solitude: "'Bee solitarie, yett favour mee soe much as that I may butt attend you. When you waulke in deserts and woods, I will serve you as a guard to keepe you from all harmes may proceed from serpents and venimous beasts. I will keepe att what distance you please, butt still in your sight, els how shall I serve you?'" (II.272). Describing Pamphilia's consent to the match, the narrator carefully splits Rodomandro's public thoughts on his nuptials from her private thoughts about Amphilanthus, which Pamphilia cannot publicize without compromising the truth of her love:

The Tartarian still hastens the receaving of his hapines, soe as urging Very much, and such business abroad, as called all men to severall ways and as many fortunes. Every one were reddy for concluding of businesses, soe as hee gained a fitt time and as brave a solem triumph for his greatest blessing (as hee termed it), and indeed was to bee prised inestimable as ever man beefor injoyed. For now Pamphilia against her her owne minde (yett nott contstrain'd, for non durst attempt that) had sayd '[aye]', though not in soule contented. (II.274)

The wedding is an item of "business" to be concluded before Rodomandro attends to political matters – namely, aiding the enchanted true Sophy of Persia, the usurpation of whose throne had been announced in the space between Rodomandro's declaration of his love and Pamphilia's reluctant acceptance. Rodomandro's character is, like the form of *Pamphilia to Amphilanthus*, saturated with publicness in tension with Pamphilia's privatizing impulses.

According to the narrator, Pamphilia attempts to foster a wider public knowledge of her true feelings at the wedding, or at least tries to convey her feelings to Amphilanthus. She rather unconventionally, at least in the Queen of Naples's opinion, wears her hair up and dons a black dress, and she offers the explanation that she is mourning the death of her brother Philarchos:

"For how can I Joye, having lost my deerest brother," sayd shee, "and truest freind. Why showld I bee triumphant, when hee is nott?"

With those words, her eyes hapened (itt may bee) by chance, butt I thinke rather truly ment, on Amphilanthus, who blusht, then wept bitterly, turning him self to a window close by, as desiring non should bee wittness of his loss and shame. (II.275)

Amphilanthus senses he is the true cause of her mourning, but her assembled family members cannot be fully sure of the implications of her actions. Even the narrator – whose ability to track Pamphilia's eyes and Amphilanthus's half-hidden reaction suggests a privileged view of these events – must guess in interpreting Pamphilia's behavior, so mired are her affections in the private sphere. Whether by chance or intentionally, Pamphilia looks at Amphilanthus, and he withdraws in order to reprivatize the shame that his blush exposed. The narrator needs intention – "truly ment" – rather than randomness – "by chance" – so that Pamphilia and Amphilanthus's true feelings can register publicly. That is, unless Pamphilia "truly ment" to cast a sidelong glance at Amphilanthus, the narrator cannot interpret her as subtly publicizing her feelings at this crucial moment. The narrator's intentionality supplements Pamphilia's inscrutability and Amphilanthus's concealment in order to clear a path toward publicness – and, ultimately, privileged status in the intimate economy of the romance – for them. Like a detective or a gossip, the narrator invests in the mystery surrounding the connection between Pamphilia and Amphilanthus rather than the bond between Rodomandro and Pamphilia that is being publicly created through marriage. This moment exemplifies how, within the romance's heterosexual economy, Pamphilia's private love for Amphilanthus challenges marriage as a privileged site of affection.

Pamphilia and Amphilanthus's relationship dominates the sonnets' representational economy, but in the romance, it has to force its way to the center of intimate life. Despite its apparent oppositionality, this relationship takes its cues almost entirely from marriage and then privatizes the relation so that her affection can be constructed as authentic even as it fades into unrepresentability. Amphilanthus's fickleness remains to trouble the authenticity of their intimacy. His sister Urania doubts whether Pamphilia's version of constancy represents strong, virtuous affection or foolishness and obstinacy:

"Tis pittie," said Urania, "that ever that fruitlesse thing Constancy was taught you as a vertue, since for vertues sake you will love it, as having true possession of your soule, but understand, this vertue hath limits to hold it in, being a vertue, but thus that it is a vice in them that breake it, but those with whom it is broken, are by the breach free to leave or choose againe where more staidnes may be found; besides tis a dangerous thing to hold that opinion, which in time will prove flat heresie." (1.470)

Urania charges that Pamphilia threatens to position constancy in opposition to marriage by taking constancy as the principle of her subjectivity. Referring to a future "heresie," Urania foreshadows that Pamphilia will eventually marry another man, and then her constancy to Amphilanthus will be adultery.

Although it does not prevent Pamphilia's marriage to Rodomandro from being publicly recognized, Rodomandro's blackness prevents Pamphilia's constancy from bearing the full stigma of adultery. As Hall notes, he "operates within a color/race schema that from the beginning marks him as unfavored and in some ways peripheral even though he wins Pamphilia's hand."[31] In fact, Rodomandro's racialization makes the adulterous affection between Pamphilia and Amphilanthus seem more like marriage than her marriage does. Rodomandro's name means "man from Rhodes," which positions him geographically further west than Pamphilia, who, though descended from the King and Queen of Morea, or the Peloponnesus, shares her name with the territory in south central Asia Minor that she comes to govern after it is bequeathed to her by her childless uncle. Yet Rodomandro's name belies his eastern origins as King of Tartaria, and references to blackness construct his otherness from the various Mediterranean and European royals who pepper the romance. When he first arrives, the narrator ambivalently praises him: "though black, yett he had the true

parfection of lovlines" (II.42). While this remark seems to appreciate a black
aesthetic, the narrator is anxious about the desire Rodomandro arouses
because its object is black. His blackness is remarkable – that is, excep-
tional and meriting commentary – because of its "parfection of lovliness."
If he were white, the narrator would not have to elaborate on his loveliness;
in the romance's Eurocentric aesthetic, white beauty is not marvelous or
miraculous in the way black beauty is.

The mixed attitude – both desire and differentiation – encoded in the
narrator's remarks about Rodomandro's "loveliness" is reflected throughout the romance in its ambivalence about him and his interactions with
other characters in the romance's affective sphere. The narrator situates
Rodomandro's affection for Pamphilia in his eyes, the blackness of which
underscores his racial status. When Rodomandro woos Pamphilia, the
narrator comments, "All the while thos words were speaking, his eyes
darts shuting sparckling affection in black, butt brightest shining, like tow
pointed diamounds sett in black foiles, for indeed most excellent eyes hee
had" (II.272). This passage, ending with the narrator's aesthetic appreciation of Rodomandro's eyes, contains an apt simile, for his black but
shining affection is used as a foil to substantiate Pamphilia and Amphilanthus's affection. Indeed, Pamphilia appropriates his blackness to provide
signification for her love of Amphilanthus at the very moment in the narrative, her marriage to another man, when it seems most impossible to
speak her true love. When she wears a black wedding dress, his blackness
becomes prosthetic, allowing her to express her resistance because her heart
still belongs to the man who has betrayed her. As Wroth deploys it, blackness can prove useful in shifting the center of the romance's heteroerotic
economy from the public to the private sphere without entirely cutting
that economy off from representation.

Rodomandro's displacement continues in the narrative's treatment of
Faire Designe, for encoded in his name is his whiteness and his potential to
allow Pamphilia and Amphilanthus's affection to preside over the narrative
closure that the romance makes so elusive. He is the narrative's "great
white hope." Racially, he is the "faire" or white substitute for the ethnically
marked child whom Pamphilia bears for Rodomandro and whose death is
announced a few words after his existence is first mentioned. The key to
Faire Designe's never-revealed real name, the cipher on his shield, connects
him to two earlier episodes in the romance that foreshadow his parentage:
one where Amphilanthus takes on a disguise as the Knight of the Cipher
and another where Pamphilia carves a cipher into a tree that encodes the
name of her beloved Amphilanthus. Faire Designe appears as the Knight

of the Cipher redux to suggest that Amphilanthus is his father, but his connection to Pamphilia is a little more obscure. During a hunt in part one, Pamphilia, lost in love, ignores a stag that takes offense at her neglect. Instead of paying attention to it, she

> in the rine of an Oake insculped a sypher, which contained the letters, or rather the Anagram of his name shee most and only lov'd. By that time the Stagge came by, grieved at her unkindnesse that she would not honor his death with her presence; which shee by his pittifull countenance perceiving, tooke her horse againe, and came in to his death. (1.325–326)

Pamphilia's use of the cipher may suggest that she is the mother of Faire Designe, but this discursive connection also points to his displacement of Rodomandro. Rodomandro first meets Pamphilia during a hunting episode that equates Rodomandro with the black stag that Pamphilia and Amphilanthus are hunting (11.43–44). Rodomandro is analogous to the stag from part one because Pamphilia neglects it in favor of her love for Amphilanthus. In turn, their "faire" or white offspring, like the carving of the cipher, encodes their relationship while further marginalizing Rodomandro, for Pamphilia and Amphilanthus have in Faire Designe a connection to the second generation whose histories come to occupy the second part of the romance. If he is to be taken as the visible, public sign of Pamphilia and Amphilanthus's union and as a signal of that union's potential continuation into the future, he contributes to the narrative structure, or "designe," by bridging the gap between the public space of representation and the unpublicizable affection between Pamphilia and Amphilanthus. Thus, even his illegitimacy does not radically revise the dominance of the reproductive couple form in the romance. Through Faire Designe, Pamphilia and Amphilanthus can continue to ground their understanding of intimacy in narrative (and reproductive) futurity and in uncompromisingly private interiorized desire – the aspects of marriage that underwrite its dominance over the intimate sphere.

Faire Designe's identity, however, is never fully revealed in the text. Pamphilia and Amphilanthus, therefore, remain suspended; their affection, no matter how great, lacks access to representation, as the narrator inadvertently emphasizes when they celebrate their *de praesenti* marriage: "What hapines they both conseaved when this was dunn, non butt such a paire (if any such the world hath) can express; others must onely admire, and for want of expression sitt dumbe ore speake to testify boldnes, nott judgment" (11.45). The narrator uses the language of heterosexual reproduction to describe the formation of their happiness. If Faire Designe is the literal result of that conception, not even the narrator can tell the reader because of the inexpressible quality of their affection. Yet, while the gap between intimacy and representation appears to foster the ineffability of true affection to the detriment of other potentially speakable forms of relationality, this aporia also provokes a sense that the ineffability of affection actually masks a vacancy of affection.

To address this skepticism, the romance does not provide evidence for the content of Pamphilia and Amphilanthus's affection; instead, it looks to other bonds that can be falsified in order to foster the illusion of authenticity. One target of this process, female-female bonds offer a potential alternate economy of affection in the romance. Throughout both volumes, Urania is depicted providing advice to Pamphilia, much of which she seems to ignore to her detriment as she deals with Amphilanthus's repeated infidelities and the other vicissitudes of their relationship. Wroth seems to advance their relationship as an exemplary female friendship within a general economy of supportive female-female relations, but, as Miller points out, "Mary Wroth represents bonds between women as both troubled and enduring, at once potentially restrictive and liberating."[32] One way Wroth differentiates among types of relationships between women is through a deployment of a racialized motif of blackness.

This differentiation is familiar from Jonson's *Masque of Beauty*, where black Night menaces the four nymphs who seek to join the original twelve daughters of Niger and, in contrast, the recently whitened daughters of Niger, "in pietie mov'd and kind" (90), come to rescue their sisters. In a key example of this differentiation from the *Urania*, Pamphilia apostrophizes the absent Amphilanthus, "I rather would wish to be a Black-moore, or any thing more dreadfull, then allure affection to me, if not from you" (1.465). At the same time as Pamphilia opposes blackness to constancy, her identification with blackness also would guarantee constancy; she imagines her blackness would precipitate her displacement as the object of other men's affection, a status which makes her appear inconstant even though she has done nothing to encourage such attention. Her syntax here opens up a space of possibility that she then forecloses on. She mentions the desired identification with blackness first, giving it primacy, and then only later suggests that it is not what she wants at all. She qualifies that it would be better than attracting the attention of men, and then she qualifies her qualification by excepting Amphilanthus from the men from whom she would not want to "allure affection." Pamphilia briefly imagines her own identification with blackness but then disavows it in order to give her relationship with Amphilanthus intimate content and underscore the importance of her primary identification as a constant lover. Still, the route to loving Amphilanthus seems contorted, in contrast to her spontaneous identification with blackness in this passage. The intimate microeconomy of the sentence works in the same way as the intimate macroeconomy of the romance: the space that Pamphilia opens up for the desire for blackness is never quite closed through her repeated disavowals.

These moments of identification challenge the centrality of Pamphilia and Amphilanthus's affection while also offering an opportunity for Wroth to use race to reassert that centrality. Wroth repeatedly depicts characters identifying with the desire of others in order to foster their own development, a pattern that Amelia Zurcher has identified.[33] When female characters identify with other female characters in the romance, however, Wroth sometimes brings in blackness as a way to guard against a potential erotic charge. We have seen how, in *The Masque of Blackness* and *The Masque of Beauty*, same-sex desire is rerouted into a heteroerotic economy and desire for blackness yields to the desirability of whiteness. Though less tied to discourses of the natural and unnatural than it was in Jonson, a similar process occurs in *The Urania*, but Pamphilia's originary homoerotic desire for blackness is under erasure and what she expresses are only the effects of the rerouting of desire. José Esteban Muñoz has recently argued that a queer approach to documenting the past should involve "suturing [evidence] to the concept of ephemera . . . the remains, the things that are left, hanging in the air like a rumor."[34] While Muñoz focuses on "the historical fact of queer lives," this sentiment also applies to literary representation and, in this case, the reconstitution of cross-racial same-sex desires in *The Urania*.[35] When she declares her desire to become black to protect her chastity, Pamphilia assumes that blackness might make her undesirable enough for other men to lose interest in her, and this assumption comes from imagining what it might be like for a man to desire blackness in a woman, but this moment of cross-gender identification reveals traces of a woman's desiring blackness in a woman. That is, within this identification and disavowal is Pamphilia's prior, unspoken (perhaps even unspeakable), and imagined desire for a black woman. Yet such a furtive moment of desire leads to heteroerotic appropriation rather than erotic union.

Before we are tempted to dismiss such symptomatic reading as lacking in evidence, we might look into the role that fantasy played in discourses of sexuality and race in the period. Though the effects of maternal impression, wherein images and fantasies during copulation, pregnancy, and childbirth affect potential offspring, were debated, there was at least some acceptance that even the most furtive fantasy can have powerful, lasting effects.

Thommaso Buoni's *Problemes of Beautie and All Humane Affections* (1606) indicates that it is customary to surround pregnant women with beautiful pictures to take advantage of maternal impression. Acknowledging the "great force of imagination and conceipt in the act of generation," Buoni writes that "great women by contemplating or gazing on serpents, and *Moores* in their chambers in the act of generation, have brought forth monstrous birthes, in some figure, and proportion like unto them."[36] In these stories of maternal impression, the difference between fantasy and sexual activity is collapsed. Such cautionary tales were presumably told to police women's thoughts for the sake of reproduction, and they use racial others as raw material, denying them desires of their own, in order to work out problems within, in this case, the sexual organization of white Europe. While inextricably caught up in patriarchal and colonialist projects, these fantasies can be read against the grain as opportunities for refiguring the kinds of relationships possible within Renaissance culture, challenging us to rethink what constitutes evidence when dealing with fantasies of forbidden intimacies in Renaissance texts.

Tropes of blackness in the romance lend support to the hierarchized differences that inhere in economies of heteroerotic desire, but Wroth also reveals through her characters' identifications with the desires of others how such a hierarchy promotes heterosexual coupling's co-optation of intimacy. We have seen how the text constructs Amphilanthus's desirability by emphasizing Rodomandro's blackness, but the romance's use of blackness divides and disempowers women in much the same way that the patriarchal marriage economy does. As Pamphilia's articulation of blackness as a means for men to discern the relative desirability of women indicates, these differences hierarchically position men as subjects and women as objects of desire, and they also institute a hierarchy of desirability among women. This latter hierarchy, as it is established by way of the deployment of tropes of blackness throughout the romance, in turn fosters an economy of female-female relations based on competition over male desire. For example, when Urania's maid becomes enchanted, she "beheld as she beleev'd Allimarlus . . . kissing and embracing a Black-moore: which so farre inraged her, being passionately in love with him, as she must goe to revenge her selfe of that injurie" (1.49). For her imagination to create this image of Allimarlus's infidelity, she first must entertain the possibility that the "Black-moore" is desirable by a man, but, in order to verify such a possibility, she must inhabit the pleasure that she imagines him experiencing and that provokes her to seek revenge. Within the logic of the apparition itself, Allimarlus's desire for the black woman represents his straying from Urania's maid; within the logic of the image's production entirely within her fancy, it is the maid's own understanding of the black woman as desirable that threatens her relationship with Allimarlus.

In the absence of an anti-black aesthetic, articulating the desirability of whiteness appears as difficult as figuring out the parentage of Faire Designe. After Amphilanthus excessively praises an early rival of Pamphilia named Antissia, Pamphilia responds:

"For truly my lord," said she, "me thinks there is not that beautie in her as you speake of, but that I have seene, as faire and delicate as shee; yet in truth shee's very white, but that extreame whitenesse I like not so well, as where that (though not in that fulnesse) is mix'd with sweete lovelines; yet I cannot blame you to thinke her peerlesse, who viewes her but with the eyes of affection." (1.61)

Pamphilia struggles to articulate that her additional qualities – such as love-liness – make her more desirable, even though she and Antissia are equal in fairness. Yet because Pamphilia insists on privatizing her desire for Amphilanthus, this passage remains ostensibly about her response to another woman's beauty, though he notices their rivalry and calls her "Womanish" for her envy (1.61). Wroth tries to position female homoeroticism so that it will make heteroeroticism articulable, but this positioning cannot do so in the absence of other signs of difference, since Wroth's texts predate modern attempts to impose an irreducible difference between homo- and heteroeroticism.

True intimacy, in Wroth, is relentlessly private and representation inexorably public. Wroth articulates a distinction between same-sex and cross-sex affections only by importing other models of difference, and she mines early modern racial discourse to provide an axis for this distinction. Nevertheless, she produces only a publicly representable simulacrum of heteroerotic affection because, instead of depicting the thing itself – that is, the affection governing the heterosexual couple form – Wroth's texts attempt to deny signification to affections not heteroerotic. More generally and in broader historical terms, the way Wroth positions and valorizes different forms of intimacy may anticipate the modern homosexual-heterosexual binary. It may then not be entirely possible or desirable in an analysis of Wroth's work to separate identity from the forms of affection she represents, as I have been doing with other texts, but we can still keep these two axes of inquiry in tension with her work. Neither Wroth nor her contemporaries could have possibly foreseen the installation of this binary, and thus they do not have a straightforward relationship with modern identity categories, relationality, and intimacy. Still, *Pamphilia to Amphilanthus* and

The Countess of Montgomery's Urania are two texts in which white women are allowed to imagine, albeit furtively, desire for black women. As such, they are part of a canon – one that we should expand – of texts that represent the alternative paths and possibilities that readers can transform into their own scripts when long-term monogamous heterosexual coupling itself fails as intimacy.

Epilogue: Invitation to a queer life

In the preceding chapters, I have insisted that many more intimate possibilities, especially those detached from an interiorized sense of embodiment, were imagined throughout Renaissance texts than appeared to be authorized at their moments of closure. Insofar as these texts circulate, readers who follow the cues that separate textual endorsement from narrative closure can recover their value and make use of them. Along the way, I have tried to emphasize the defamiliarizing aspects of Renaissance texts and show how these aspects are forms of protest to a cultural shift in the definition of intimacy. In my last chapter, I discussed how Lady Mary Wroth emphasized interiority and privacy in affection, and how her narrative's trajectory in part established these two aspects of affection as the basis for distinguishing privileged heteroerotic bonds from subordinated homoerotic ones. These distinctions are part of a terrain that is, arguably, familiar to the modern reader, but the boundary in Wroth's work is inchoate and permeable, making it possible to read her texts against the grain of their own narrative tendencies to delimit the intimate sphere. Thus, though my discussion of Renaissance texts concludes with a resemblance to modernity in which the intimate is remarkably homogeneous and centralized around abiding coupledom, I have tried to argue throughout that this historical trajectory was not inevitable. Instead, the contraction of the intimate sphere around coupling was hotly contested through these texts' representations of alternative possibilities for affective relations. Even in Wroth's narratives, other voices disturb the texts' ostensible orientation toward a narrower understanding of intimacy. In the context of the arguments of the earlier chapters of this book, this orientation seems more like a departure from polyvocality than a progression because I did not start with modernity as a given. More generally, then, when these representations circulate among readers and audiences in print, in manuscript, and in performance, the possible alternative lives that authors imagine for their characters circulate as persistent reminders, not of a world to which we can or should return, but of the avenues of resistance to dominant ideologies that the circulation of texts opens up.

In the years since the Renaissance, the contest over the signifying power and authority of intimacy has itself changed significantly. Now, it is often tacitly assumed that the most desirable form of relationality is long-term monogamous coupling; the question we now ask is usually whether certain kinds of long-term monogamous coupling have a right to society's official sanction through marriage, with its attendant economic, social, and political benefits. The modern debate over intimacy has no room for the experimental alternatives imagined in Renaissance texts, except insofar as alternatives reaffirm the value of long-term monogamous coupling. Even when they are still practiced, these possibilities are regarded as failed approximations of intimacy at best, and, at worst, perversions of it; as such, their undesirability is no longer a matter of question. This historical shift in the debate can be seen in the way that texts from the Renaissance and from modernity differently constitute the task of "building a life" when a character or a poetic persona is motivated to do so by an affective relation. In my discussion of the invitation poem now known as Christopher Marlowe's "The Passionate Shepherd to His Love" and the reply poem, Walter Ralegh's "The Nymph's Reply to the Shepherd," I argued that the invitation poem invites the addressee to a "life" that the speaker of the reply rejects, understanding intimacy as the experience of interiorized desire over the long term. Four hundred years later, the nymph seems to have prevailed. Now, temporary, situational relations like those the invitation poem imagines are often compromises – in the negative sense – made when long-term monogamous coupling is somehow unavailable. That is, the unassailable propriety and desirability of long-term monogamy always shadows the experience of temporary affective relations, no matter how pleasurable. The short story "Brokeback Mountain" by Annie Proulx and its motion picture adaptation by Ang Lee can demonstrate this shift from questioning what constitutes intimacy to questioning who should be allowed access to the one true form of intimacy available.[1] A homophobic society prevents the protagonist shepherds, Ennis del Mar and Jack Twist, from building a life of long-term monogamy together, but, having internalized the dictates of heteronormative culture, they persist in wanting that life together. At a structural level, these texts do not imagine any alternatives to the typical tragic love plot in which a couple's deep and potentially abiding affection is not afforded protection from social intrusion and, consequently, their relationship ends prematurely in the death of one or both of the lovers. In "Brokeback Mountain" heteronormativity and homophobia work together to ensure that Ennis and Jack's love story can only end in failure. Within heteronormativity, success in intimacy by definition requires the achievement of long-term monogamy, and homophobic culture prevents them from ever achieving it.

Proulx's story chronicles the difficulty and disappointment that, despite the spectacular omnipresence of natural beauty, characterizes rural life in the western United States in the late twentieth century. Ennis and Jack meet in Wyoming in 1963 when they both take jobs herding sheep on Brokeback Mountain. Life with the sheep is difficult; Jack and Ennis survive exposure to the elements, threats from animals, and even lack of food. The story's representation of a harsh natural world resembles more that of the nymph's reply poem than the idealized pastoralism of the invitation of the "Passionate Shepherd," though the cinematography of the film reintroduces the grandeur of nature as a replacement. Yet like "The Passionate Shepherd" and other homoerotic Renaissance pastorals, such as Richard Barnfeld's *Affectionate Shepherd* and Edmund Spenser's *Shepheardes Calender*, "Brokeback Mountain" contains an invitation to a life. The pastoral context of these texts suggests that such invitations to alternatives often accompany movement to some other place more hospitable to the relationship, and in some of the Renaissance texts I have discussed, this place has ranged from a rural setting, to a convent, to even the court. A geographical space in these texts often symbolizes the imaginative space of possibility that the narrative opens up for rethinking the boundaries of intimate sphere, which is itself a geographic image for relational life.

While shepherding, Jack and Ennis have sex and fall in love, but, once they come down the mountain, they return to their ostensibly heterosexual lives. After four years, Jack contacts Ennis and they meet for sex in a motel. In their post-coital pillow-talk, Jack tells Ennis, "'Listen, I'm thinkin, tell you what, if you and me had a little ranch together, little cow and calf operation, your horses, it'd be some sweet life.'"[2] In this invitation, Jack hopes that sharing property and running a ranch will give them good standing in capitalist society, which will, in turn, guarantee the privacy and normalcy of their relationship as it might for a heterosexual couple. By starting a ranch, they will live out Jack's earlier sentiments and hopes about the privacy of their relation, "'Nobody's business but ours'" (262). The Renaissance pastoral invitation poem and the other texts I have discussed, contrastingly, have not always required solitude for their visions of alternate forms of intimacy. Whereas Jack invites Ennis to withdraw, the speaker of "The Passionate Shepherd" asks the addressee to move to a rural landscape not devoid of other people. Lapet's courtier masochism in *The Nice Valour* also requires a populated court. Indeed, Renaissance texts often void the intimate content of a form of relationality by representing the place in which that relationship occurs as unpopulated. This was certainly the case in the texts that represent female-female intimacy in convents.

The privacy that makes the invitation in "Brokeback Mountain" different from these Renaissance texts turns out to be elusive anyway. A business, no matter how successful, cannot make others mind their own business when it comes to same-sex intimacy in a homophobic world. Even when they are herding on Brokeback, the remote setting does not guarantee their privacy, as their boss, Joe Aguirre, sees them having sex and does not rehire Jack the following year because of it. Ennis rejects Jack's invitation to a life knowing that they would not be afforded the privacy guaranteed heterosexual couples. It is a lesson he learned from his father:

"There was these two old guys ranched together down home, Earl and Rich – dad would pass a remark when he seen them. They was a joke even though they was pretty tough old birds. I was what, nine years old and they found Earl dead in a irrigation ditch. They'd took a tire iron to him, spurred him up, drug him around by his dick until it pulled off, just bloody pulp. What the tire iron done looked like pieced a burned tomatoes all over him, nose tore down from skiddin on gravel."

"You seen that?"

"Dad made sure I seen it. Took me to see it. Me and K.E. [Ennis's brother]. Dad laughed about it. Hell, for all I know he done the job. If he was alive and was to put his head in that door right now you bet he'd go get his tire iron." (270)

Even in the motel, Ennis cannot get away from the idea that he is being watched. He summons the specter of his father, the same enforcement arm of homophobia that took him to see the violent spectacle of what happens when even "pretty tough old birds" flout the proscriptions of heterosexual culture, in order to demonstrate that running a ranch would provide only illusory protection from prying eyes and tire irons.

Though he rejects Jack's invitation, Ennis, like Jack, desires to pattern their intimacy on normative coupling. Ennis reacts in anger at the mere thought that Jack goes to Mexico to have sex with men when Ennis is not available. He threatens Jack, "'all them things I don't know would get you killed if I should come to know them'" (277). Much like Ennis's wife Alma, who, having discovered his affair with Jack, divorces Ennis after years of resentment, Ennis feels he ought to be able to expect monogamy from Jack. The strength of their connection should require it, it would seem.

Also like Alma, at least in the years between her discovery of the affair and the divorce, Ennis can lie to himself in order to salvage the bond between them from the destructive force of his expectation.

Jack and Ennis's situation is all the more tragic because of how similar what they want is to what heterosexual couples, such as Ennis and Alma and Jack and his wife Lureen, are allowed and expected to want for themselves, at least when these relationships begin. Ennis reminds us of the marriage vows at the end of the story when he says "Jack, I swear" (285), but Jack is dead and thus it is impossible to turn that utterance into a marriage vow. In the movie version of the short story, Ennis's final words come after his daughter, Alma Jr., announces she is getting married and leaves his trailer. Here, the movie further emphasizes how tragically unfair it is that heterosexuals, through marriage, are allowed to build a life and imagine a future in a way that Jack and Ennis never can despite the intensity of their connection to one another. Yet both marriages are failures: Ennis's ends in divorce and Jack and Lureen stay together but drift apart emotionally. So, why do the men continue to feel pressured to pattern their own relationship on heterosexual coupling? Simply put, it is the only valid pattern available to them in the heteronormative culture in which their love takes place. Whenever the men get together, both, but primarily Jack, seem pressured to figure out the future of their relationship. Jack tells Ennis: "'we got a work out what the fuck we're goin a do now'" (268). Ennis, rejecting Jack's invitation to start a ranch, suggests an alternative that strangely forgets that they are not protected from the binoculars of people like Joe Aguirre even in the wilderness: "'Two guys livin together? No. All I can see is we get together once in awhile way the hell out in the back a nowhere'" (270). These words do not have the playful, experimental, and optimistically resistant quality that characterizes Renaissance representations of alternate forms of intimacy. The short story and film characterize alternatives to long-term monogamy and shared property as compromises with homophobic culture and concessions to its power to regulate their sexuality. The dominance of long-term coupling can seem so totalizing within modern heteronormative culture that any alternatives to it that could be imagined are always already cast as not only failures of intimacy but also failures of political resistance. As Ennis stoically says, "if you can't fix it, you got a stand it" (271).

"Standing it" represents different things for each man, but the way each man "stands it" does not satisfy the other because it is not long-term monogamy, the desirability of which is unquestionable. Increasingly dissatisfied with the arrangement that they get together whenever they can get away, Jack tells Ennis, "'I'm not you. I can't make it on a couple a high-altitude fucks once or twice a year'" (278). The narrator reports that during their first four-year separation, Jack "had been riding more than bulls" (268), and he fills the time between their encounters with sexual tourism to Mexico. "Brokeback Mountain" briefly imagines alternatives to normative coupling, but unlike the Renaissance texts I have discussed, Proulx's story cannot imagine them as potential forms of intimacy on their own and they are never available, even momentarily, to the story's readers in these terms. They are alternatives to both coupling and intimacy, which seem coextensive in modern culture. Since the former is impossible for Jack and Ennis, so is the latter.

If we look at "Brokeback Mountain" as the story of love thwarted by an unforgiving homophobia that cannot tolerate same-sex coupling, we only see part of the ideology that produces Jack and Ennis's tragedy. This intolerance indeed makes scripts for love between two men scarce, and Ennis has sought them: "'Shit. I been lookin at people on the street. This happen a other people? What the hell do they do?'" (271). The literary texts I have discussed in this book answer this question for an early modern Ennis who seeks an alternative with which he can identify, but the modern Ennis goes unsatisfied. Furthermore, when Ennis "look[s] at people on the street" for signs of how they conduct their intimate lives, he mimics the scrutiny that he senses when he is with Jack. Because of the association of intimacy and the private sphere, the search for alternatives can only be conducted furtively in the public space of the street, as it is prohibited as a violation of privacy. Jack and Ennis briefly invent their own models, but in their improvisation they never fully abandon the model of long-term coupling that is supposed to characterize normative heterosexual relations. They are not wrong to want what they want, but what they want is also structured by the norms of the culture that seeks to prevent them from having it. If the alternate pattern of intimacy that they call "standing it" in this story amounts to conceding to a repressive homophobia, then "fixing it" – that is, building a life based on long-term monogamy – similarly involves conceding to a repressive heteronormativity. Whether or not Jack dies in a homophobic assault, as Ennis suspects, their tragedy is that homophobia does not allow them to have the long-term monogamous coupling that they want with each other, and heteronormativity does not allow them to imagine wanting any other type of relationship.

In the double operation of these two ideologies, resistance to one form of oppression often seems to empower the other; getting out from under the force of normative proscriptions on intimate life is thus fraught with political difficulty. Some politicized forms of sexual empowerment rely implicitly on the derogation of alternate ways of living and loving. One form of intimacy thus represents the path to "fixing it" and all the rest constitute "standing it." For example, arguments for the legalization of gay marriage in the US often proceed by way of further marginalizing certain experiences of pleasure, such as S/M or promiscuity. By rethinking the very structures of the stories that we tell ourselves about what constitutes building a life, the cycle of political empowerment through the abjection of others can be interrupted.

In the Renaissance, texts imagined alternative forms of relationality that disrupted or dilated their narratives' ostensible trajectory toward long-term monogamy. By thinking of these interruptions as imaginative possibilities, I have mapped these texts' representations of resistance to the organization of intimacy around long-term monogamous coupling. A similar kind of re-envisioning based on an aesthetic of interruption rather than on one of development would enable a re-imagining of the intimate sphere at a representational level. Moreover, these possibilities circulate with these texts to challenge the assumed value of long-term monogamy. Assembled as a necessarily expandable canon, they help readers and audiences know that, to expand the intimate sphere, they need to repurpose and reimagine scripts for their own intimate lives and invite others to join in, if they so desire.

Notes

INTRODUCTION

1 Philip Stubbes, *The Anatomy of Abuses* (London, 1583) sig. L8v.
2 Michel Foucault, *The History of Sexuality: An Introduction*, vol. 1, trans. Robert Hurley (New York: Vintage, 1990) 38.
3 Jonathan Goldberg and Madhavi Menon, "Queering History," *PMLA* 120.5 (2005): 1612.
4 Lauren Berlant and Michael Warner, "Sex in Public," *Critical Inquiry* 24.2 (1998): 555.
5 *Ibid.* 556.
6 See also Michael Warner, *The Trouble with Normal: Sex, Politics, and the Ethics of Queer Life* (Cambridge, MA: Free Press, 1999). I would not deny that gay men and lesbians have been at the forefront in resisting the dominance of the couple form and have a unique interest in resisting heteronormativity.
7 Madhavi Menon, *Unhistorical Shakespeare: Queer Theory in Shakespearean Literature and Film* (Basingstoke: Palgrave, 2008) 1.
8 *Ibid.* 14.
9 Cornelius Tacitus, *The Histories* (Harvard University Press, 1925) 120, emphasis mine.
10 Cornelius Tacitus, *The Ende of Nero and Beginning of Galba: Fower Bookes of the Histories of Cornelius Tacitus*, trans. Henry Savile (London, 1598) sig. D5v, emphasis mine.
11 Daniel Juan Gil, *Before Intimacy: Asocial Sexuality in Early Modern England* (University of Minnesota Press, 2006) 3.
12 Brian Melbancke, *Philotimus: The Warre betwixt Nature and Fortune* (London, 1583) sig. T2v.
13 John Barclay, *Barclay His Argenis, or the Loves of Poliarchus and Argenis*, trans. Kingsmill Long (London, 1625) sig. G1r.
14 John Milton, *Samson Agonistes, The Riverside Milton*, ed. Roy Flannagan (Boston: Houghton Mifflin, 1998) 224.
15 Lawrence Stone, *The Family, Sex, and Marriage in England, 1500–1800* (New York: Harper and Row, 1977) 23; 44–46.
16 *Ibid.* 8.

17 Valerie Traub, *The Renaissance of Lesbianism in Early Modern England* (Cambridge University Press, 2002) 265.

18 *An Homily of the State of Matrimony*, 1563, in *Daughters, Wives, and Widows: Writings by Men about Women and Marriage in England, 1500–1640*, ed. Joan Larsen Klein (University of Illinois Press, 1992) 13.

19 Jeffrey Masten, *Textual Intercourse: Collaboration, Authorship, and Sexualities in Renaissance Drama* (Cambridge University Press, 1997) 281; see also Alan Bray, *The Friend* (University of Chicago Press, 2003) and Laurie Shannon, *Sovereign Amity: Figures of Friendship in Shakespearean Contexts* (University of Chicago Press, 2002).

20 Francis Beaumont and John Fletcher, *The Coxcomb*, ed. Irby B. Cauthen, in *The Dramatic Works in the Beaumont and Fletcher Canon*, vol. 1, ed. Fredson Bowers (Cambridge University Press, 1966) 2.1.152–156.

21 Edmund Tilney, *The Flower of Friendship*, 1568, ed. Valerie Wayne (Cornell University Press, 1992) 128–129.

22 Frances E. Dolan, *Marriage and Violence: The Early Modern Legacy* (University of Pennsylvania Press, 2008) 4.

23 Tilney, *Flower of Friendship* 112.

24 Traub, *Renaissance* 265.

25 Traub, *Renaissance* 269.

26 Michel Foucault, *The Use of Pleasure, The History of Sexuality*, vol. II, trans. Robert Hurley (New York: Vintage, 1990) 5.

27 See Francis Barker, *The Tremulous Private Body: Essays in Subjection*, 2nd edn (University of Michigan Press, 1995); Catherine Belsey, *The Subject of Tragedy: Identity and Difference in Renaissance Drama* (London: Methuen, 1985); Jonathan Dollimore, *Radical Tragedy: Ideology and Power in the Drama of Shakespeare and His Contemporaries*, 2nd edn (Duke University Press, 1989); Stephen Greenblatt, "Psychoanalysis and Renaissance Culture," in *Literary Theory/Renaissance Texts*, ed. Patricia Parker and David Quint (Johns Hopkins University Press, 1986) 210–224; and Julian Yates, *Error, Misuse, Failure: Object Lessons from the English Renaissance* (University of Minnesota Press, 2003).

28 Thomas Wright, *The Passions of the Minde* (London, 1601) sig. B6v.

29 David Hillman, *Shakespeare's Entrails: Belief, Scepticism, and the Interior of the Body* (Basingstoke: Palgrave, 2007) 2.

30 Wright, *Passions of the Minde* sig. E7r.

31 *Ibid.* sig. H7r.

32 Hillman, *Shakespeare's Entrails* 6.

33 Katharine Eisaman Maus, *Inwardness and Theater in the English Renaissance* (University of Chicago Press, 1995) 24.

34 Barker, *Tremulous Private Body* 41.

35 Sigmund Freud, *Three Essays on the Theory of Sexuality*, 1905, in *The Standard Edition of the Complete Psychological Works of Sigmund Freud*, vol. VII, ed. and trans. James Strachey *et al.* (London: Hogarth Press, 1953) 149.

36 Freud, *Three Essays* 234.

37 Freud, *Three Essays* 150.

38 Leo Bersani and Adam Phillips, *Intimacies* (University of Chicago Press, 2008) vii.

39 G. R. Quaife, *Wanton Wenches and Wayward Wives: Peasants and Illicit Sex in Early Seventeenth Century England* (Rutgers University Press, 1979) 165.

40 Henry Abelove, *Deep Gossip* (University of Minnesota Press, 2003) 26.

41 Anthony Giddens, *The Transformation of Intimacy: Sexuality, Love, and Eroticism in Modern Societies* (Stanford University Press, 1992) 44–45.

42 Roland Barthes, *A Lover's Discourse: Fragments*, trans. Richard Howard (New York: Hill and Wang, 1978) 23.

43 Lauren Berlant, "Intimacy: A Special Issue," in *Intimacy*, ed. Lauren Berlant (University of Chicago Press, 2000) 5.

44 D. A. Miller, *Narrative and Its Discontents: Problems of Closure in the Traditional Novel* (Princeton University Press, 1981) xiii.

45 Peter Brooks, *Reading for the Plot: Design and Intention in Narrative* (New York: Knopf, 1984) 96.

46 Freud, *Three Essays* 149.

47 Miller, *Narrative and Its Discontents* 267.

48 Freud, *Three Essays* 150.

49 Freud, *Three Essays* 149.

50 Lee Edelman, *No Future: Queer Theory and the Death Drive* (Duke University Press, 2004) 3–4. See also Judith Halberstam, *In a Queer Time and Place: Transgender Bodies and Subcultural Lives* (New York University Press, 2005).

51 Edelman, *No Future* 3.

52 Edelman, *No Future* 4.

53 Alan Sinfield, *Shakespeare, Authority, Sexuality: Unfinished Business in Cultural Materialism* (London: Routledge, 2006) 20.

54 On *bricolage* as the repurposing of the products of dominant culture by the marginalized, see Michel de Certeau in *The Practice of Everyday Life*, trans. Stephen Rendall (University of California Press, 1984) 29–42; Richard Dyer, "Introduction," in *Gays and Film* rev. edn (New York: Zoetrope, 1984) 1; and Dick Hebdige, *Subculture: The Meaning of Style* (New York: Methuen, 1979) 102–105. My use of *bricolage* is similar to the "reparative reading" that Eve Kosofsky Sedgwick advocates in *Touching Feeling: Affect, Pedagogy, Performativity* (Duke University Press, 2003) 123–152.

55 See Gregory W. Bredbeck, *Sodomy and Interpretation: Marlowe to Milton* (Cornell University Press, 1991) 149; Bruce R. Smith, *Homosexual Desire in Shakespeare's England: A Cultural Poetics*, 2nd edn (University of Chicago Press, 1994) 92; and Gregory Woods, "Body, Costume, and Desire in Christopher Marlowe," in *Homosexuality in Renaissance and Enlightenment England: Literary Representation in Historical Context*, ed. Claude J. Summers (New York: Haworth Press, 1992) 82.

56 For the sake of clarity, I will refer to the poems in *England's Helicon* using the titles supplied by the miscellany. I do not, however, wish to suggest that they are authorial or have no ideological effects.

57 Douglas Bruster, "'Come to the Tent Again': 'The Passionate Shepherd,' Dramatic Rape, and Lyric Time," *Criticism* 33.1 (1991): 52.

58 From this reading practice, we might abstract an editorial practice that, rather than privileging the *England's Helicon* version and casting the *Passionate Pilgrim* version as textual corruption, would approach each version on its own terms and would also attend to the variety of definitions of intimacy that were imaginable in the Renaissance.

CHAPTER 1

1 Stephen Orgel, "Tobacco and Boys: How Queer Was Marlowe?" *GLQ* 6.4 (2000): 555–576.

2 Lawrence Stone, *The Family, Sex, and Marriage in England, 1500–1800* (New York: Harper and Row, 1977) 55–56.

3 *Ibid.* 117.

4 Alan Macfarlane, *Marriage and Love in England: Modes of Reproduction, 1300–1840* (Oxford: Blackwell, 1986) 238.

5 Christopher Marlowe, *Hero and Leander: A Facsimile of the First Edition, London 1598*, ed. Louis L. Martz (Washington, DC: Folger Shakespeare Library, 1972) 143–144. Subsequent references will appear parenthetically in the text.

6 Gregory Woods, "Body, Costume and Desire in Christopher Marlowe," in *Homosexuality in Renaissance and Enlightenment England: Literary Representations in Historical Context*, ed. Claude J. Summers (New York: Haworth Press, 1992) 73. See also Gregory Bredbeck, *Sodomy and Interpretation: Marlowe to Milton* (Cornell University Press, 1991) 110.

7 Lorna Hutson, "Fortunate Travelers: Reading for the Plot in Sixteenth-Century England," *Representations* 41 (1993): 85.

8 *Ibid.* 83. See also Patricia Parker, *Inescapable Romance: Studies in the Poetics of a Mode* (Princeton University Press, 1979).

9 Roland Barthes, *The Pleasure of the Text*, trans. Richard Miller (New York: Hill and Wang, 1975) 52. See also Patricia Parker, "Deferral, Dilation, Différance: Shakespeare, Cervantes, Jonson," in *Literary Theory/Renaissance Texts*, ed. Patricia Parker and David Quint (Johns Hopkins University Press, 1986) 182–209.

10 Bruce R. Smith, *Homosexual Desire in Shakespeare's England: A Cultural Poetics* (University of Chicago Press, 1991) 135, 136.

11 Judith Haber, *Desire and Dramatic Form in Early Modern England* (Cambridge University Press, 2009) 43.

12 See Marion Campbell, "*Desunt Nonnulla*: The Construction of Marlowe's *Hero and Leander* as an Unfinished Poem," *ELH* 51.2 (1984): 241–268; and Louis L. Martz, "Marlowe's 'Amorous Poem': Triadic Design in *Hero and Leander*," in *From Renaissance to Baroque: Essays on Literature and Art* (University of Missouri Press, 1991) 87–99.

13 In *Unhistorical Shakespeare: Queer Theory in Shakespearean Literature and Film* (Basingstoke: Palgrave, 2008), Madhavi Menon argues that Shakespeare's *Venus*

and Adonis challenges the linkage of sexuality and teleology that often informs modern interpretive strategies (27–50). Marlowe's *Hero and Leander* registers this challenge and responses to it at the material level of the printed text as well.

14 Henry Abelove, *Deep Gossip* (University of Minnesota Press, 2003) 26.

15 Sigmund Freud, *Three Essays on the Theory of Sexuality*, 1905, in *The Standard Edition of the Complete Psychological Works of Sigmund Freud*, vol. VII, ed. and trans. James Strachey *et al.* (London: Hogarth Press, 1953) 149.

16 See Michel Foucault, *The History of Sexuality: An Introduction*, vol. I, trans. Robert Hurley (New York: Vintage, 1990) esp. 36–49.

17 Lauren Berlant and Michael Warner, "Sex in Public," *Critical Inquiry* 24.2 (1998): 558.

18 Adapted by Lauren Berlant from Gilles Deleuze and Felix Guattari's term "minor literature," the term "minor intimacy" refers to alternate plottings of affective relations outside long-term monogamous coupling. See Lauren Berlant, "Intimacy: A Special Issue," *Intimacy* (University of Chicago Press, 2000) 1–8.

19 See Edward Coke, *The Third Part of the Institutes of the Laws of England* (London, 1644) 59, and *The Twelfth Part of the Reports of Sir Edward Coke* (London, 1656) 37.

20 Coke, *The Third Part of the Institutes* 59.

21 *The Tryal and Condemnation of Mervyn, Lord Audley, Earl of Castle-Haven* (London, 1699) 12.

22 *Ibid.* 25.

23 Smith, *Homosexual Desire* 52–53.

24 On the limits of an exclusive focus on legal discourses in understanding the Renaissance sexual imaginary, *ibid.* 14–18.

25 Ian Frederick Moulton, *Before Pornography: Erotic Writing in Early Modern England* (Oxford University Press, 2000).

26 Clark Hulse, *Metamorphic Verse: The Elizabethan Minor Epic* (Princeton University Press, 1981) 118–119.

27 Thomas Elyot, *The Boke Named the Governour* (London, 1531) sig. G4r.

28 A. R. Braunmuller, "Marlowe's Amorous Fates in *Hero and Leander*," *Review of English Studies* 29.113 (1978): 61.

29 Gordon Braden, *The Classics and English Renaissance Poetry: Three Case Studies* (Yale University Press, 1978) 146.

30 Leo Bersani and Adam Phillips, *Intimacies* (University of Chicago Press, 2008) 41.

31 Freud, *Three Essays* 169.

32 W. L. Godshalk, in *"Hero and Leander*: The Sense of an Ending," in '*A Poet and a Filthy Play-Maker': New Essays on Christopher Marlowe*, ed. Kenneth Friedenreich *et al.* (New York: AMS Press, 1988) 293–314, argues that though the narrator is unreliable, our access to the poem is largely impossible without his mediation.

33 Foucault, *History of Sexuality* vol. I, 94.

34 Foucault, "The Ethics of the Concern of the Self as a Practice of Freedom," in *Ethics, Subjectivity, and Truth*, ed. Paul Rabinow, trans. Robert Hurley *et al.* (New York: New Press, 1997) 287, 288.

35 Elizabeth Harvey, "The Touching Organ: Allegory, Anatomy, and the Renaissance Skin Envelope," in *Sensible Flesh: On Touch in Early Modern Culture*, ed. Elizabeth Harvey (University of Pennsylvania Press, 2003) 87.

36 While penetration and non-monogamy are not mutually exclusive, an ethical non-monogamous praxis is not available to the penetrative erotic bonds in this poem.

37 On the homoeroticism of the tale, see Bredbeck, *Sodomy and Interpretation* 132–134 and Smith, *Homosexual Desire* 132–136.

38 Haber, *Desire and Dramatic Form* 39.

39 George Chapman, *Hero and Leander,* in *Christopher Marlowe: The Complete Poems and Translations*, ed. Stephen Orgel (London: Penguin, 1971) 6.137–141. Subsequent references will be cited parenthetically in the text.

CHAPTER 2

1 References to Shakespeare's plays will be taken from the *The Oxford Shakespeare: The Complete Works*, ed. Stanley Wells and Gary Taylor (Oxford University Press, 1988), and they will be subsequently cited parenthetically. In my discussion of *All's Well*, I have departed from the Oxford edition by returning the second "l" to Parolles's name because its presence does not obscure the connection of his name with "words" and the three syllables of "Parolles" is occasionally metrically justified.

2 Susan Snyder, *Shakespeare: A Wayward Journey* (University of Delaware Press, 2002) 141–142.

3 Sujata Iyengar, "'Handling the Soft Hurts': Sexual Healing and Manual Contact in *Orlando Furioso, The Faerie Queene, and All's Well That Ends Well*," in *Sensible Flesh: On Touch in Early Modern Culture*, ed. Elizabeth Harvey (University of Pennsylvania Press, 2003) 53.

4 John Arderne's *Treatises of Fistula in Ano* was appended to Francisco Arceo's *Most Excellent and Compendious Method of Curing Woundes in the Head and in Other Parts of the Body* (London, 1588). On Shakespeare's echoes of Arderne, see Frank Whigham, "Reading Social Conflict in the Alimentary Tract" *ELH* 55.2 (1988): 333–350.

5 Arderne, *Treatises* sig. AA2r.

6 Michael C. Schoenfeldt, *Bodies and Selves in Early Modern England: Physiology and Inwardness in Spenser, Shakespeare, Herbert, and Milton* (Cambridge University Press, 1999) 96.

7 Gail Kern Paster, *The Body Embarrassed: Drama and the Disciplines of Shame in Early Modern England* (Cornell University Press, 1993) 133.

8 On Freud's phallocentric understanding of the anus, see Lee Edelman, *Homographesis: Essays in Gay Literary and Cultural Theory* (New York: Routledge, 1994) 173–191.

9 Jonathan Goldberg, "The Anus in *Coriolanus*," in *Historicism, Psychoanalysis, and Early Modern Culture*, ed. Carla Mazzio and Douglas Trevor (New York: Routledge, 2000) 266. See also Jeffrey Masten, "Is the Fundament a Grave?" in *The Body in Parts: Fantasies of Corporeality in Early Modern Europe*, ed. David Hillman and Carla Mazzio (New York: Routledge, 1997) 128–145.

10 Helkiah Crooke, *Mikrokosmographia: A Description of the Body of Man* (London, 1616) 77, 79.

11 *Ibid.* 165.

12 *Ibid.* 166.

13 *Ibid.* 166, 167.

14 Leo Bersani, in "Is the Rectum a Grave?" *October* 41 (1987): 197–222, discusses the threat to interiorized selfhood underscored in modern, often homophobic, understandings of anal penetration.

15 Phineas Fletcher, *The Purple Island* (1633) in *Giles and Phineas Fletcher: Poetical Works*, vol. ii, ed. Frederick S. Boas (Cambridge University Press, 1909) 2.15.3–4.

16 *Ibid.* 2.43.1–7.

17 Guy Hocquenghem, *Homosexual Desire*, trans. Daniella Dangoor (Duke University Press, 1993) 99.

18 In a similar vein, Masten points to Fletcher's assertion that the anus is a "gate endow'd with many properties" (Fletcher, *Purple Island* 2.43.5) to argue that it might be possible to "dislodge the rectum or anus from any definitive transcultural meanings," (140) including antisodomitical ones.

19 Fletcher, *Purple Island* 3.6.1–7.

20 See also Jonathan Gil Harris, "All Swell That End Swell: Dropsy, Phantom Pregnancy, and the Sound of Deconception in *All's Well That Ends Well*," *Renaissance Drama* 35 (2006): 169–190.

21 Janet Adelman, *Suffocating Mothers: Fantasies of Maternal Origin in Shakespeare's Plays*, Hamlet *to* The Tempest (New York: Routledge, 1992) 82.

22 Crooke, *Mikrokosmographia* 154.

23 Marcus Tullius Cicero, *The Familiar Epistles of M. T. Cicero*, trans. Joseph Webbe (London, 1620) sig. X6v.

24 Marvin Herrick, *Comic Theory in the Sixteenth Century*, 2nd edn (University of Illinois Press, 1969) 123. Though Aristotle's influence over English Renaissance drama was not as prescriptive as in other periods and nations, the directional and psychological aspects of this theory of comic resolution nevertheless informed Renaissance dramatic practice on a general level as playwrights adapted forms, such as New Comedy, from classical theater.

25 Daniel Punday, *Narrative Bodies: Toward a Corporeal Narratology* (New York: Palgrave, 2003) 15.

26 See Patricia Parker, "Preposterous Events," *Shakespeare Quarterly* 43.2 (1992): 186–213 and "Preposterous Reversals: *Love's Labour's Lost*," *Modern Language Review* 54.4 (1993): 435–482.

27 David Hillman, *Shakespeare's Entrails: Belief, Skepticism, and the Interior of the Body* (Basingstoke: Palgrave, 2007) 44.

28 Hocquenghem, *Homosexual Desire* 111.

29 H. B. Charlton, *Shakespearean Comedy* (New York: MacMillan, 1938) 217.

30 Crooke, *Mikrokosmographia* 166.

31 Hocquenghem, *Homosexual Desire* 101.

32 *Ibid.* 105.

33 On Parolles as an ass, see Will Stockton, "'I am made an ass': Falstaff and the Scatology of Windsor's Polity," *Texas Studies in Literature and Language* 49.4 (2007): 356–357.

34 Paster, *Body Embarrassed* 126 n23.

35 Jonathan Dollimore, *Sexual Dissidence: Augustine to Wilde, Freud to Foucault* (Oxford University Press, 1991) 56.

36 Philip Sidney, *The Defence of Poesy*, in *Sir Philip Sidney: Selected Prose and Poetry*, 2nd edn, ed. Robert Kimbrough (University of Wisconsin Press, 1983) 129.

37 Jonathan Sawday, *The Body Emblazoned: Dissection and the Human Body in Renaissance Culture* (London: Routledge, 1995) 2.

38 I have reverted to the traditional name, Iachimo, which the Oxford edition, modernizes to Giacomo, while I accept the Oxford editors' change of "Imogen" to "Innogen."

39 Crooke, *Mikrokosmographia* 214. See also John Banister, *The historie of man sucked from the sappe of the most approued anathomistes* (London, 1578) sig. BB4v.

40 In *Making Sex: The Body and Gender from the Greeks to Freud* (Harvard University Press, 1990), Thomas Laqueur argues that gender in the Renaissance was conceived according to a Galenic one-sex model in contrast to a modern model of polarized sexual difference, rendering the boundaries between the sexes threateningly permeable (63–113). This model is nevertheless based on polarized difference as it organizes the body into genital and non-genital zones. In "*Romeo and Juliet*'s Open Rs," in *Queering the Renaissance*, ed. Jonathan Goldberg (Duke University Press, 1994), Jonathan Goldberg notes that the anus, as an organ that is shared by both sexes and that situates erotic pleasure outside reproductive genitality, breaks down even further the notions of difference inscribed by gender discourse on the body (218–235). In *Homographesis: Essays on Gay Literary and Cultural Theory*, Lee Edelman pursues this topic in psychoanalytic terms as he discusses how anal sex repudiates the castration complex that informs gender difference and the heterosexualization incumbent upon such difference. See also "Is the Rectum Straight?" in her book *Tendencies* (Duke University Press, 1993), where Eve Kosofsky Sedgwick critiques psychoanalytic accounts that recast anal pleasure in terms of the gender difference and heterosexuality that are undermined by libidinal investment in the anus.

41 In "Queer Money" *ELH* 66.1 (1999): 1–23, Will Fisher traces the connection of sodomy and counterfeiting as illegitimate modes of reproduction in Renaissance thought.

42 William Shakespeare, *Sonnets*, ed. Stephen Booth (Yale University Press, 1977) 20.4.

43 Shakespeare, *Sonnets*, 20.9–14.

44 For accounts of the ambiguity of the final lines of Sonnet 20, see Gregory W. Bredbeck, *Sodomy and Interpretation: Marlowe to Milton* (Cornell University Press, 1991) 175–180; Stephen Orgel, *Impersonations: The Performance of Gender in Shakespeare's England* (Cambridge University Press, 1996) 56–57; and Eve Kosofsky Sedgwick, *Between Men: English Literature and Male Homosocial Desire* (Columbia University Press, 1985) 35–39.

45 A rather germane example of a contemporaneous use of "to prick out" to refer to making indentations into a body can be found in *Locrine* (1595) in *The Shakespeare Apocrypha*, ed. C. F. Tucker Brooke (Oxford: Clarendon Press, 1908), where Thrasimachus offers the following threat to Strumbo and Trompart: "Tell me, you villaines, why you make this noise, / Or with my launce I will prick your bowels out" (2.3.45–46).

46 Mario DiGangi, *The Homoerotics of Early Modern Drama* (Cambridge University Press, 1997) 50.

47 Valerie Wayne, "The Woman's Parts of *Cymbeline*," in *Staged Properties in Early Modern English Drama*, ed. Jonathan Gil Harris and Natasha Korda (Cambridge University Press, 2002) 288–297.

48 Michael Shapiro, *Gender in Play on the Shakespearean Stage: Boy Heroines and Female Pages* (University of Michigan Press, 1996) 180.

49 On the connections of the anus and narrow openings in Renaissance texts, especially around sewer conduits, see Jonathan Gil Harris, *Foreign Bodies and the Body Politic: Discourses of Social Pathology in Early Modern England* (Cambridge University Press, 1998) 79–106.

50 Richard Rambuss, "After Male Sex," *South Atlantic Quarterly* 106.3 (2007): 586.

51 Parker, "Romance and Empire: Anachronistic *Cymbeline*," in *Unfolded Tales: Essays on Renaissance Romance*, ed. George M. Logan and Gordon Teskey (Cornell University Press, 1989) 205. See also Heather James, *Shakespeare's Troy: Drama, Politics, and the Translation of Empire* (Cambridge University Press, 1997) 151–188.

CHAPTER 3

1 Sir John Davies, "In Francum," in *The Poems of Sir John Davies*, ed. Robert Krueger (Oxford: Clarendon Press, 1975) 143.

2 Ian Frederick Moulton, "'Printed Abroad and Uncastrated': Marlowe's *Elegies* with Davies' Epigrams," in *Marlowe, History, and Sexuality: New Critical Essays on Christopher Marlowe,* ed. Paul Whitfield White (New York: AMS Press, 1998) 86.

3 *Ibid.* 85.

4 William Shakespeare, *Antony and Cleopatra*, in *The Oxford Shakespeare: The Complete Works*, ed. Gary Taylor and Stanley Wells (Oxford University Press, 1988) 5.2.290–291.

5 Jonathan Goldberg, "Margaret Cavendish, Scribe," *GLQ* 10.3 (2004): 435.

6 Gary Taylor, in "Thomas Middleton, *The Nice Valour*, and the Court of James I," *The Court Historian* 6 (2001): 1–27, argues for Middleton's authorship and for the 1622 date of the play. I am grateful to Taylor for letting me make use of the edition of the play that he and Susan Wiseman prepared prior to its publication.

7 Sigmund Freud, *Beyond the Pleasure Principle*, 1920, in *The Standard Edition of the Complete Psychological Works of Sigmund Freud*, vol. XVIII, ed. and trans. James Strachey *et al.* (London: Hogarth Press, 1955) 16. Leo Bersani, in *The Freudian Body: Psychoanalysis and Art* (Columbia University Press, 1986) 51–80, and Jean Laplanche, in *Life and Death in Psychoanalysis*, trans. Jeffrey Mehlman (Johns Hopkins University Press, 1976) 85–102 and *Essays on Otherness* (New York: Routledge, 1999) 201–217, chronicle how unevenly Freud grants agency to the masochist.

8 Kaja Silverman, *Male Subjectivity at the Margins* (New York: Routledge, 1992) 213. See also Karmen MacKendrick, *Counterpleasures* (State University of New York Press, 1999) esp. 107.

9 Gilles Deleuze, "Coldness and Cruelty," trans. Jean McNeill, in *Masochism* (New York: Zone Books, 1989) 22.

10 *Ibid.* 77.

11 See Havelock Ellis, *Studies in the Psychology of Sex*, vol. 1.2 (New York: Random House, 1937) 130–131. See also Ian Gibson, *The English Vice: Sex and Shame in Victorian England and After* (London: Duckworth, 1978) 1–47.

12 One might use the term "algolagnia," but then one loses masochism's particularity in describing pleasure from receiving, as opposed to inflicting, pain as well as the term's connection to the literary through Sacher-Masoch and to contemporary S/M.

13 Walter Cohen, "Prerevolutionary Drama," in *The Politics of Tragicomedy: Shakespeare and After*, ed. Gordon McMullan and Jonathan Hope (New York: Routledge, 1992) 127.

14 Francis Beaumont and John Fletcher, *Philaster, or Love Lies A-bleeding*, ed. Andrew Gurr (Manchester University Press, 2003) 1.2.83. Subsequent references will be cited parenthetically in the text.

15 Jeffrey Masten, "Editing Boys: The Performance of Genders in Print," in *From Performance to Print in Shakespeare's England*, ed. Peter Holland and Stephen Orgel (Basingstoke: Palgrave, 2006) 121.

16 Deleuze, "Coldness and Cruelty" 89.

17 Silverman, *Male Subjectivity* 189.

18 On the parallelism between the Country Fellow and the citizens, see Philip J. Finkelpearl, *Court and Country Politics in the Plays of Beaumont and Fletcher* (Princeton University Press, 1990) 159.

19 In the likely censored Q1 of *Philaster* (1620), Bellario accepts the King's offer and marries the courtier Trasiline.

20 On absolutism in the play, see Finkelpearl, *Court and Country Politics* 183–211.

21 Francis Beaumont and John Fletcher, *The Maid's Tragedy*, ed. T. W. Craik (Manchester University Press, 1988) 5.1.47–52. Subsequent references will be cited parenthetically in the text.

22 Kathleen McLuskie, *Renaissance Dramatists* (Atlantic Highlands: Humanities Press, 1989) 193.

23 *Ibid.* 195. On male-male relations in the play, see Stephen Guy-Bray, *Homoerotic Space: The Poetics of Loss in Renaissance Literature* (University of Toronto Press, 2002) 179–197.

24 Theodore Reik, *Masochism in Sex and Society*, trans. Margaret H. Beigel and Gertrude M. Kurth (New York: Grove Press, 1962) 145.

25 Lee Bliss, "Tragicomic Romance for the King's Men, 1609–1611: Shakespeare, Beaumont, and Fletcher," in *Comedy from Shakespeare to Sheridan: Change and Continuity in the English and European Dramatic Tradition*, ed. A. R. Braunmuller and J. C. Bulman (University of Delaware Press, 1986) 151.

26 Jennifer Low, *Manhood and the Duel: Masculinity in Early Modern Drama and Culture* (Basingstoke: Palgrave, 2003) 147.

27 Thomas Middleton and William Rowley, *A Fair Quarrel*, ed. Suzanne Gossett, in *Thomas Middleton: The Collected Works*, ed. Gary Taylor *et al.* (Oxford University Press, 2007) 1.1.44.

28 *Ibid.* 1.1.84, 85.

29 For a recent discussion of the implications of the eroticism of boys on the early modern stage, see Masten, "Editing Boys."

30 Middleton and Rowley, *A Fair Quarrel* 1.1.121.

31 Mario DiGangi, *The Homoerotics of Early Modern Drama* (Cambridge University Press, 1997) 143.

32 Thomas Middleton, *The Nice Valour*, ed. Gary Taylor and Susan Wiseman, in *Thomas Middleton: The Collected Works*, ed. Gary Taylor *et al.* (Oxford University Press, 2007) 3.2.11–12. Subsequent references appear parenthetically.

33 See Mervyn James, *Society, Politics, and Culture: Studies in Early Modern England* (Cambridge University Press, 1986) 313–378; V. G. Kiernan, *The Duel in European History: Honour and the Reign of Aristocracy* (Oxford University Press, 1988); Markku Peltonen, *The Duel in Early Modern England: Civility, Politeness, and Honour* (Cambridge University Press, 2003); and Lawrence Stone, *The Crisis of the Aristocracy, 1558–1641* (Oxford University Press, 1965) 223–245.

34 Silverman, *Male Subjectivity* 206.

35 See Deleuze, "Coldness and Cruelty" 32–33; Laplanche, *Life and Death in Psychoanalysis* 85–102; Reik, *Masochism* 44–58; and Silverman, *Male Subjectivity* 209.

36 Michel Foucault, "Sex, Power, and the Politics of Identity," in *Ethics, Subjectivity, and Truth*, ed. Paul Rabinow, trans. Robert Hurley *et al.* (New York: New Press, 1997) 165.

37 Sigmund Freud, *Three Essays on the Theory of Sexuality*, 1905, in *The Standard Edition of the Complete Psychological Works of Sigmund Freud*, vol. VII, ed. and trans. James Strachey *et al.* (London: Hogarth Press, 1953) 169.

38 See Freud, *Three Essays* 149.

39 *Ibid.* 193.

40 Celia R. Daileader, "Back Door Sex: Renaissance Gynosodomy, Aretino, and the Exotic," *ELH* 69.2 (2002): 308–309.

41 Elizabeth D. Harvey, "The Touching Organ: Allegory, Anatomy, and the Renaissance Skin Envelope," in *Sensible Flesh: On Touch in the Early Modern Period*, ed. Elizabeth D. Harvey (University of Pennsylvania Press, 2003) 82.

42 On the early modern book-body connection, see Margreta de Grazia and Peter Stallybrass, "The Materiality of the Shakespearean Text," *Shakespeare Quarterly* 44.3 (1993): 255–283 and Elizabeth Pittenger, "Explicit Ink," in *Premodern Sexualities*, ed. Louise Fradenburg and Carla Freccero (New York: Routledge, 1996) 223–242.

43 Laplanche, *Life and Death in Psychoanalysis* 93.

44 Elizabeth D. Harvey, "Introduction: The 'Sense of All Senses,'" in *Sensible Flesh: On Touch in Early Modern Culture* (University of Pennsylvania Press, 2003) 2. In *The Inarticulate Renaissance: Language Trouble in an Age of Eloquence* (University of Pennsylvania Press, 2009), Carla Mazzio discusses the vexed status of touch – at once the lowest among the senses, the basis of other senses, and capable of making meaning when the other senses fail (175–214).

45 Patricia Fumerton, *Cultural Aesthetics: Renaissance Literature and the Practice of Social Ornament* (University of Chicago Press, 1991) 1.

46 Frank Whigham, *Ambition and Privilege: The Social Tropes of Elizabethan Courtesy Theory* (University of California Press, 1984) 18.

47 Freud, "'A Child Is Being Beaten': A Contribution to the Study of the Origin of Sexual Perversions," 1919, in *The Standard Edition of the Complete Psychological Works of Sigmund Freud*, vol. XVII, ed. and trans. James Strachey *et al.* (London: Hogarth Press, 1955) 189.

48 Deleuze, "Coldness and Cruelty" 60.

49 David Scott Kastan, "Is There a Class in This (Shakespearean) Text?" *Renaissance Drama* 24 (1993): 106.

50 DiGangi, *The Homoerotics of Early Modern Drama* 144.

51 Silverman, *Male Subjectivity* 186.

52 See Gary Taylor, *Thomas Middleton and Early Modern Textual Culture: A Companion to the Collected Works*, ed. Gary Taylor *et al.* (Oxford University Press, 2007) 1073.

53 Michael Warner, *The Trouble with Normal: Sex, Politics, and the Ethics of Queer Life* (Harvard University Press, 1999) 171.

CHAPTER 4

1 Frances E. Dolan, "Why Are Nuns Funny?" *Huntington Library Quarterly* 70.4 (2007): 514.

2 Kate Chedgzoy, "'For Virgin Buildings Oft Brought Forth': Fantasies of Convent Sexuality," in *Female Communities 1600–1800: Literary Visions and*

Cultural Realities, ed. Rebecca D'Monté and Nicole Pohl (Basingstoke: Macmillan, 2000) 56.

3 Wendy Wall, *Staging Domesticity: Household Work and English Identity in Early Modern Drama* (Cambridge University Press, 2002) 146.

4 Theodora Jankowski, *Pure Resistance: Queer Virginity in Early Modern Drama* (University of Pennsylvania Press, 2000) 172.

5 Valerie Traub, *The Renaissance of Lesbianism in Early Modern England* (Cambridge University Press, 2002) 15.

6 *The Rule of the Most Blissed Father Saint Benedict* (Ghent, 1632) sig. E2v.

7 *Ibid.* sig. C6v. In *Medieval English Nunneries, c. 1275–1535* (Cambridge University Press, 1922), Eileen Power long ago noted that convent architecture was being altered in the High and Late Middle Ages to give nuns more privacy by subdividing their sleeping quarters, which had formerly been large, undivided halls, and not strictly enforcing communal refection (315–322). Yet, as Marilyn Oliva points out in *The Convent and the Community in Late Medieval England: Female Monasteries in the Diocese of Norwich, 1350–1540* (Rochester: Boydell Press, 1998), these changes were uneven in England, and in individual convents private cells were often only available to nuns at the top of the hierarchy (102–103).

8 See Orest Ranum, "The Refuges of Intimacy," in *A History of Private Life*, vol. 3, ed. Roger Chartier, trans. Arthur Goldhammer (Cambridge: Belknap Press, 1989) 207–264.

9 Nicky Hallett, *Lives of Spirit: English Carmelite Self-Writing of the Early Modern Period* (Aldershot: Ashgate, 2007) 39.

10 *Ibid.* 24.

11 Judith M. Bennett, "'Lesbian-Like' and the Social History of Lesbianisms," *Journal of the History of Sexuality* 9.1–2 (2000): 9–10.

12 William Whately, *A Bride-Bush* (London, 1623) sig. D2r.

13 *Ibid.* sig. D2r.

14 Alan Stewart, *Close Readers: Humanism and Sodomy in Early Modern England* (Princeton University Press, 1997) xliv.

15 John Bale, *The first two partes of the Actes or unchaste examples of the Englyshe Votaryes* (London, 1560) 11, sig. D2r. Subsequent references will appear parenthetically in the text.

16 As Margaret Cavendish's *The Convent of Pleasure* and Andrew Marvell's "Upon Appleton House" show, the concerns about marriage, the nation, and convents were still being rehearsed in the 1650s. In "The Enclosure of Virginity: The Poetics of Sexual Abstinence in the English Revolution," in *Enclosure Acts: Sexuality, Property, and Culture in Early Modern England*, ed. Richard Burt and John Michael Archer (Cornell University Press, 1994), John Rogers rightly cautions that Elizabethan representations of powerful virgins differ from mid-seventeenth century ones due to the latter's English Civil War contexts and historical distance from the Virgin Queen (229–250).

17 Peter Stallybrass, "Patriarchal Territories: The Body Enclosed," in *Rewriting the Renaissance: The Discourses of Sexual Difference in Early Modern Europe*, ed. Margaret W. Ferguson *et al.* (University of Chicago Press, 1986) 129.

18 *Ibid.* 134.
19 Robert Greene, *Friar Bacon and Friar Bungay*, ed. Daniel Seltzer (University of Nebraska Press, 1963) 2.66. Subsequent references will appear parenthetically in the text.
20 William Harrison, *The Description of England* (1587), ed. Georges Edelen (Cornell University Press, 1968) 116–117.
21 Edelen glosses "suspicious" as "promising," for Harrison criticizes merchant greed, not the voyages themselves.
22 Harrison, *Description of England* 117.
23 Richard Hakluyt, *The Principal Navigations, Voyages, Traffiques, and Discoveries of the English Nation*, vol. 1, ed. John Masefield (London: J. M. Dent, 1907) 3.
24 Jonathan Gil Harris, *Sick Economies: Drama, Mercantilism, and Disease in Shakespeare's England* (University of Pennsylvania Press, 2004) 164.
25 William Shakespeare, *Richard II*, in *The Oxford Shakespeare: The Complete Works*, ed. Stanley Wells and Gary Taylor (Oxford University Press, 1988) 2.1.66.
26 See Elizabeth I, "Her Answer to [the Commons'] Petition that She Marry," in *Elizabeth I: The Collected Works*, ed. Leah Marcus *et al.* (University of Chicago Press, 2000) 59.
27 Shakespeare, *Richard II* 2.1.47–49.
28 On the textual problems of *The Merry Devil of Edmonton*, see Laurie Maguire, *Shakespearean Suspect Texts: The 'Bad' Quartos and Their Contexts* (Cambridge University Press, 1996) 282–284, 331–332.
29 Traub, *Renaissance* 174.
30 *The Merry Devil of Edmonton*, in *The Shakespeare Apocrypha*, ed. C. F. Tucker Brooke (Oxford: Clarendon Press, 1908) 3.1.76, 85–86. Subsequent references will appear parenthetically in the text.
31 Philips van Marnix van St. Aldegonde, *The Beehive of the Romish Church*, trans. George Gylpen (London, 1579) sig. U7r.
32 Perhaps the best-known literary allusion to poaching in the early modern period occurs in *The Merry Wives of Windsor*, where Shallow accuses Falstaff of poaching his deer. See Jeffrey Theis, "The 'ill kill'd' Deer: Poaching and Social Order in *The Merry Wives of Windsor*," *Texas Studies in Literature and Language* 43.1 (2001): 46–73.
33 Enfield Chase was inherited by Mary de Bohun, whose marriage to Henry IV brought this property into royal ownership, and thus it had only been a royal forest from the beginning of the fifteenth century. See David A. Pam, *The Story of Enfield Chase* (Enfield: Enfield Preservation Society, 1984) 17.
34 Roger B. Manning, *Hunters and Poachers: A Social and Cultural History of Unlawful Hunting in England, 1485–1640* (Oxford: Clarendon Press, 1993) 135.
35 *Ibid.* 55.
36 Thomas Brewer, *The Life and Death of the Merry Devill of Edmonton* (London, 1631) sig. A4r.
37 W. W. Greg, "*The Merry Devil of Edmonton*," *Library* 25.3–4 (1944): 131. See also David Kathman, "Peter Fabell," in *The Oxford Dictionary of National Biography*

vol. 18, ed. H. C. G. Matthew and Brian Harrison (Oxford University Press, 2004) 870.

38 The biographical data about the Dukes of Norfolk derive from G. E. Cock-ayne's *The Complete Peerage of England, Scotland, Ireland, Great Britain, and the United Kingdom*, ed. H. A. Doubleday *et al.* (London: St. Catherine's Press, 1936) 608–624.

39 Robert Burton, *The Anatomy of Melancholy* (London, 1628) sig. BB3v.

40 Traub, *Renaissance* 197.

41 See Jonathan Dollimore, "Transgression and Surveillance in *Measure for Measure*," in *Political Shakespeares: Essays in Cultural Materialism*, 2nd edn, ed. Jonathan Dollimore and Alan Sinfield (Cornell University Press, 1994) 73.

42 William Shakespeare, *Measure for Measure*, in *The Oxford Shakespeare: The Complete Works*, ed. Stanley Wells and Gary Taylor (Oxford University Press, 1988) 5.1.312–313. Subsequent references will appear parenthetically in the text.

43 Thomas Robinson, *Anatomy of the English Nunnery at Lisbon* (London, 1622) sig. C3r.

44 "A Protestation of Allegiance made by thirteen Missioners to Queen Elizabeth, January 31, 1603," rpt. in M. A. Tierney, *Dodd's Church History of England*, vol. III (London, 1840) cxc–cxci.

45 John Bossy, *The English Catholic Community, 1570–1850* (London: Darton, Longman & Todd, 1975) 40–41.

46 Samuel Harsnett, *A Declaration of Egregious Popish Impostures*, 1603, in F. W. Brownlow, *Shakespeare, Harsnett, and the Devils of Denham* (University of Delaware Press, 1993) 319.

47 *Ibid.* 198.

48 "The Catholics' Supplication unto the King's Majesty, for toleration of Catholic Religion in England," 1603, in M. A. Tierney, *Dodd's Church History of England*, vol. IV (London, 1841) lxxiii.

49 *Ibid.*

50 Stat. 1 Jac. I c.4.

51 See Lena Cowen Orlin's *Private Matters and Public Culture in Post-Reformation England* (Cornell University Press, 1994).

52 Lauren Berlant and Michael Warner, "Sex in Public," *Critical Inquiry* 24.2 (1998): 553.

53 Edmund Tilney, *The Flower of Friendship*, 1568, ed. Valerie Wayne (Cornell University Press, 1992) 105.

54 Lee Edelman, *No Future: Queer Theory and the Death Drive* (Duke University Press, 2004) 3.

55 Jonathan Goldberg, *James I and the Politics of Literature: Jonson, Shakespeare, Donne, and Their Contemporaries* (Johns Hopkins University Press, 1983) 232.

56 Michel Foucault, *The History of Sexuality: An Introduction*, vol. 1, trans. Robert Hurley (New York: Vintage, 1990) 61.

57 Mario DiGangi, "Pleasure and Danger: Measuring Female Sexuality in *Measure for Measure*," *ELH* 60.3 (1993): 591.

58 Gail Kern Paster, *The Idea of the City in the Age of Shakespeare* (University of Georgia Press, 1985) 207.

59 Kathleen McLuskie, "The Patriarchal Bard: Feminist Criticism and Shakespeare: *King Lear* and *Measure for Measure*," in *Political Shakespeare: Essays in Cultural Materialism,* 2nd edn, ed. Jonathan Dollimore and Alan Sinfield (Cornell University Press, 1994) 97.

60 McLuskie, "The Patriarchal Bard" 97.

61 Julia Reinhard Lupton, *Citizen-Saints: Shakespeare and Political Theology* (University of Chicago Press, 2005) 154, 141.

62 *The Rule of the Holy Virgin S. Clare* (London, 1621) sig. A5v-A6r, B1v.

63 *The Rule of the Holy Virgin S. Clare* sig. A5r.

64 Janet Adelman, *Suffocating Mothers: Fantasies of Maternal Origin in Shakespeare's Plays,* Hamlet *to* The Tempest (New York: Routledge, 1992) 94.

65 Some of the seventeenth-century Carmelites nuns mention that they were lucky to have avoided the convent of Poor Clares at Gravelines because of that order's reputation for austerity (Hallett, *Lives of Spirit* 44, 68, 74).

66 Katharine E. Maus, *Inwardness and Theater in the English Renaissance* (University of Chicago Press, 1995) 180.

67 Harsnett, *Egregious Popish Impostures* 319.

CHAPTER 5

1 This is not to say that the difference between homosexuality and heterosexuality works the same way as racial difference, but instead that these systems of difference do work for each other. See Janet E. Halley, "'Like Race' Arguments," in *What's Left of Theory?: New Work on the Politics of Literary Theory,* ed. Judith Butler *et al.* (New York: Routledge, 2000) 40–74.

2 Philip Sidney, *Astrophil and Stella,* in *Sir Philip Sidney: Selected Prose and Poetry,* 2nd edn, ed. Robert Kimbrough (University of Wisconsin Press, 1983) 69.9–10. Subsequent references, cited by poem number and line, appear parenthetically in the text.

3 I refer only to the 1621 print version of *Pamphilia to Amphilanthus.* The Folger manuscript has a different arrangement and includes additional poems.

4 Wroth, *Pamphilia to Amphilanthus,* in *The Poems Of Lady Mary Wroth,* ed. Josephine A. Roberts (Louisiana State University Press, 1983) P1.14. Subsequent references will appear parenthetically in the text.

5 Josephine A. Roberts, "The Biographical Problem of *Pamphilia to Amphilanthus,*" *Tulsa Studies in Women's Literature* 1.1 (1982): 51.

6 Daniel Juan Gil, "The Currency of the Beloved and the Authority of Lady Mary Wroth," *Modern Language Studies* 29.2 (1999): 77; and Jeffrey Masten, "'Shall I Turne Blabb?': Circulation, Gender, and Subjectivity in Mary Wroth's Sonnets," in *Reading Mary Wroth: Representing Alternatives in Early Modern England,* ed. Naomi J. Miller and Gary Waller (University of Tennessee Press, 1991) 67.

7 Reference to *Hamlet* is from *The Oxford Shakespeare: The Complete Works*, ed. Gary Taylor and Stanley Wells (Oxford University Press, 1988) 1.2.84, 85.

8 Philippe Ariès, Introduction, in *A History of Private Life*, vol. 3, trans. Arthur Goldhammer, ed. Roger Chartier (Cambridge: Belknap, 1989) 9.

9 Jürgen Habermas, *The Structural Transformation of the Public Sphere: An Inquiry into a Category of Bourgeois Society*, trans. Thomas Burger *et al.* (MIT Press, 1991) 11.

10 Francis Barker, *The Tremulous Private Body: Essays on Subjection*, 2nd edn (University of Michigan Press, 1995) vi.

11 Lauren Berlant and Michael Warner, "Sex in Public," *Critical Inquiry* 24.2 (1998): 553.

12 *Ibid.* 562.

13 Barbara Kiefer Lewalski, *Writing Women of Jacobean England* (Harvard University Press, 1993) 254 and Wendy Wall, *The Imprint of Gender: Authorship and Publication in the English Renaissance* (Cornell University Press, 1993) 332.

14 Valerie Traub, *The Renaissance of Lesbianism in Early Modern England* (Cambridge University Press, 2002) 6.

15 The argument that Renaissance verse's amatory content is a metaphoric rendition of its political content can be traced to Arthur F. Marotti's influential "'Love is Not Love': Elizabethan Sonnet Sequences and the Social Order," *ELH* 49.2 (1982): 396–428.

16 Berlant and Warner, "Sex in Public" 553.

17 Naomi J. Miller, *Changing the Subject: Mary Wroth and Figurations of Gender in Early Modern England* (University Press of Kentucky, 1996) 183.

18 Michael Warner, *Publics and Counterpublics* (New York: Zone Books, 2002) 23.

19 Kim F. Hall, *Things of Darkness: Economies of Race and Gender in Early Modern England* (Cornell University Press, 1995) 9.

20 One notable exception is Valerie Traub's "Mapping the Global Body," in *Early Modern Visual Culture: Representation, Race, and Empire in Renaissance England*, ed. Peter Erickson and Clark Hulse (University of Pennsylvania Press, 2000) 44–97.

21 Ben Jonson, *The Masques of Blackness and of Beauty*, in *Ben Jonson*, vol. VII, ed. C. H. Hereford *et al.* (Oxford: Clarendon Press, 1941) 143, 144, 163–164. Subsequent references will appear parenthetically in the text.

22 Kathryn Schwarz, *Tough Love: Amazon Encounters in the English Renaissance* (Duke University Press, 2000) 119.

23 See Richmond Barbour, "Britain and the Great Beyond: *The Masque of Blackness* at Whitehall," in *Playing the Globe: Genre and Geography in English Renaissance Drama*, ed. John Gillies and Virginia Mason Vaughan (Fairleigh Dickinson University Press, 1998) 129–153.

24 John Leo Africanus, *A Geographical Historie of Africa*, trans. John Pory (London, 1600) sig. N2v.

25 *Ibid.* sig. N3r.

26 *Ibid.*

27 Hall, *Things of Darkness* 107.

28 Joyce Green MacDonald, *Women and Race in Early Modern Texts* (Cambridge University Press, 2002) 4.

29 Lady Mary Wroth, *The Second Part of the Countess of Montgomery's Urania*, ed. Josephine A. Roberts *et al.* (Tempe: Arizona Center for Medieval and Renaissance Studies, 1999) 1. Subsequent citations will appear parenthetically in the text by volume and page number. Volume I, the printed version, refers to *The First Part of the Countess of Montgomery's Urania*, ed. Josephine A. Roberts (Binghamton: Center for Medieval and Early Renaissance Studies, 1995) and Volume II, the edition of the manuscript continuation as cited in this note.

30 Roberts, "'The Knott Never to Bee Untide': The Controversy Regarding Marriage in Mary Wroth's *Urania*," in *Reading Mary Wroth: Representing Alternatives in Early Modern England*, ed. Naomi J. Miller and Gary Waller (University of Tennessee Press, 1991) 111. See also Maureen Quilligan, *Incest and Agency in Elizabeth's England* (University of Pennsylvania Press, 2005) 164–212.

31 Hall, *Things of Darkness* 206.

32 Miller, *Changing the Subject* 182.

33 Amelia Zurcher, *Seventeenth-Century English Romance: Allegory, Ethics, and Politics* (New York: Palgrave, 2007) 57–58.

34 José Esteban Muñoz, *Cruising Utopia: The Then and There of Queer Futurity* (New York University Press, 2009) 65.

35 *Ibid.*

36 Thommaso Buoni, *Problemes of Beautie and All Humane Affections*, trans. Samson Lennard (London, 1606) sig. E10r.

EPILOGUE

1 For more on the way the film's narrative domesticates homoerotic desire, see D. A. Miller, "On the Universality of *Brokeback Mountain*," *Film Quarterly* 60.3 (2007): 50–60.

2 Annie Proulx, "Brokeback Mountain," *Close Range: Wyoming Stories* (New York: Scribner, 1999) 270. Subsequent references will be cited parenthetically in the text.

Index